Crime, Courts and Community in Mid-Victorian Wales

Crime, Courts and Community in Mid-Victorian Wales

Montgomeryshire, People and Places

Rachael Jones

UNIVERSITY OF WALES PRESS
CARDIFF

www.uwp.co.uk

British Library Cataloguing-in-Publication Data.
A catalogue record for this book is available from the British Library.

ISBN   978–1-78683–259–7
eISBN   978–1-78683–260–3

Funding for this publication by the Marc Fitch Fund is gratefully acknowledged.

Typeset by Mark Heslington Ltd, Scarborough, North Yorkshire.
Printed by CPI Antony Rowe, Melksham.

For my parents
Who never let me down

CONTENTS

ACKNOWLEDGEMENTS

Appreciation goes to Richard Ireland for invaluable advice, and to Clive Emsley, Peter King, Richard Moore-Colyer, Keith Snell, Sujitha Subramanian and Thomas Glyn Watkin for important constructive criticism. I acknowledge the public library in Newtown, Powys, for its wonderful local history resources, and helpful and knowledgeable staff. I am grateful for the freely available access to the Ancestry website at local authority libraries, which enabled the start of this project.

I am very grateful to the Marc Fitch Fund and to Mrs D. L. Jones whose generous support enabled publication.

Finally, and most importantly, I give my appreciation to the people of nineteenth-century Montgomeryshire and the heritage they left.

LIST OF FIGURES

LIST OF TABLES

ABBREVIATIONS

DNB	*Dictionary of National Biography*
HMIC	Her Majesty's Inspector of Constabularies
ME	*Montgomeryshire Express*
Mont. Colls	*Montgomeryshire Collections*
NLW	National Library of Wales
NWE	*Newtown and Welshpool Express*
PCA	Powys County Archives
TNA	The National Archives

INTRODUCTION

AIMS, STRUCTURE AND METHODOLOGY

This book is a study of the public and personal experiences of Montgomeryshire people in the criminal courts, from aristocrats to paupers, male and female, the elderly and the very young, agriculturalists and industrialists. It examines social relations through the medium of the criminal justice system in mid-Victorian Wales, stressing social interaction and the comparative experiences of women, to see how these influenced and were reinforced by established legal procedures. A main intention is to understand local administration of justice through investigating the motivations and contributions of participants in law enforcement. It uses testimonies and courtroom interaction to uncover lives and the social significance of events. The localised environment within mid-Wales is a constant theme, and much reference is made to topography, including architecture, roads, watercourses and woodland. The book aims to highlight the study of landscape in relation to both offending and detection, whether in urban or rural situations.[1] Crowd responses to law enforcement are considered at a local level,[2] and much of the method of this book thus involves a form of local history now often termed microhistory: where local areas and personalities are used to explore wider themes; and where broader issues become understandable only via the lens of close 'micro' study of people who are known individuals and their immediate surroundings.[3]

Seminal work in the 1970s introduced the idea that a study of the courts could access the experiences of people about whom little hitherto had been written.[4] The fact that wider society was seen in court meant that the history of the criminal justice system 'was central to unlocking the meanings of eighteenth-century social history',[5] and herein lies the basis of the present work set in the later nineteenth century. While recognising that the class system was played out in court, the procedures of justice were shown to protect the interests of the general public throughout England and Wales,[6] and the importance of jury discretion will be built upon here.[7] Courts have a many-faceted nature, and a diversity of persons can affect the outcome of a case. Some historians have confined their investigative studies to small elite groups, but the present book is not limited in that way. Rather, it examines offenders, victims and witnesses and encompasses a wide range of offending, by considering over 5,000 cases.[8]

The ground-breaking work of E. P. Thompson, while being 'of the people', nevertheless concentrated on men.[9] This left a space that started to be filled by feminist writers from the 1970s.[10] The work presented here investigates the whole community and makes comparisons between the experiences of men and women. It includes a chapter which specifically considers gender-related differences, looking particularly at how physicality affected the getaway part of the offence. It also considers a call for a study of 'history from below interacting with history from above',[11] and an 'end to segregation of urban from rural' and for expansion of 'gender-shaped experiences of the working classes'.[12] Women could use the law themselves, even taking men to court to resolve issues and demonstrating an impressive, perhaps surprising, knowledge of the legal system.[13]

This book is a history from all sides. The nineteenth-century restriction of the administration of law to men only, in the form of judges, lawyers, magistrates and police, means that a study of crime and community will contain a sizeable focus on this part of society.[14] Analyses of many events will occur here, with a scrutiny of the associated activities of the Montgomeryshire Constabulary and Bench of magistrates,[15] filling large spaces in the knowledge of this county's legal procedures. The selection of Montgomeryshire was for several reasons. In classic works such as David Jones's *Crime in Nineteenth-century Wales*, the county receives scant attention,[16] and studies of Wales usually concentrate on industrialised areas, mainly in the south.[17] However, in a paper presented to *Llafur* – the Welsh People's History Society, which studies history from below – Jones, did use 300 cases from early 1860s Montgomeryshire for an investigation. In this, he concentrated on rural offences, mainly arson, poaching and vagrancy, with a decided leaning towards men's experience of crime.[18] There are some detailed studies of crime in Montgomeryshire by other historians but set in earlier time periods.[19] There is thus need for a study of crime and the whole community in the later nineteenth century in mid-Wales. The current work is, in many ways, a mid-Victorian extension of Melvin Humphreys's book on Montgomeryshire, in that the whole community is studied without an overall focus on one social or gendered group.[20] The important features of the county are that it had both English and Welsh characteristics from its long border, approaching 150 miles, with Shropshire and with four Welsh counties. Montgomeryshire also had dual agricultural and industrial features from its rich farming heritage and revolutionary factory presence.[21] This study will address the well-justified concern that Welsh labour history, and the history of Welsh people, has been concentrated on the heavily industrialised areas.[22]

The first two chapters set the scene for the investigation, describing the county and its features. The geography of the area, linguistic dimensions and demography are discussed, along with an exploration of the available employment opportunities and religiosity. The face of the justice system seen in the courtroom is then considered by examining personalities in the local legal system, namely the magistrates and policemen. Their backgrounds are investigated, looking at life histories and identifying hierarchies within the diverse groups of men. Conclusions are made about possible motivations for joining the Bench and police force, and how far the identified hierarchies were represented in the landscape.

The central chapters provide a close-up study of the work of the courts and constabulary, looking first at how far the police force was an agent of the public, and to what degree the men were accepted by the lower orders. Their methods of law enforcement and the response of the community to their actions are analysed, and an early forensic investigation is considered. The work of magistrates in petty sessions, and their sentencing patterns, are scrutinised. Much is uncovered about motivations and methods, and the influence of the chief constable. We will also look at the use of the courts by the public. Later chapters move away from the administrators of justice, to the contributions of court users. First, there are the roles and actions of decision-makers in the form of prosecuting individuals and the juries in quarter sessions, then the court witnesses. In a study of the assize court, the highest judicial forum, we look into the differences resulting from outsiders' input, and evaluate whether the system subjugated participants, particularly women defendants. Status and reputation are priorities here, touching upon issues such as court protocol in relation to personal reputation.

The concluding two chapters investigate particular types of offending. In a study of theft, its gendered nature is evaluated. First-hand evidence from depositions sheds light on motivations and experiences, along with the part played by the landscape in criminal offending. Gendered involvement is further discussed in the final chapter on prostitution and its relation to public houses and alcohol. These life stories and experiences of women have hitherto been unstudied for Montgomeryshire, and here they are linked to an assessment of police attitudes and involvement. How were prostitutes handled by the legal system, and did their apparent status disadvantage them?[23]

CHRONOLOGY AND METHODOLOGY

The mid-Victorian age was chosen for study for several reasons. Initial investigations began at this point because the local newspaper, *The Newtown and Welshpool Express,* a starting point for gathering material, is available from 1869. The new police had been present for some thirty years in the county and was now ingrained within its justice system. A new chief constable was appointed in 1868, allowing his methods to be studied from the start. Social changes at this time had many implications for the administration of justice, as increasing numbers of newly rich individuals bought country properties, rose to become new gentry and joined the Bench of magistrates.[24] Women were not enfranchised, and yet by 1894 an established women's movement existed within some sections of the community, allowing us to view the effects of this emergent pressure group.[25] The Montgomeryshire flannel industry, once widely known throughout Britain and beyond, had suffered a long decline, almost from the point of police force origination, and this textile de-industrialisation had implications for offending and the financial penalties imposed. Despite that decline, Montgomeryshire was about to feature strongly in a retail revolution that much benefited the county economy: mail-order purchasing was launched by local entrepreneur Pryce Pryce-Jones in the 1870s.[26] We will see his influence as a resident of the county's most populous town.

The book's especial methodological focus on the decade from 1869 allows us to study evidence in greater detail than might otherwise be the case.[27] Over this period, *The Newtown and Welshpool Express* reported many court cases in detail, with names, places and minutiae given. Reports were supplied from summary courts around the county, highlighting cases that reflected the differing areas of Montgomeryshire. It is possible that some details may have been missed, and all sessions in all divisions may not have been covered. Occasional detail may have been reported wrongly, especially if the reporter was reading back from shorthand notes, and as records of summary and assize courts no longer exist, the evidence of the newspapers cannot be checked.[28] Most of the quarter sessions records are held at the county record office but there are gaps. Caution is always necessary as to veracity of reporting, for reporters and editors may have been biased, possibly pursuing their own agendas.[29] Despite such caveats, it has been noted that some convictions went unrecorded except in a newspaper.[30] Such reporting was public and fairly immediate, which was an obvious consideration disposing towards accuracy and correct reportage, with the reporter's job at stake.

Much of this book examines the constabulary, and for this the newspaper is the primary source. However, there are other sources that are important. At the National Library of Wales, there exists a Montgomeryshire policeman's note-book for this period, against which detail from the newspaper can be checked.[31] Powys County Archives holds the chief constable's reports to quarter sessions, and much further documentation is within quarter sessions bundles, such as depositions, financial records and the clerk's records of police activity.[32] Other archives around the country contain relevant material, such as the National Archives at Kew (for records of prisoners), and Denbighshire Record Office and Shropshire Archives supply information on neighbouring Benches and courts.

Given the centrality of Montgomeryshire people in this work, it was crucial to understand personal circumstances affecting motivations and events. This approach is very apparent in, for example, Barry Godfrey's work on Crewe, and Brian Short's fascinating work on so-called 'lifepaths'. Short observed that there was a constant 'ebb and flow' of younger men across the countryside in Victorian Sussex, and such migration and corresponding family history will be a feature of this book.[33] The internet has revolutionised this kind of research, and the Ancestry website allows the national censuses to be readily examined. Information on personal circumstances can be gathered in this way from 1841 to 1911, though again caution must be exercised as data may be incorrect or missing. For example, young offender Walter Ruscoe's place of birth was Guilsfield, Montgomeryshire, but was given as Glamorganshire in 1891 and Staffordshire in 1901. Names may be incorrect or spelled wrongly in the censuses, and this makes using the search facility problematic, and often names or places have been transcribed wrongly. For example, Kerry in Montgomeryshire was often transcribed as Kerry, Ireland. Harriet Chandler, who lived in Llanidloes in 1911, has been transcribed as Farriers Chandler. Women who changed their surnames upon marriage commonly disappeared, and in a region where names such as John Jones or Mary Evans occurred frequently, it was often only men with distinctive names who could be traced. Other electronic resources were of great utility to this research, particularly database and spreadsheet software. The data gathered from newspapers and court records were entered into a database from which sub-tables and so-called 'queries' could be generated. Entries were then sorted and interrogated with ease, and exported to spreadsheets where numerical analyses were performed. The embedding of formulae within the spreadsheets allowed much further analysis.

Comment and analysis is made here on actions well over a hundred years before our time. Sensibilities have changed. There have been considerable improvements in living standards; religious beliefs have significantly altered and often diminished; the boundaries of Welsh-language use and the morality, doctrines and popular hold of Nonconformity in Wales have altered; social and class attitudes have become very different; we no longer share many norms about crime and authority which prevailed in the Victorian period; and beliefs about gender roles have altered drastically. We are faced with questions and theory about the historic role of class and kinship in rural Wales, indeed in the same county that was studied in Alwyn Rees's famous book *Life in a Welsh Countryside*, one of the most pioneering and enduring masterpieces of mid-twentieth-century 'community studies'.[34] 'When was Wales?', the forthright historian Gwyn Williams asked, while other historians even question 'Why Wales Never Was',[35] and whatever their controversial verdicts we need to enquire how distinctive *was* Wales, and *this* region of rural mid-Wales? Does it fit into more predictable English historical models of society, conflict and social change, and if not, why not? Did it then comprise 'communities', and of what sort? How viable are Marxist theories of class and economic change as ways of interpreting criminal offending, justice and punishment in a Welsh county like this? Should one be looking more to post-Weberian theories of status or organisational behaviour, or social interpretations of religion, or anthropological understandings of kinship, or insights from community or gender studies, and how might theories of social capital and individualised respect be accommodated as ways of thinking about Welsh rural conduct and bureaucratic systems of regulation or arbitration? How did the knowable communities and structures of feeling of countryside and town compare and interact in this region, to re-phrase Raymond Williams, into a Welsh region not far north of his own?[36]

We are indeed concerned with many wider theories or interpretative frameworks of social formation and conflict, about how the criminal justice system may have been an adjunct to, or a major player in, a history of social control, status ascription, class suppression, or gendering patriarchy – and all such rival concepts or expressions involve and imply different and contested theories of history and of social change. The choice of Victorian Montgomeryshire and its justice system to explore these issues breaks ground abruptly from many established areas of nineteenth-century history. Indeed, it is also different from many of the geographical regions where key concepts of historical interpretation were formed historiographically by famous British and Irish scholars. This county is most certainly and informatively not, for example, the West Riding, or south Lancashire, or the Welsh industrial valleys, or the East End of London, or Glasgow and Clydeside; nor in a rural dimension is it the agrarian south-east of England, or the Highlands, or the famine-struck regions of Ireland.

Our own time is now very far removed from the Victorian period studied here. We need to be aware of the values and priorities of mid-Victorian Wales, notably of its religious and gendered cultures, let alone its small-farm and textile economy and related forms of technology, and caution should be exercised when bringing twenty-first-century sensibilities to bear analytically on attitudes, behaviour and experience from this period. Such history is always an exercise in empathetic understanding, close source exploration and carefully imaginative replication of footsteps, in this case through a hilly Welsh-named landscape that can be difficult to reconnoitre. However, Barry Godfrey and his co-workers drew upon modern surveys of court practices in their historical work on sentencing patterns,[37] a method of comparison shared by many other historians of justice, and similarly *Crime, Courts and Community in Mid-Victorian Wales* will at times make comparisons and contrasts with modern courts. As with much historical research, one worthwhile aim – among many others – is to place our modern concerns and practices into a historical perspective, to see how they have evolved, to judge them in the light of the past, and so to help explain why they changed.

Chapter 1 now follows, painting in the background of Montgomeryshire to illuminate the setting for subsequent investigations. We turn our attention to how the eastern and western sides of this most attractive county had differing characteristics, and to how the industrialised nature of the central Severn valley opened up different criminal opportunities compared to the agricultural, and poorer eastern side.

1

MONTGOMERYSHIRE

PEOPLE, PLACES AND OCCUPATIONS

The focus of this study is the county of Montgomeryshire. This chapter will set the scene for forthcoming investigations, describing the main features of this part of Wales, namely the land, industries and people. There will be a description of the topography and changes that occurred in the countryside as industrialisation took place in hitherto market towns. Demographic features including occupational status and sizes of labour forces will be noted, and the justice system seen by people in court will be interpreted.

THE COUNTY

Montgomeryshire is now part of the modern county of Powys, but before local government changes in 1974 it was a county in its own right. It was the largest county in north and mid-Wales, and the second largest in Wales as a whole (Figure 1.1). Flat land pushes into the hills in the north-east forming a gateway into the area, and the low-lying land that accompanies the rivers Banwy and Vyrnwy provides routes westwards. Another way into Montgomeryshire is also from the north-east, but this time following the valley of the river Severn in a south-westerly direction past Welshpool, Newtown and Llanidloes (Figure 1.2).

OCCUPATIONAL NATURE OF THE COUNTY

During the nineteenth century, the main industry in Montgomeryshire was agriculture, and approximately one-tenth of the produce of Wales came from the county. In the 1871 census, 11,004 persons aged over twenty years were of the agrarian class, which constituted a little over a quarter of that

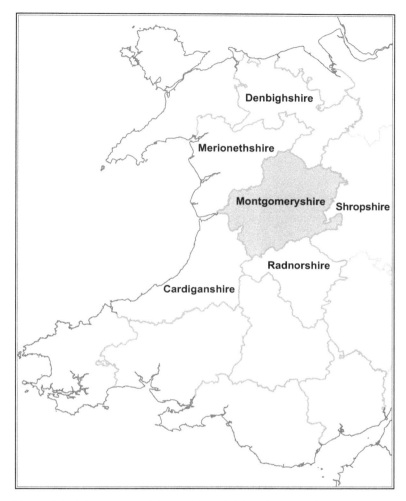

Figure 1.1 Montgomeryshire and its neighbouring counties.

age group.[1] In modern times, much of the western side of the county has been classified by the government as 'severely disadvantaged', being wetter and less fertile than the east.[2] The same situation existed during earlier periods as John Marius Wilson wrote in 1874:

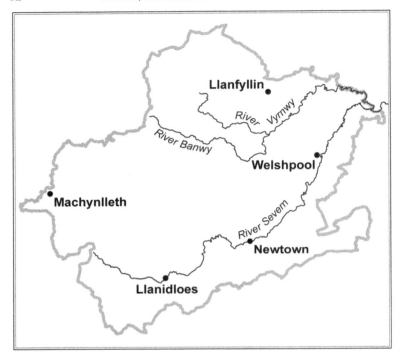

Figure 1.2 Montgomeryshire: the valleys of the Severn, Banwy and Vyrnwy.

The surface, in most of the east, to the mean breadth of about 5 miles, is a mixture of rich vale and pleasant hill, luxuriant, warm and low; but the surface, all elsewhere, is prevailingly mountainous, moorish, bleak and wild.[3]

He did concede, however, that many western hills were wooded and surrounded by vales that afforded unexpected fertility. The main crops were oats, wheat and barley, with the first of these being the most produced, although by 1870 land under the plough was decreasing as stock breeding increased. New varieties of sheep were trialled, and dairy shorthorn and Hereford cattle became popular.[4] Wilson wrote that about one-eighth of the land was arable, about one-third pasture and about half was common or waste. He observed a further disparity between the east and west:

Yet the farmhouses, in other parts than the east, are aggregately far from good – many of them timbered, and the cottages are very poor. The native cattle, a small, brindled short-legged breed, deep in the carcase, are kept on the inferior farms. The Devonshire and Herefordshire breeds abound on the best farms.[5]

Two examples of the well-off farmers in the east were widow Susan Powell of Buttington Hall, near Welshpool, and her neighbour William Beckerton. Both these farms were of over 300 acres and gave employment to a total of fifteen residential workers. The survival of this live-in form of labour was a feature of the county, a more traditional form of labour that had been lost in many English regions by this time.[6]

HEAVY INDUSTRY

Along with agriculture, manufacturing was present in the county, the chief business being the production of woollen items which had been ongoing since the middle ages.[7] Originally, the trade was a cottage industry, with all the preparatory processes carried out by hand, and only the final 'fulling', or washing, of the cloth being done at a fulling mill (*pandy* in Welsh).[8] It is said that in Montgomeryshire 'nearly every farm had its weaving contingent and rents were half made from the making of flannel'.[9] Daniel Defoe's account of his traverses through the county during the 1720s does not mention any factories:

> The River Severn is the only beauty of this county, which rising I say, out of the Plymlymon [sic] Mountains, receives instantly so many other rivers into its bosom, that it becomes navigable before it gets out of the county, namely at Welch Pool,[10] on the edge of Shropshire. This is a good fashionable place, and has many English dwelling in it, and some very good families, but we saw nothing further worth remarking. The vales and meadows upon the banks of the Severn are the best of this county, I had almost said, the only good part of it.[11]

Fifty years later, Thomas Pennant observed the effects of the flannel industry while on his tour of Wales:

Llanidloes, a small town, with a great market for yarn, which is manufactured here into fine flannels, and sent weekly, by wagonloads to Welshpool ... Welshpool, a good town, is seated in the bottom, not far from the castle [Powis Castle, seat of the Earl of Powis]. Great quantities of flannel, brought from the upper country, are sent from hence to Shrewsbury.[12]

The reference to Shrewsbury is very telling. The town had a monopoly on buying and selling Welsh cloth that began in Tudor times by an Act of 1565,[13] and by the eighteenth century Montgomeryshire producers were totally dependent on the Shropshire drapers – a reflection of the poverty of the mid-Wales countryside, where the quick sale of cloth for ready cash meant the difference between existence and starvation. As well as this, the drapers helped weavers to buy raw materials, in some cases buying yarn for them and paying only for the weaving. By the end of the eighteenth century, local drapers emerged and eclipsed the Shrewsbury traders. When the Revd J. Evans travelled in the area at the end of the eighteenth century, he observed of Newtown:

It contains several streets and is in a flourishing condition. An extensive manufactory of flannel is carried on in the town, and in the parts adjacent. This article is got up in a masterly manner and employs the numerous poor of the town and neighbourhood ... All the flannels here are the effect of manual labour: machinery has not found its way into north Wales.[14]

However, mechanisation did arrive, and investors in new machinery became powerful manufacturers.[15] In 1818 John Aitkin noted: 'Newton [sic] on the Severn, is the centre of a considerable woollen manufacture, especially of flannels of all qualities.'[16]

In 1871, about 22 per cent of the population aged over twenty years was involved in this industry, only a few percentage points less than agriculture.[17] The manufacturing heartland was along the Severn the towns of Llanidloes, Newtown and Welshpool, facilitated by the accessibility of the valley. Indeed, both the county's only canal and the railway line to Aberystwyth, were constructed along this route.[18] Of the three centres of production, Newtown was the

greatest, and was known as 'the Leeds of Wales' owing to the
success of its factories.[19] In 1833, Robert Parry wrote a ballad
extolling its success and the prosperity it brought:

> Oh what a blissful place! By Severn's banks so fair,
> Happy thine inhabitants, and wholesome is thine air.
> Nine years long since last I've seen thee fled,
> Ah! When departing my heart in grief has bled!
> Thy lasses fair, and thy young men as kind,
> Thy flannel fine and generous every mind,
> But now, 'tis now I wonder most,
> I see thy improvements; well can thy townsmen boast;
> To London great, in short by the canal,
> Thy flannel goes, as quick as one can tell,
> And thence from there the flannel's quickly hurled
> To every part of Britain and the world.
> Thy gaslight's bright, thy new built houses high,
> Thy factories lofts seem smiling on the sky.[20]

Although there had been a downturn in the industry's
prosperity after the 1830s, it was still a major employer in the
town at the beginning of the 1870s.[21] Investigation of the
1871 census show 300 woollen-cloth producers and 152
flannel manufacturers, and flannel workers living all around
the town.[22] There were pockets where the workers in these
trades lived, generally in those quarters containing yards,
sometimes known as shuts or courts. One of the main thor-
oughfares in Newtown was Park Street, and several yards were
concealed behind it with access via narrow passages. Ten of
these yards were investigated and 34 per cent of residents
worked in the woollen or flannel industries. Across the town
in a northerly direction was Russell Square, a small enclosed
area with thirty-four residents stating an occupation.
Eighty-eight per cent of them were flannel and wool workers.
West of Russell Square, on the far side of the main shopping
street was Kinsey Yard. Here 50 per cent were flannel and
wool workers. Many of these areas have been demolished,
but old photographs, maps and the remaining houses show
building types that expanded during the Industrial Revolution. Some contemporaries considered them to be a cause of
crime and vice, including close-packed, back-to-back, small

terraced houses.[23] The people of the Park Street yards had access to three wells and two pumps, and those living in Russell Square shared one well. Although the location of Kinsey Yard is not on any existing map, an idea about its whereabouts can be deduced from the census revealing that its residents had access to one pump. To the north of the town, across the river, lay Llanllwchaiarn and the industrial quarter known as Penygloddfa. Three yards were investigated here and it was found that 71 per cent of residents worked in the flannel or wool industries.

The flannel industry for which Newtown was famous also existed in Welshpool. A visitor to the town wrote in 1832 that it was: 'A large and populous town and the appearances of opulence are very predominant throughout the place perhaps owing to the trade in Welsh flannel which is carried on here to a very great extent.'[24]

During the first half of the nineteenth century, housing for the workers grew up in parts of the town formerly occupied by gardens. The prosperity of the industry did not last and Table 1.1 shows the change in numbers of flannel manufacturers and merchants featured in trade directories.[25] The demise of the industry in Welshpool has been attributed to strong competition by mills in Newtown and Llanidloes, although by the 1840s the industry was also failing in those towns.[26] Robson's *Directory of North Wales* (1840) gives 'the centrality of Newtown' as the reason for its superseding Welshpool.[27]

Severn Street lies to the south-west of Welshpool. During the prosperous years of the flannel industry, a mill was situated on the northern side of the road, and the adjacent Red Lion Passage was occupied mainly by mill workers. In 1851 there were 76 persons living in the passage and of the 37 people in employment, 27 had mill occupations. The mill

	1829	1850	1868
Flannel manufacturers	9	3	0
Flannel merchants	2	2	0

Table 1.1 Number of flannel manufacturers and merchants in Welshpool

brought in workers from outside the area: out of all 37 workers, only eight were Welshpool born and three of these eight were Welshpool-born offspring of incomers. Eight workers had been born outside the county. Looking at the census for 1871, the effects of the collapsed flannel industry are clear as the total population of this passage had fallen from 76 to 59 and the flannel workers had mainly gone. What happened to the former occupants of the passage? It has been possible to trace some of the 1851 residents through the censuses and other records. Spinner John Hodgekiss moved to nearby Berriew Street and lost his wife. By 1871 he was remarried to a Liverpool woman and working as a gardener. Abraham Thomas, a weaver originating from Radnorshire, moved with his family to work in the industry in Newtown. His eldest son continued living with the family but did not follow in his father's footsteps, but became a carpenter. Another Radnorshire-born weaver was John Hammond. By 1861 he, his wife and eldest son were working as handloom weavers in the Penygloddfa part of Newtown. Thomas Swancott gave up weaving, moved his family to Staffordshire and became a labourer. Evan Andrews, also a weaver, moved to Liverpool where by 1861 he was aged 63 and no longer working. Weaver Isaac Astley appeared in court in 1854, was convicted of larceny and received six months' imprisonment. Neither he nor his wife appear in any subsequent census. In 1851, twelve-year-old Mary Ann Gough had been a servant to her spinner aunt in Red Lion Passage, possibly looking after her baby cousin. Mary Ann had been born into a weaving family living on the other side of town and had at least seven siblings. By 1861, her mother Elizabeth had remarried and moved with some of her children, including Mary Ann, to Ladywell Street in Newtown. She was now a currier's wife with the surname Hetherington. Her new husband was not present on the night of the census, but living with the family was Mary Ann's cousin from Red Lion Passage, now aged eleven years. Mary Ann was aged twenty-two years, but no occupation was given for her.

A picture thus emerges of fluctuating employment, an unstable resident population and, possibly, significantly high levels of unemployment.[28] Local trade directories provide an indication of the work opportunities available across the county. Worrall's *Directory of North Wales* (1874) shows that the flannel industry was gone from Welshpool but still existed in Machynlleth on the western edge of Montgomeryshire.[29] As expected, the two most populous towns had the greatest business diversity. However, business people probably had to pay for entries, so the directories may not give an accurate account of contemporary commercial enterprise. These figures may be better regarded as an indicator of the numbers present.[30]

An element of squalor existed in the working-class areas of industrialised Newtown. Correspondence in *The Newtown and Welshpool Express* showed this, for example in a letter published on 23 February 1869:

> The bulk of the dwellings upon Penygloddfa are not drained at all … the sewer in Commercial Street intercepts rather than assists the natural drainage, it acts as a receptacle for a certain amount of decaying animal and vegetable matter as well as human excreta which cannot and does not run off during the greater portion of the year … emptying as it does beneath the windows of dwelling houses, grossly offensive to the senses of vision and smell of the whole town, is a disgrace to the civilisation of the times.[31]

Closer to the centre of town, near Kinsey Yard, there were two more sources of extreme insanitation which were discussed by Newtown Local Board:

> There is a nuisance on the way leading to the Wesleyan chapel, on the corner of Wesley Street. There is an ash pit, indeed, I may say a cesspool, of stagnant filth, continually lodged there. The parties empty slops, chamberware, ashes and all other refuse, and this on the road leading to a public place of worship, and it is continually complained of. There is another nuisance question which has occupied my attention for the last few days. It is in respect to the emptying of privies into the public drains in different parts of the town. I am of the opinion that the drains were never meant for such a purpose.

We have Mr Davies pointing out to us the terrible state the drains are in … It is worthy of consideration of the Board to say whether they are not disposed to issue an order to prevent the issue of such a quantity of night soil from their petties into the drains where there is not a sufficient supply of water to carry it away … It will be some time before the evil which exists will be removed. I believe in some parts of town the drains are nearly choked up.[32]

The Park Street area began to be developed early in the nineteenth century and the accommodation was described as 'little more than hovels'. The properties were often tiny, back-to-back, two-roomed houses (one up, one down), sometimes with weaving rooms above.[33] Picton's Row, for example, off Park Street, no longer exists but measurements and calculations made from the 1902 1-inch Ordnance Survey map show that the rooms in the houses were about 10 feet square, as in some parts of East End London. Lying parallel to Park Street and connected to it by Picton's Row, was Ladywell Street. In 1874, the town's medical officer sent a report to the local board which said:

> Since my last report, eight cases of scarlet fever have to my knowledge occurred within the district – three in Ladywell Street, three in Albion Yard [off Park Street], and two in the High Street. Of these, two have proved fatal. When I visited the houses in Ladywell Street and Albion Yard I found that in two instances the inmates were sleeping in the room with the dead body waiting burial. In one case a woman dying of pulmonary consumption and a boy ill with scarlet fever were lying near the corpse.[34]

Thus, in some respects the conditions in Newtown resembled those in the larger towns and cities. Another indicator of deprivation seen commonly in working-class areas of towns and cities was the pawnshop, where personal items could be exchanged for small quantities of cash. An advertisement for such an establishment appeared in *The Newtown and Welshpool Express* in 1871. The proprietor's name was Cornelius Owen, a licensed pawnbroker who would advance money on any type of goods including wearing apparel, gold and silver, and

watches. Several traders, not pawnbrokers as such, put advertisements into the newspaper offering payment for 'any sort
of goods'. Newtown was the only town showing a pawnbroker
in Worrall's *Directory* of 1874. In nineteenth-century east
London, there was a large trade in second-hand goods, and
such an outlet was a common way of fencing stolen goods,
with some people making a living out of stealing clothes.[35] In
Newtown, a Mrs Hibbott trading in Old Church Street, which
was just around the corner from Russell Square, put a prominent note in her advertisement 'Secrecy strictly guaranteed'.
Was this to reassure potential clients that they would not be
humiliated by their dire need, or because she knew that some
goods would have been stolen?

The picture of deprivation did not extend to all parts of
the town. To the west of Penygloddfa lies Milford Road which
was, and still is, a leafy and desirable area. It was described by
J. B. Willans in 1905 as 'one of the prettiest roads leading out
of the town.[36] It leads to a fulling mill known as Milford
Factory, built by a wealthy London wholesale draper.[37] A
magistrate, a supervisor of Inland Revenue and a large
proportion of domestic servants lived on this thoroughfare –
23 per cent compared to 2 per cent in the Park Street yards.
The magistrate's name was Major John Drew, and he will
feature prominently in forthcoming chapters. Squalor also
existed in Welshpool at the time when the flannel industry
was strong, as suggested by the seventy-six persons in narrow
Red Lion Passage. *The Newtown and Welshpool Express,* however,
as in the reports of the local health board, shows central
Newtown as being on its own in Montgomeryshire in terms of
deprivation in the 1870s.

INCOMERS

Nineteenth-century economic migration is extremely well
documented.[38] As Newtown boomed during the first half of
the century, people moved in from other areas, as is clear
from the census. Analysis of population data from 1871
produces interesting results. The areas of Penygloddfa and
Russell Square, where there was a high percentage of wool
and flannel workers, shows that around 90 per cent of heads

of households were Montgomeryshire-born. By comparison, in the retail area of Broad Street, middle-class Milford and multi-occupation Park Street, the figure was around 72 per cent. This shows that non-flannel occupations were attracting more people from outside the county than the textile districts, pointing to class and occupational differentials affecting migration.[39]

The origins of people in Newtown were very much like Machynlleth, on the western side of the county, and Montgomery in the east. The origins of heads of households in arbitrarily chosen streets in the centres of these towns were investigated. In all three towns they were overwhelmingly locally born, with the figures for Newtown being virtually the same as for non-factory Montgomery. In Machynlleth, six persons born outside Wales were the Marquess of Londonderry's Scottish-born gardener and his family, and they did not stay in Wales. By the time of the 1881 census, they had all dispersed to locations throughout England, perhaps reacting to living among a Welsh population where their dialectal difference was conspicuous. Welshpool also received migrants, as a study of randomly chosen areas shows. For example, near the centre of town lay Red Lion Passage. Nineteen persons occupied the passage in 1871, seven of whom were Welshpool-born, with not one born outside the county. Severn Street itself was a generally middle-class area with most of the houses built for prosperous men. The residents of the street included a magistrate, a solicitor, an auctioneer and two army officers' widows. On the other side of town from Severn Street was an area noted for the presence of a watercourse known as the Lledan brook. A leat drawn from it powered a corn mill, and near to the mill was a row of fifteen back-to-back cottages known as Mill Place. In 1871 all the properties were occupied. The miller and his family lived there along with ten other households. These households included skilled tradespeople such as a watchmaker and shoemaker, and only a very small proportion of unskilled workers. Most of the heads of household were incomers, and several came from a significant distance away. The miller originated in northern Montgomeryshire, about 10 miles away from Welshpool and his wife came from Oswestry. The watchmaker, who had come to Welshpool from Liverpool, was clearly an itinerant, as the 1861 census shows him living in the Lake District, and in 1881 he was living in Lancashire with children born in Kendal and Birmingham. Near to Mill Place was an armoury, home to the Montgomeryshire militia. The effect of this establishment is clear from the occupations and places of origin of its residents, namely seven sergeants and their wives and children, with only some children and one sergeant being born locally. All the others were born in disparate parts of the British Isles, including Ireland. The wife of the locally born sergeant was Irish, and his daughter was born in the West Indies. In 1861, the armoury had been even more cosmopolitan with residents' origins including America, and in the 1850s the area was known as 'Ireland'.[40] This analysis shows that, as in Newtown, non-flannel industries attracted immigrants from outside the county.

THE MIDDLE AND UPPER CLASSES

The trade directories include lists of each town's resident gentry or so-called 'private residents'. For example, Worrall's *Directory* of 1874 lists sixty-five of these householders in Machynlleth, including the Marquess of Londonderry. In Welshpool, there were nearly one hundred nobility, gentry and clergy, and it has been possible to trace some of them through the censuses. Charlotte Clive was living in Elmshurst on the edge of Powis Castle Park, one of the houses Defoe spoke of approvingly. From her name and place of birth it appears that she was related closely to the Earl of Powis, who was a descendant of the first Lord Clive. She remained unmarried throughout her life and lived much of it in Welshpool with a retinue of servants. In 1841, two of her near neighbours were builder John Baggaley and his wife Martha. John Baggaley was dead by 1851, but on the census Martha describes herself as master builder's widow, and was living in a large house named Dolanag, adjacent to Charlotte Clive's house. William Yearsley spent his childhood in Severn Street. He was the son of a solicitor and became a lawyer himself. He was living with his widowed mother in 1861 but by 1871 was living in the plush Golfa area, neighbour to a baronet's widow.

Newtown had over a hundred private residents listed, and Llanidloes had forty-two. Montgomery, perhaps the most genteel of the towns, with its elegant Georgian architecture and absence of heavy industry, featured seventy-one, including the Earl again, as he owned a property in that town too. Investigation of names around the county shows that many were the new rich, including those who had made fortunes in industry elsewhere and had come to live in Montgomeryshire. Among these were Lancashire-born John Dugdale, a former calico printer now living in Llanfyllin, and William Fisher, a Liverpool druggist now with a smart mansion near Welshpool. It is clear that a man would know he had arrived in society when he achieved a listing in the directory, and there is a sense of the so-called *arrivistés* who 'renewed the gentry class' as one old family left and another took its place.[41] An indication of the aspiring middle classes was the existence of private schools. In Welshpool there was a tone of professionalism created by a commercial academy held in the High Street, and a commercial and collegiate school further along the road. Both produced impressive advertisements advocating their quality and the successes of their students. The advertisements give an insight into the curricula offered. Older boys were offered studies in scripture, reading, arithmetic, geography and bookkeeping, and could be prepared for university entrance and civil service examinations. French and Latin were offered at an additional cost. The Misses Oakley and Hodges boarded three young boys with four older girls, in a school established in her coal-dealer father's house. One of the children had a distinctive name that can be traced easily: Edward E. W. Ebrall, the son of a Shrewsbury gunsmith. Miss Oakley herself was well educated, having attended a boarding school in Shrewsbury in her teens, and her school in Welshpool went on to thrive, still running into the 1880s. The same array of private educational enterprise was found in all the Montgomeryshire borough towns, and the provision of private education attracted at least five school proprietors who were non-natives of the county. Their origins included Shropshire, Derbyshire, Warwickshire and Oxford. Boarding pupils arrived not only from Great Britain but also from many parts of the world including Switzerland and the USA.[42]

OUTSIDE THE BOROUGH TOWNS

The urban areas of the county have been highlighted. A comparative settlement is Berriew, located between Newtown and Welshpool, which shows both rural, industrial and commercial features. The village is five miles south-west of Welshpool at the confluence of the rivers Severn and Rhiw, and is a preserved, pre-industrial village.[43] The church of St Beuno is early nineteenth century, built on the site of a much earlier church and the village has several examples of timber-framed cottages. There are also medieval farmhouses situated around the wider parish and four drinking establishments, which are all very old. As Berriew village is small, the nearby hamlets of Garthmyl and Efail Fach were also included. In future discussions, 'Berriew' will mean the three localities together.

Berriew was originally a land of strip cultivation, waste and commons but at the end of the eighteenth century, under pressure from landholders, it began to be enclosed.[44] The lord of the manor was the Earl of Powis, and other major landholders were the Winder family of Vaynor Hall, Arthur Owen of Glansevern and the trustees of a school charity. A parliamentary Act of 1796 enabled the enclosure of most of Berriew, and an Act of 1801 enclosed the remainder. The earlier Act gave a measure of protection to squatters but none was provided in Berriew in 1801. The Earl was given 174 acres as compensation for his loss of rights, and several owners took the opportunity of transferring sections of land to consolidate holdings. Common land in certain areas on either side of the river Rhiw was shared, meaning that persons living in one area had rights in another.[45] The new gentry, with their purchasing of small estates, and the enclosure Acts which consolidated private, enclosed parcels of ground, suggest that poaching may have become a serious issue in areas such as Berriew. Poaching can be a good index of social tension, sometimes being revenge attacks or demonstrations against poor-law provision, evictions and enclosure of common land. Sometimes enclosure awards, which gave proprietors a monopoly of game and fishing rights, were often bitterly resented.[46] The issue will be discussed further in forthcoming chapters.

INDUSTRY AND INCOMERS TO BERRIEW

There were four mills within a short distance of the village, and study of the 1841 census shows that there was a flannel industry with a wool spinner and two weavers. The village was once thriving: the 1861 census shows people moved in from all over the country including Scotland. The presence in 1861 of eight carpenters and joiners, a brick maker, two plumbers, a timber merchant, a lath cleaver (splitter of timber), an architect, a mason and a plasterer shows that Berriew was growing, and although in 1861 there were only 315 residents, the village merited a policeman. A notable feature in the statistics is the huge rise in labourers by 1871. The number had jumped by 400 per cent, suggesting plenty of available work. The result of the building work was obvious because by 1871 the population had risen to 396, a rise of over a quarter. Some of the farms listed on the 1871 census were new; others were restored, previously unoccupied ones.[47] The building work, however, appears to have largely stopped by the early 1870s as the group of workers involved in the building trade now consisted of four carpenters only. As well as the loss of builders, the number of different occupations overall had fallen by over 50 per cent, from 56 to 24. The proportion of people aged under siteen years stayed virtually the same: 35 per cent in 1871 compared to 37 per cent in 1861. Six people had arrived in Berriew from Welshpool; two of these were small children, two were women who had married relatively prosperous men, viz. a maltster and a farmer, one was a labourer and the other gave no occupation but was living on her grandparents' small farm. Analysis indicates clearly how Montgomeryshire-born persons dominated the social mix, with a small representation of incomers. A picture thus emerges of locally born farmers maintaining and cultivating land rented from wealthy landlords, with scattered properties largely occupied by Montgomeryshire people, with a few incomers who were often labourers.

IMPLICATIONS FOR THE WELSH LANGUAGE IN THE COUNTY[48]

At the time of Defoe's visit to Montgomeryshire in the 1720s, a sizeable proportion of the local population spoke Welsh as their first language. Returns from parish clergy in the following century showed that Welsh, English and bilingualism were all represented, although there were clear-cut parts of the county where each predominated.[49] Parishes in the north and west were virtually monoglot Welsh; eastern communities within the flood plain of the Severn were almost completely English, and a narrow 'transition zone', or bilingual zone, lay between.[50] Newtown contained many English, and the 1847 education reports, denounced by many as being Anglo-centric and ignorant, confirmed the overwhelming Welshness of western districts, and the considerable presence of English in the east at that time.[51] In 1824 printer Jackson Salter produced the rules for Newtown Welsh Society showing that there was representation of the language in the town, although the formation of the society means that Welsh was not the norm.[52] At the time of change from Welsh predominance to English, the manufacturing centre along the Severn valley had emerged. The transport routes identified earlier served as a language route also, with English entering the county. Direct contact with Shropshire influenced English characteristics of eastern Montgomeryshire, but it was noted in 1882 that if 'constant migration of Welsh-speaking people from the hill country [in] the north into the more fertile valley land' had not occurred, 'the Welsh language would have died out much faster'.[53] The earlier town analyses confirm that a small number of people from the Welsh heartlands of the west and north were resident in Montgomeryshire, but a language survey showed that by 1871 in eastern Montgomeryshire, only 4.4 per cent of the population spoke Welsh either mono- or bilingually.[54] A private school with a boarding department was founded in Llanidloes in 1877 with a distinct Welsh ethos. Its proprietor was Hugh Jerman – noted artist, musician and winner of a prestigious prize at a national eisteddfod.[55] Jerman advertised his school in Welsh-language newspapers published in north Wales, and promoted his eisteddfod success.[56] The school brought in Welsh-speakers from the north, and in Llanidloes there was a sizeable Welsh-speaking middle class. This affected the workings of the courts in Llanidloes, where many magistrates were Welsh-speakers. In the higher courts, too, when juries included men from the Llanidloes area, verdicts could reflect Welshness. More will be said on these aspects of the justice system in later chapters.

Anglicanism was bolstered in Wales by the translation of the Bible into Welsh in the sixteenth century. In Montgomeryshire, later diversion of tithes to north Wales and England, and victimisation of Dissenters caused deep divisions between the established Church of England and those who would not conform.[58] These rifts became deeper during the eighteenth century when absentee clerics allowed Dissenters to gain a foothold in previously loyal Church of England areas.[59] By the 1850s, they often outnumbered members of the established Church by four or five to one, being particularly strong in industrial areas, and the characteristics of their beliefs coloured modern Welsh history.[60] Nonconformists, by the mid-nineteenth century, were part of mainstream Welsh life.[61] Their chapels became widespread, and the 1850s–60s was a critical period which launched a new wave of Nonconformist building.[62] By the period of study here, these buildings were scattered liberally across the county. The large parish of Llangurig, for example, contained one church and seven Nonconformist chapels.[63] Religion contributed to education in the form of Sunday schools, and by mid-century over 250 of these existed in the county, of which 90 per cent were run by Nonconformists, providing teaching mainly in Welsh.[64] Many Anglican clerics were Welsh-speakers too. For example, among members of the committee of the Newtown Welsh Society were the vicar of Kerry and the rector of Manafon.[65] Well into the nineteenth century, Anglican services were often in Welsh because many worshippers could not understand any other language.[66] From Tudor times a bishop could refuse to institute a clergyman in a parish where the common language was Welsh if the candidate could not speak the language.[67] About 30 per cent of clergy in the Established Church were from a Nonconformist background but had taken orders with the Church of England because of its stipendiary posts.[68] Nevertheless, Anglican clergy were sometimes wealthy English-speaking landowners, and occasionally related to aristocratic families, as for example the Reverend R. J. Harrison who was related to Viscount Hereford, and Canon John Herbert, who inherited his mansion on the edge of Newtown from his mother.[69] As early as 1795, parishioners in the village of Bettws Cedewain near Newtown (part of Lord Sudeley's Gregynog estate) had to attend services in English because of the appointment of an English-speaking curate.[70] The English bishops of the two dioceses, which controlled most of Montgomeryshire, also sometimes appointed their English relatives and friends to benefices.[71] This contributed to the idea of some that the Church of England in Wales was in a privileged position propped up by English property owners.[72] It was proposed in a House of Commons debate in 1869 that 'there never was such a time in the history of the country when the upper classes and the Church of England were so unpopular in Wales'.[73] This debate came one year after the Conservatives had been defeated in a general election and two years after the second Reform Act, which gave the vote to many lower middle-class and working-class men. Conservatives were seen to be supporting the Crown and Anglican Church, while Liberals often endorsed Nonconformity, religious tolerance and electoral reform. Two active politicians in Montgomeryshire were Charles Hanbury-Tracy (later Lord Sudeley) and the Earl of Powis. They were Liberal and Conservative respectively, and such men often encouraged their tenants to support their respective allegiances.[74] Hanbury-Tracy had been one of the so-called 'Adullamites' who had voted against his own party's Reform Bill in 1866,[75] a decision which returned to haunt him in due course and helps explain why, in the following decade, he actively courted the new breed of voting tenants by building Nonconformist chapels and better housing.[76] There were implications for the courtroom too. It is worth noting here that both these aristocratic men had major roles on the Bench, being lord lieutenant and chairman respectively, and many of their tenants were eligible for jury service.

In an overwhelmingly Protestant county, there was one element of Roman Catholicism. This was in Welshpool where, possibly due to Irish militiamen, railway building and emigration from the famine in Ireland, a church was established in the town by the 1850s and listed in Worrall's *Directory* of 1874.[77] The number of adherents at this church was only twenty according to the religious census of 1851.[78] At this time, Irish immigrants in Wales were on the margins of 'respectability' owing to their Catholicism. The Irish were believed to inhabit the worst areas of towns, such parts often gaining the epithet 'Little Ireland', and there was a part of Welshpool known as 'Ireland'. As well as this, people, including some Protestant clergymen, blamed the Irish for the poor findings of the compilers of the 1847 education reports.[79] Specific trouble had occurred in the early 1860s in southern Montgomeryshire when rioting broke out because Welsh railway navvies were losing their jobs to Irish who accepted lower wages.[80] Thus there were, in 1870s Welshpool and the wider county, inevitably strong anti-Irish tensions and incidents.[81]

CONCLUSION

Until the last quarter of the eighteenth century, Montgomeryshire had been an agricultural county with flannel making carried on only as a cottage industry, or as a supplement to a farming income. The nature of the county changed to an extent as the flannel industry became factory-based along the Severn valley. In linguistic terms, a division that had existed since earlier times with Welsh in the west and English in the east became more pronounced. Court users will have heard Welsh spoken around them, but in eastern courtrooms the majority will have been using English. There was a rich mixture of accents as Montgomeryshire residents originated from a wide range of geographical locations. The county population was a mix of agricultural and factory workers with others including shop workers and labourers, washerwomen, clerks and artisans. The proportion of the upper orders in the community was small and few of this class will have been seen in court apart from those on the Bench. Some of the justices will have been bilingual and had roles within the Established Church of England.

There was poverty and squalor in many urban quarters, with contrasting architecture in middle- and upper-class locations. In the farming community, too, division existed between well-off farmers and poorer ones, and further divides between farmers and their servants. There was agricultural prosperity in the east, although a comfortable living could be found on some western farms.

The following chapter investigates the men most often seen handing out justice in the community, namely the magistrates and the police

2

THE LEGAL SYSTEM

MEN, MOTIVATION AND STATUS

An investigation now begins into the courts and the system of law enforcement that existed during the period under study. There is an exploration of the nature of the county Bench of magistrates and how far they conformed to the countrywide pattern of appointment. There will be consideration of whether their social position and daily lives had a bearing on their judgements in court. The work of policemen will be examined and, for both magistrates and police, an exploration of possible motivations for their execution of duty will be made. Finally, a survey of the justice system as seen in the landscape, in the form of infrastructure, will be undertaken.

THE COURTS OF PETTY AND QUARTER SESSIONS

The courts have been described as the 'heart of the criminal justice system',[1] and were the public face of the laws of the land.[2] Petty and quarter sessions dealt with most criminal matters, presided over by magistrates who were drawn from the community.[3] These men owned property worth at least £100 per annum, and therefore were not representative of the general public.[4] As well as administering justice, quarter sessions constituted a form of local government, with responsibility for, among other things, administering the poor law and maintenance of bridges and roads.[5]

THE MONTGOMERYSHIRE BENCH IN THE 1870s

From examination of newspaper reports of sessions and justices' qualification rolls,[6] seventy-two magistrates on the Commission during the 1870s were found, and their backgrounds explored through the censuses.[7] The men were mainly from the landowning class and the Anglican clergy.[8] However, the steady curtailment of the upper class's monopoly on wealth, education and widely travelled experience is seen,[9] as a small number of those on the Bench had paid employment, viz. three surgeons (one of whom had noble connections), two lawyers and a wine merchant. Six had been army officers.[10] Several of the magistrates were on the Bench by way of ownership of land in Montgomeryshire although they resided in other counties.[11] One of these out-of-county justices had been MP for a Shropshire constituency but lost his seat in 1868, and one was MP for Peterborough. One was a Chester industrialist, and one – a clergyman normally resident in Staffordshire – had inherited land from an industrialist relative.[12] Six of the justices lived solely on an income from land (other than by being farmers),[13] and several did not have an identified source of income. A number were involved with the Montgomeryshire militia. The list includes five members of the aristocracy who took their positions on the Bench only at quarter sessions. The justices could sometimes be found on holiday, visiting out of county or receiving visitors. It was common for their sons to receive a university education and to enter the professions, and for their wives and daughters to have ladies' maids. Most of the justices ended their days retired and living on annuities and many of their surviving residences are now listed buildings and feature in *The Buildings of Wales* series.[14] This description of the county Bench, with fewer than a hundred men from the nobility, landowning and new-gentry classes, sitting in judgement on a population of some 68,000,[15] reinforces the idea of a mutual interest in the preservation of rule by men of influence and high local standing.[16] It paints a picture of a deferential community with the 'rude classes' at the bottom.[17] This picture is one that will be examined in forthcoming chapters.[18]

HIERARCHIES

The 'rude classes' may well have regarded any man on the Bench as upper class,[19] but among the magistrates there were divisions. The most obvious of these was between county and borough justices. Most of the Welshpool magistrates for example – who were on the Bench as elected members of the town corporation and not necessarily occupiers of £100 estates – lived in town houses with gardens, not country piles.[20] They might employ a live-in maid, but there would be no butler, lady's maid or coachman; and whereas a landed gentleman relied on income from his tenants and from investments,[21] mayor and surgeon Thomas Barrett was reliant on the patients who paid his fees, and merchant Griffith Parker on the customers who bought his wine. Pointedly, these men worked for their livings, and were the sort of men from whom the old gentry expected deference, not a seat at a shared table.[22] In borough towns, the mayor and immediate ex-mayor were *ex-officio* magistrates. This led to conflicts of interest but, as a protracted case of encroachment in Welshpool shows, neither members of the town corporation nor the magistrates were in each other's pockets. These borough magistrates were justices who supported themselves from earnings, and the encroachment case shows that fellow traders and ratepayers afforded the magistrates no more respect than they would other tradesmen living in town. Samuel Powell was the proprietor of a flourishing currying and leather business near the centre of Welshpool. Some new buildings that he had put up were extending too far onto the pavement. The matter was discussed at Local Board meetings, headed by fellow magistrate and chairman of the Bench in his capacity as mayor, surgeon Edward Harrison. Powell put his side across determinedly in a letter to the clerk of the Board:

> In reply to your communication from the Local Board with a copy of two resolutions passed at their last meeting, I have to state I do not recognize the authority of the Board to interfere with any erection of mine upon private property. As regards the surface water, I do not consider myself liable to convey the same into the sewer at the direction of the Board.
>
> S. Powell.[23]

The last report on this business appeared in the newspaper at the end of March, and the affair petered out as Powell agreed to address the problem.[24] Powell was answerable to his fellow townsmen, unlike John Winder at the Vaynor Estate who brought forward the wall of his mansion by several feet without any outside interference,[25] or Lord Sudeley who extended the mansion at Gregynog to suit his own wishes.[26] Powell, like all people inhabiting town houses, had to abide by the provisions of the 1835 Highways Act, which allowed urban authorities to fine a person for bringing forward the frontage of a house or for not providing adequate sewerage.[27] The borough magistrates' activities had a visibility that was not suffered by the landed gentry on their estates, and were bound in a way that the country gentlemen were not. Forthcoming investigations of court cases show that being accustomed to doing as they pleased affected old-gentry magistrates' behaviour on the Bench.

THE COUNTY BENCH AT QUARTER ESSIONS

The Bench, once restricted to the greater county gentry, was by the middle of the nineteenth century, displaying the mix of lesser gentry, clergy and working justices described earlier. Near the end of the previous century, average attendance per session was 4.4; six or seven justices were regular attendees and another six attended once a year.[28] Now the total number of justices in attendance on day one at the first sessions of 1869 was fifteen, including the Earl of Powis and Sir Charles Watkin Williams- Wynn, who were chairman and deputy chairman respectively. Criminal proceedings began at 10 a.m. on day two, and the previous century's trend of reduced numbers of magistrates is visible: seven of the previous day's attendees did not show, although three new faces appeared. Overall, the number was down by four to only 17 per cent of the total number of justices at that time. Study of the composition of the Bench across the decade shows several regular and frequent attendees at quarter sessions – Capt. Crewe-Reade, Arthur Humphreys Owen, Capt. Mytton, John Bayard and Richard Woosnam for example. The same men were consistent petty sessions attendees. The Earl of Powis, as chairman of the Bench, was also a frequent attendee at quarter sessions, but often only on day one, and rarely during the summer months.[29] Some of the Anglican clergy magistrates were reliable in their attendance,[30] but there may have been a feeling of discrimination among the general population as to the absence of Nonconformist ministers on the Bench. Religious dissent was the first major challenge to established authority, and was a factor in the Rebecca uprisings a generation earlier.[31] People will have remembered the fiasco of 1838 when the magistrates of Bala in neighbouring Denbighshire refused to sit with a former shopkeeper and Methodist who had been appointed to the Bench.[32] However, many of these dissenting men did not fulfil the property requirements required for being on the Bench, and many did not want to be associated with the legal system, as there was a long history of Dissenters being tried and sent to prison.[33] Discussions regarding eligibility criteria and the nature of representation inevitably raised issues about religious diversity on decision-making bodies. Such debates were common in Wales during this period, and may have arisen over the magistracy. George Hammond Whalley, one of the Montgomeryshire Bench, was a staunch anti-Catholic and, as MP for Peterborough, made tirades against members of the Roman Catholic church, particularly against the Pope.[34]

ATTENDANCE AT SESSIONS

Travel to sessions was problematic for magistrates living a distance from the court.[35] At the Hilary sessions in 1869,[36] Major John Pryce, on behalf of Earl Vane who was not present, requested that the timing of the first day be changed. The Earl was to become the fifth Marquess of Londonderry and his wife's family owned Plas Machynlleth at the western extremity of the county, where the couple lived. His message was that travel from the far reaches of the county was too lengthy and meant that those magistrates did not arrive back home until the evening.[37] The chairman of sessions, the Earl of Powis, objected at length to any idea of change, but nevertheless the timing of some matters was altered to be more accommodating. At the midsummer sessions of 1869, Vane again sent a representative, magistrate Charles Thruston, to ask that a new meeting place for justices to be erected in

Machynlleth.[38] Vane eventually attended sessions in October 1870, twenty months after court timings were changed at his request.[39] The change of timings seems hardly to have improved attendance: magistrates from the Llanidloes area in particular are noticeable by their absence.[40] Some magistrates were living miles away from their Montgomeryshire houses or away on holiday. Hunting also occupied their time during winter months,[41] but despite the attractions of the sporting field, attendance at Michaelmas and Hilary quarter sessions was higher than at other times. Attendance levels could increase when there were political anxieties or worries about law and order,[42] and it was during the winter months that poaching offences were most likely to occur, as well as burglaries and assaults under the cover of darkness. This helps to explain the increased attendance at this time. A few of the magistrates also sat on the Shropshire Bench because of their ownership of property in that county, giving them more opportunities of being seen with the nobility, as the Earl of Bradford sat regularly in Shrewsbury.[43]

When residences of justices are traced, most of them follow the line of the river Severn. Large parts of the county, particularly the centre and north, were poorly served by resident magistrates. The same situation existed in Anglesey in north Wales and restricted the justice available to people living in those areas as there was less opportunity for individuals or policemen to apply for warrants.[44] A key feature of total magisterial attendances at the Montgomeryshire quarter sessions across the decade is that the number rose from around seventy-five during the first few years to over one hundred, an increase of about 30 per cent, in 1873. The figure dropped back subsequently. The reason for the sudden improvement in attendance in 1873 is unclear, but it is possible that a directive had been issued, perhaps by the Lord Chancellor, or Lord Sudeley as lord lieutenant, or the Earl of Powys as chairman of the Bench, to increase attendance.[45]

OTHER COUNTY POSITIONS

The most prestigious role was that of lord lieutenant, the first Montgomeryshire lieutenant being appointed in 1761.[46] The lord lieutenant was the sovereign's representative in the county, and played a significant role in the legal system, suggesting persons for the Bench, and appointing the clerk to the quarter sessions.[47] A list of names of those lieutenants who served during the nineteenth century has the appearance of a 'closed shop', accessible only to the aristocracy. It was also a 'job for life'.[48] It is notable that the former industrialist, the first Baron Sudeley, was eligible for this role only after he changed class by being raised to the peerage.[49] Another prestigious role in the county was that of high sheriff, not least because of the large amount of ceremony associated with it. The man appointed also had the task of selecting jury members. It was a Crown appointment but did not have the same degree of exclusivity as the lord lieutenant and was more accessible to the new gentry.[50] The censuses from this period show that the men who served as sheriff all occupied substantial properties and kept several servants. A few employed a live-in coachman or groom, and none of them was a town-based, borough magistrate. Several were, or formerly were, in trade, however. It has been said that the office of high sheriff was only really attractive to the relative newcomers of landed society, who saw it as the first step towards social and political acceptance.[51]

The man selected as high sheriff was most visible when the assizes were held, as his duties included receiving the judge, accompanying him to the pre-assize church service, and sitting with him during proceedings. The whole event was meant to be impressive.[52] One of the requirements of the role was to deliver the judge to his lodgings and to court in his own coach. This, therefore, meant that the position of high sheriff was restricted to those men who kept such a vehicle. The job of under-sheriff carried with it similar pomp. This man was charged with the administrative tasks necessary for the assizes, and court reports show that during the 1870s the appointee was county coroner Robert Harrison, and later his son, solicitor George Harrison. So, a member of the new-gentry class knew that he would never be the lieutenant but he might become the sheriff, providing he occupied a country house and owned a coach.[53] Without a coach he may have become under-sheriff. There were three quarter session committees that met four times per year and provided reports to the court prior to the criminal cases being heard. These were the constabulary, finance and prison-visiting committees, and a small number of justices sat on each. Study of the proceedings of the groups shows that it was the same handful of men every time.[54]

PETTY SESSIONS BENCHES

Counties were divided into petty sessional divisions, with justices assigned to particular divisions. However, when court cases were reported in the local newspaper, they were usually given the name of the largest settlement in the area.[55] The courts were usually held at a regular time and place, with generally two magistrates in attendance, and could be in a justice's own home. Occasionally, so-called 'special sessions' could be convened when an out-of-the-ordinary offence had occurred.[56] There were also the 'police courts' at which police officers prosecuted the cases.[57] First appearing in the fifteenth century, their growing existence reflected the increase in local business and appreciation by central government of the importance of local knowledge.[58] During Tudor times they had been notable for dealing with vagrancy,[59] and the association of petty sessions with the 'lower sorts' still existed as the courts dealt with lesser offences such as drunkenness, low-value thefts and trespass.[60] The cases appearing at Montgomeryshire petty sessions were often those involving tramps, labourers, apprentices, farmers, shopkeepers and craftsmen, often drunk and often having been in fights. Magistrates here also heard cases that were dealt with ultimately at quarter sessions or assizes as they conducted preliminary hearings in felony cases and decided whether the accused should be released, dealt with informally, imprisoned for further examination, bailed or committed to gaol to await jury trial in the major courts.[61]

BACKGROUNDS OF PETTY JUSTICES

The petty sessional Benches at Newtown and Welshpool were dominated by the new gentry. All but two of these men were frequent petty sessions attenders as well as being quarter sessions stalwarts.[62] The aristocratic justices, Lords Powis, Vane and Sudeley, and baronet Sir Watkin Williams-Wynn, never sat in the summary courts. Most of non-aristocratic magistrates lived and worked among ordinary, working people at some points during their lives. Particularly noticeable is that the borough magistrates of Welshpool mostly lived in the centre of town where they daily encountered the sorts of people who appeared before them in court, and where they would have been aware of street disturbances. Whereas an aristocratic justice could issue a warrant for serving on a tenant he had never seen, the borough magistrate would often sign warrants for serving on regular customers. Town-based justices with these backgrounds were in a better position to judge the cases in court, but others on the Bench would have considered them vulgar. Living in close proximity to many defendants and witnesses would leave the court proceedings open to accusations of unfairness, as in a Glamorganshire case where an ironmaster magistrate was said to have used the law to subjugate his employees.[63] It is noticeable that many of the members of the Montgomeryshire Bench never attended court, either petty or quarter sessions. One wonders why they joined. One possibility is that membership of the Bench provided themselves and family members with access to social occasions, which helped to further business interests, or to find marriage suitors for their daughters. The social capital possessed by an individual depended on the network of connections he could effectively mobilise and on the economic, social and symbolic capital possessed by the other members of his network.[64] This analysis illuminates the magisterial networks and conduct. A hierarchy existed in the magistracy, and men were marked out by their places of abode, title, source of income and family connections. A model can be made for the Bench which shows the social strata within the Bench. (Figure 2.1). Movement between strata was possible by marriage, knighthood or elevation to the peerage.[65] Using this model, the different layers within the Bench are obvious, and particularly remarkable is the differentiation between men at the extreme ends. Patronage was viewed as an

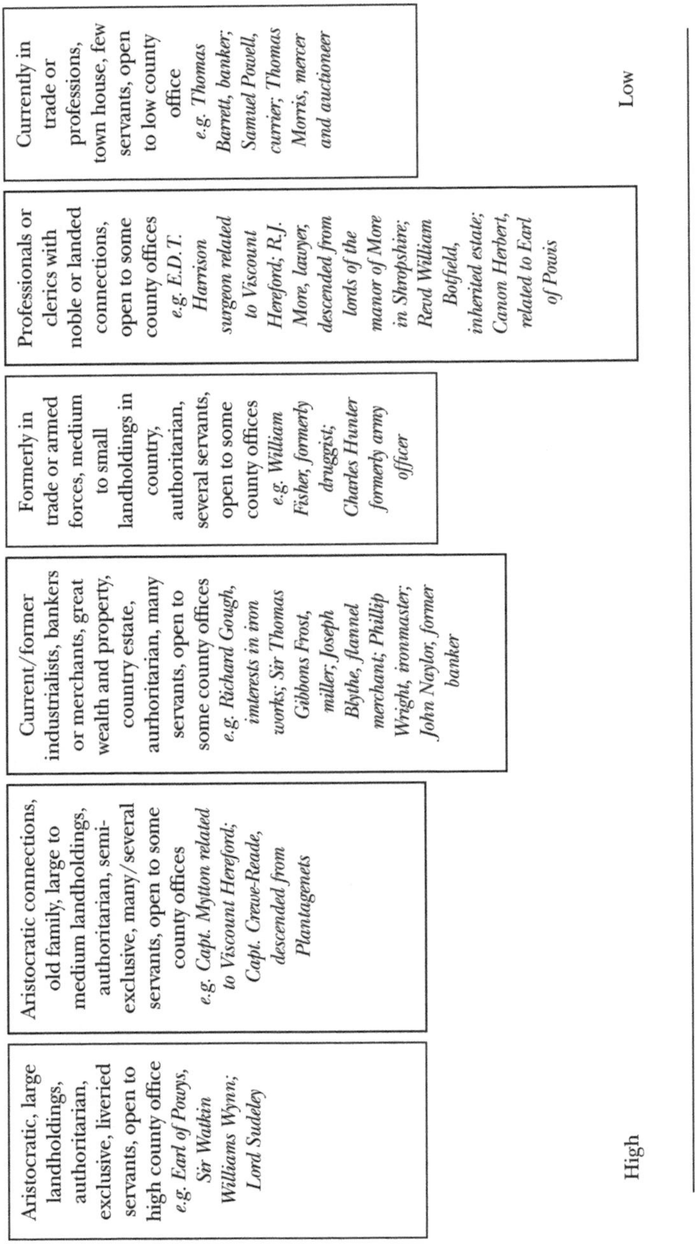

Aristocratic, large landholdings, authoritarian, exclusive, liveried servants, open to high county office e.g. *Earl of Powys, Sir Watkin Williams Wynn; Lord Sudeley*

Aristocratic connections, old family, large to medium landholdings, authoritarian, semi-exclusive, many/several servants, open to some county offices e.g. *Capt. Mytton related to Viscount Hereford; Capt. Creuve-Reade, descended from Plantagenets*

Current/former industrialists, bankers or merchants, great wealth and property, country estate, authoritarian, many servants, open to some county offices e.g. *Richard Gough, interests in iron works; Sir Thomas Gibbons Frost, miller; Joseph Blythe, flannel merchant; Phillip Wright, ironmaster; John Naylor, former banker*

Formerly in trade or armed forces, medium to small landholdings in country, authoritarian, several servants, open to some county offices e.g. *William Fisher, formerly druggist; Charles Hunter formerly army officer*

Professionals or clerics with noble or landed connections, open to some county offices e.g. *E.D.T. Harrison surgeon related to Viscount Hereford; R.J. More, lawyer, descended from lords of the manor of More in Shropshire; Revd William Botfield, inherited estate; Canon Herbert, related to Earl of Powis*

Currently in trade or professions, town house, few servants, open to low county office e.g. *Thomas Barrett, banker; Samuel Powell, currier; Thomas Morris, mercer and auctioneer*

High

Low

Figure 2.1 Social stratification of the Montgomeryshire Bench.

essential duty of a gentleman and motives for patronage included 'the compelling need to maintain social status'.[66] Motivation for joining the judiciary probably included an element of striving for social prestige, but within the Bench each man knew his place. Focus now turns to a different section within the legal system.

THE LEGAL SYSTEM SEEN ON THE STREETS: DEVELOPMENT OF THE POLICE FORCE

Most of the people who appeared in court already had some experience of law enforcement through encounters with the police, who were answerable to the magistrates. The service the officers gave will be studied in depth in later chapters, but here their backgrounds will be examined, as was done for the magistrates. Like much of Great Britain, many Welsh boroughs and counties established paid police forces in the first half of the nineteenth century.[67] Montgomeryshire magistrates had decided to adopt the terms of Home Secretary Lord John Russell's 1839 County Police Act soon after it became law. This was influenced by Chartist troubles, notable in Llanidloes and Newtown,[68] but other crime had as much, or more, influence, particularly crime related to the implementation of the new poor law. In 1836, Edwin Chadwick had argued for a strong rural police force for the suppression of tumults connected with the administration of poor relief,[69] and many newspapers linked the proposed police reform with the 1834 Poor Law Amendment Act. In 1837, the yeomanry had gone to the aid of an assistant poor-law commissioner who was being threatened by a mob in Llanfair Caereinion, and the following year the force had been called out to deal with trouble at Caersws workhouse.[70] These events and others like them led to some Montgomeryshire people associating the new, reformed police of the 1840s with oppression of the working class.

MONTGOMERYSHIRE CONSTABULARY
AT THE BEGINNING OF THE 1870S

Thirty years had now passed since the founding of the county force. The number of constables had grown by over 100 per cent and the number of places in which the men were stationed had increased correspondingly. Some men were found by their appearance in newspaper reports and quarter sessions records, and some were tracked down by examination of the 1871 census.[71] There were clusters of officers in Newtown and Welshpool, and individuals or pairs of men at other stations. A sergeant could be found in both Newtown and Llanidloes, and inspectors in Newtown and Welshpool. The chief constable and the county's sole superintendent were based in Newtown.

Whereas there were lines of social differentiation within the magistracy, imperceptible to many people, there was no such subtlety between the Bench and the officers who brought defendants to them. It has not been possible to trace the histories of all members of the Montgomeryshire force but in some cases the occupation of the policeman's father has been found. The constables were from working-class backgrounds, as found in recruitment to forces throughout Britain, and from agricultural, labouring, retail and craftsman backgrounds.[72] To the chief constable, an agricultural labourer made the ideal candidate because of his strength and qualities of stoicism and deference, but in reality they often proved poor candidates.[73]

Magistrates had a variety of reasons for joining the Bench, but pay was not one of them. Money, however, was often the motivating factor for police recruits. Whereas farm workers could never be certain of having either work or regular pay, the opposite was the case for the police, although some described the remuneration as poor. Analysis of constables' pay has shown that in some counties real gains in wages could be made by becoming a policeman,[74] and scrutiny of Montgomeryshire constabulary pay data and the labour books from the Gregynog Estate near Newtown, enable a similar analysis.[75] Data are available to allow the pay of senior officers to be compared to white-collar workers,[76] as well as labourers

Occupation	Annual amount £
Chief constable	250
Agent's clerk	105
Superintendent	100
Inspector	84
Sergeant	65
Constable (first class)	54
Constable (second class)	49
Constable (third class)	45
Gamekeeper	42
Schoolmaster	34
Carter	30
Haymaker (male)	30
Postboy (experienced)	24
Haymaker (female)	23
Postboy (new)	12

Table 2.1 League table of pay, 1871 (seasonal pay for haymakers has been multiplied to an annual sum for comparability purposes only)

to be contrasted with constables. Much of the estate work, such as haymaking, was seasonal but if all the rates of pay are converted to annual amounts, a league table of pay can be constructed (Table 2.1). Other factors such as boot allowance and deduction for superannuation should be taken into account when considering pay,[77] and as well as this, policemen received pay for attending events and allowances for inspecting livestock under the Contagious Diseases (Animals) Act.[78] The men received half pay for a limited period during sickness, a benefit not enjoyed by other members of the uniformed working class. There was also the prospect of promotion.[79] Considering all these things, the pay and conditions of the policeman in Montgomeryshire was attractive and helps explain why 28 of the 39 of the policemen in this study stayed in the job for ten years or more.[80]

LEVELS WITHIN THE CONSTABULARY

There were distinctions among members of the county constabulary that were formalised and visible in their employment status, as with men and officers as in the army. There was the pay differential, but also terminology indicated status. A man might join as a third-class constable, achieve second-class status after twelve months and possibly first-class status five years later. He might go on to become a sergeant or, rarely, a higher rank.[81] One such recruit was innkeeper's son Edwin Crowden who joined the constabulary from Cardiff, achieved second-class status in 1871 and retired from policing after thirty years with the rank of superintendent. Dramatic progress was seen by John Danily. He joined the force in 1851 and was an inspector within ten years. He became chief constable in 1868.[82] Later, over a period of retirement that lasted twenty-eight years, he drew a total pension of £6,720.[83] Regardless of increased status, however, the poor backgrounds of some of the men could come back to haunt them. This was in the form of abuse, or goading, from those members of the public who resented the police. 'Baiting' of the police often took place, for example, a youngster threatening to kick a policeman.[84] In Newtown on Christmas night 1868, Constable Richards was baited by a drunk outside a public house, and the terms of the abuse related to his agricultural background. The assailant shouted: 'Thou art only a plough boy, I'll warm thee, I'll have thy inside out', such abuse highlighting class.[85]

Another incentive for joining the force was the availability of police accommodation. As well as providing a regular, decent income for his family, a married policeman could give his dependants a relatively comfortable house to live in. For example, farmer's son John Sibbald began as a constable living with his wife in a cottage in Berriew. Ten years on, they were in the new police house at the top end of Llanidloes, very near to the bottom of the drive leading to magistrate Richard Woosnam's estate. The 1871 census shows Constable William Breese living in the newly-built police station in Llanfair Caereinion where he, his wife and nine children lived for at least ten years.[86]

From census information, it was found that twenty-eight
men served at least ten years and twenty men served at least
twenty years. One of the most notable was James Owen who
was among the first intake of constables to the county force
in 1841, became a sergeant in Llanidloes and retired in 1875
after 35 years' service.[87] Another long-serving officer was
Henry Clayton, who achieved inspector rank by 1870. He left
the county, however, and appears on the census for Toxteth
in 1871, with the rank of constable. It is not known why he
decided to go, but even with the reduced rank, in Liverpool
the pay rates were such that (if he had been first-class
constable) he would have been earning more than he had
been as an inspector in Newtown.[88] There are indications of
the magistrates being aware of their responsibilities towards
officers. When Constable Richards was assaulted by a drunk,
the Bench stated that the police must be protected at all
costs, and imposed a heavy fine.[89] They ordered in January
1869 that hats be replaced by helmets as the latter were less
likely to be displaced during 'a row',[90] and in October of the
same year they ordered that a supply of replacement staves
be purchased as several currently in use had become 'unserviceable'.[91] In March 1877, the Bench at quarter sessions
ordered the payment of the surgeon's bill after Constable
Ashton was wounded in discharge of his duty.[92]

Just as magistrates' social status, and the way in which they
were viewed by others on the Bench, was indicated by their
residences, so the policemen's houses gave similar, unspoken
information. A document written by the surveyor-general of
prisons in 1875 describes the accommodation that a
policeman or officer could expect, depending on his rank.[93]
A single constable would receive a living room, one other
room and three bunks whereas his married counterpart
would be given, in addition, a scullery and washhouse, pantry,
coal cellar, three bedrooms and a water closet in the yard.
The list intimates that a man ranked as sergeant or above
would be married, and shows the value put on lavatory
arrangements, at a time when many town dwellers shared
poor-quality facilities.

THE PRESENCE OF THE LEGAL SYSTEM
IN THE BUILT ENVIRONMENT

In earlier centuries, the focus of justice was often the lord of the manor's residence, or even under a tree on the village green. The nineteenth-century system, with its paid police force and widespread magistracy, not only had a bearing on the detection of crime and subsequent prosecutions, it also had repercussions for the landscape, mostly in populated areas, where police stations and courts were placed. The arrival of these buildings indicated the permanent and solid establishment of the system and displayed and reinforced the hierarchy of the justice system. By the middle of the decade, the standard of police accommodation was laid down.[94] Its construction could also be requested and required by government officials. In 1874, Inspector of Constabulary, Charles Augustus Cobbe wrote to Chief Constable Danily:

6 October 1874.

Dear Mr Danily,

When I was at Newtown, I think you hinted at a prospect of the justices considering the subject of your cells at Newtown at these sessions. If the subject be brought up could you not introduce the plan of having a regular St. House [station house] built at Newtown with the cells (say three in number) in the residence provided for the officer and so have all together – public office, residence and cells. The present arrangement cannot be a desirable one for some one must be within call of persons whenever in custody and no member of your force living near, resort must be had to whoever resides in the building to answer the call of the prisoners.[95]

Divided authority over prisoners is bad and leads to insecurity and there are many strong reasons why a person in custody should, till committed to prison, be in charge of the police who in 99 cases out of a hundred have taken them into custody and who are [illegible] responsible for the person as well as the property. As we walked towards the Bridge there seemed a very suitable piece of ground which I understood – but perhaps erroneously – was available. You will remember the plot – just close to and adjoining the present cells which might be utilized by a little rearrangement and arrangement of place.

The present arrangement about your cells is not satisfactory so if the justices are considering the subject, it will be a good opportunity to submit the view of a regular St. [station] House at Newtown, [your] headquarters and [your] gaol being at a distance makes it the more desirable to have good cells where persons may be kept under remand if necessary.

Believe me, yours truly,

C. A. Cobbe[96]

Three years later, plans were in place for a new police station with the accommodation advocated in the letter.[97] The plans were approved and the building was completed in 1879. It still stands today, but renovated into flats. The entrance marked in the architect's design as 'entrance for magistrates', is finer and more decorated than the other which is marked 'public entrance'. The first-floor residential accommodation in the design shows living room, pantry and scullery; three bedrooms and a private stairway. Thus, this living space was intended for a married constable, and he and his family would enjoy privacy in highly secure accommodation with their own entrance. In comparison, most of the people he dealt with in his day-to-day work shared entrances to mean quarters. The new police station fulfilled Cobbe's recommendation for the police officer to be within easy call of the prisoners as there are four cells shown on the ground floor. It also included a fully fitted courtroom, and justices' retiring room. At Welshpool, the lock up was deemed unfit in 1848, and in February 1861 building began on a new station house with cells in the town.[98] As in Newtown, the officer and his family living here had a well-built house, security and their own entrance.

COURTHOUSES

The new police station building in Newtown also housed the court in which petty sessions were held. The magistrates entered through the separate entrance described earlier, and reached their retiring room via a separate stairway. From the retiring room was direct entry to their dais in the court-room. From there the men were elevated and looked down upon the gathered community below, and the community had to look up to the Bench.[99] Quarter sessions were held in the Public Rooms, the grandest building in the town, at the back of which were the original cells. In most of the petty sessional divisions, new court buildings were being erected, for example at Llanidloes and Llanfair Caereinion, estab-lishing the presence of the system in the community.

In Welshpool, petty sessions were held in a solicitors' chambers in Severn Street. Quarter sessions were held in the town hall which was some 65 years old and built on the site of a guild hall that had been in place since at least 1629. Quarter sessions paid rent to the local board for use of the chambers for court purposes. The administrative business, on the first day of proceedings, was held in the grand jury room situated upstairs. By the end of the 1860s, the town hall, which also housed the market on the ground floor, was considered to be too small, and discussions were taking place regularly at meetings of the local board and at quarter sessions regarding its future.[100] At the Hilary sessions of 1869, John R. Jones, chairman of the town hall committee of magistrates, read from their report:

> The existing courthouse has been the subject of constant complaint by the judges; it has no retiring room for the judge, barristers' robing room, or petty jury room and, excepting one instance, is without proper convenience … [The plans for the new court] provide on the first floor a good Assize court with judge's retiring room, grand jury room and all other accommodation for county purposes.[101]

No mention was made of witnesses, the public or prisoners, and the focus seems to be upon those court users from the higher classes. This is confirmed by the Earl of Powis's words in a discussion about the holding of quarter sessions alter-nately at Newtown and Welshpool, putting importance on the prestige of the sessions:

The competition alluded to was not for the petty sessions but to have the honour of having the quarter sessions held there. The petty sessions were paid for [to Newtown local board for use of space in the public rooms] but the quarter sessions were free.[102]

As discussions over the future of Welshpool town hall continued, a ratepayer wrote to the editor of the local newspaper expressing his concern:

Sir –

A proposal was made before the magistrates at the last quarter sessions in Welshpool that a large sum of money from the rates of the county of Montgomery should be voted for the quarter sessions and Assize buildings at Welshpool, the assizes and quarter sessions being held alternately at Newtown and Welshpool. A few years ago they were held altogether at the county town –Montgomery.[103] At the change taking place, it being then thought for the convenience of the whole county, sufficient accommodation was provided for both holding the assizes and quarter sessions at Newtown, not by the ratepayers of the county, chiefly agricultural, but by voluntary subscriptions for the fitting up and furniture, and by shares of £50 each by the inhabitants and their adjoining neighbours, for which no money interest was received for a number of years, and if this was done at the central and most convenient town, surely it may be done at Welshpool which is the richer portion of the county.

I would earnestly request the magistrates to consider well their present position. As far as it is possible to judge, there will be a change in the power of voting. A bill supported by many of both parties in the House of Commons will create a county board, elected by the general body of ratepayers.[104] At present, many of the most worthy and most useful magistrates are clergymen, having no large landed stake in the county. The fair opinion of the whole county ought to be taken. I have formally noticed that a quarter sessions held at Welshpool and at Newtown do not always take the same views in the case of motions affecting the whole county. On the present motion, both meetings are held in one place at the end of the county.[105]

Wishing to put the case fairly for consideration, I remain your obedient servant,

T. P.[106]

T. P., at least, had recognised that decisions made by magistrates from 'down the valley' could be different from the more gentrified section of the Bench, those living 'up the valley'.[107] Significantly, T. P. also noted that those men without landed interests could have noticeably different sensibilities. His words could contain a warning or veiled threat that uncooperative men might one day be voted out.

The decision to adapt Welshpool town hall was taken, and the improvements were completed in 1874. The architect's drawing of the new building shows that he, at least, was aware that the building would serve all manner of people.[108] He depicted members of the lower classes around the building, and this may have been a result of discussion with his clients, viz. the local board and the magistracy, or may have been a representation of his own thoughts about the building's future use.[109] The building's front elevation included a balcony, enabling dignitaries to observe the people from above, as was the case with the Bench in the courtroom in Newtown

CONCLUSION

Appointment to the magistracy in Montgomeryshire followed the pattern seen elsewhere in the country. The aristocracy was represented, along with members of the old county set, but the new-gentry class of former merchants and tradesmen supplemented the Bench. Anglican clergymen joined them and played an important role. There was a hierarchy that was established by a man's background, and more visibly indicated by the residence that he occupied. This was most clearly observed with borough justices and their town houses. The status of each man determined roles that he could play in the county power structure, and establishing himself in higher society was likely to have been a motivating factor for joining the Bench. Just as the Montgomeryshire magistracy reflected Benches elsewhere in the country, so appointment to the Montgomeryshire constabulary followed a pattern seen in other counties. The men were working- or lower middle-class, and the systematic pay and conditions, access to promotion and good living quarters explained why many men stayed in post for years. A hierarchy was present within the force, with each man's status established by his pay and conditions, particularly the accommodation to which he was assigned.

The criminal justice system was present in the urban landscape in the form of police stations and courts. The construction of new police buildings was subject to government directives and one inspector of constabulary, a former chief constable, highlighted the needs of prisoners when considering the construction of the headquarters in Newtown. This building's outward appearance, however, mirrored the hierarchy within the judiciary. The renovated town hall in Welshpool seemed primarily designed to suit the magistrates' desire for prestige.

The following chapter will examine the everyday work of the constabulary, and the responses of various sections of the public.

3

MONTGOMERYSHIRE CONSTABULARY

MEN, METHODS AND COMMUNITY RESPONSE

The system of a paid police force in Wales was established at a time of civil unrest. At that time crime was associated with growing towns and cities, and there were calls for political reform.[1] In Montgomeryshire, the new police were associated with suppressing tollgate riots and protests against the new workhouses.[2] The present chapter examines the work of the county's policemen three decades after their foundation, and investigates the demands made on them by the wider community, and the reactions of varying sections of the general public to their presence and actions.[3] This study will give context to later chapters by considering police methods of dealing with situations and apprehending suspects.

ORGANISATION AND WORK OF THE COUNTY FORCE

Montgomeryshire was a small constabulary compared, for example, to neighbouring Shropshire, but not when compared to other Welsh forces. Table 3.1 shows the ratios of population and acreage per constable.[4] The far greater number of constables in Denbighshire resulted in a considerably reduced area for each man to patrol in that county. Policemen were located around the Montgomeryshire periphery as well as in the interior. Easy access points into the area, including Kerry, Buttington and Cemmaes, were manned, and the usefulness of these locations as security points becomes even more apparent when considered in terms of turnpike roads.[5] Although the southern and western entry points were covered, the north east was guarded even better, but as this was the more highly populated area, more policemen would be located there in any case. Turnpike Acts began to be repealed during the second half of the

Constabulary	No. of constables	Population per constable	Acreage per constable
Radnorshire	11	1262	17,008
Montgomeryshire	26	Not given in report. In 1861 was 2,307	15,591
Merionethshire	21	1729	14,270
Cardiganshire	26	2099	12,668
Denbighshire	50	Not known. In 1861 was 1,968	5941

Table 3.1   Ratio of population and acreage per constable

nineteenth century with the last remaining trust (relating to the Anglesey portion of the Shrewsbury to Holyhead Road) expiring on 1 November 1895.[6] In Montgomeryshire in the 1870s, money was still being made from the turnpike roads, realising healthy profits for the men who leased the gates. For example, the Park gate in Newtown made a profit of £199 in 1868–9.[7] Although landowners were still making money from farmers and others in this way, the police no longer had to deal with riots at tollgates as seen thirty years earlier, but other types of offences occasionally took place. During the 1870s, ten incidents leading to court appearances occurred at tollgates, although none of these involved police intervention that was recorded.[8]

VAGRANCY AND PRESSURE FROM THE HIGHER ORDERS

Montgomeryshire roads contributed to one of the widespread key features of the 1870s, the problem of the so-called 'tramping community'.[9] As in other counties, tramps were present in great numbers,[10] exacerbated in Montgomeryshire by the guardians of Forden workhouse providing relief without the tramps having to do work. It was said that in the early 1860s vagrants flocked to Montgomeryshire, treating Forden workhouse as a hotel.[11] The decision of the chief constable to position men at entry points into the county was likely to have been to apprehend vagrants.[12] The report of her Majesty's Inspector of Constabularies spoke of the problem:

In consequence of the numerous systems adopted in different parts of the country, I am quite unable to offer any suggestion for its suppression [vagrancy] by police action. Unless the justices direct the police throughout the country to be stringent towards vagrants, the active efforts of the police, even supported by the justices in one county, will only drive the vagrants into another county or district.[13]

There was fear and prejudice against tramps among many segments of society, often the upper orders, and in response the police tended to channel resources towards the protection of propertied members of society.[14] Directives issued by justices or the chief constable, however, were restricted by the available number of officers. Both fear and prejudice, and the limited number of policemen, are illustrated by an anonymous letter and accompanying editorial that appeared in *The Newtown and Welshpool Express* in 1871:

I live in a secluded spot. The parish is about six miles long with a population of perhaps 700. The nearest police station is some half-a-dozen miles off. A police officer comes to the village, over the mountains (being nearer) about once a week; calls with the parson, and returns home invariably without a job though the district is swarming with tramps of the very worst stamp. Five have just passed in a troop and here are two more forming a rear guard. The latter have just called, asking for bread. On being refused, one of them started to argue with my sister on the ways of Providence and that it was a sin to work ... They understand the latitude and longitude of the country and are well acquainted with every building in the district even from a hen roost to a nobleman's mansion. What is to be done towards scouring the country of these vagabonds? The most effectual way by far would be for every man to take physical force and use violence, driving every tramp out of the country and allow the police officers to refer to some other source for promotion ... I am positive the support they [the tramps] get from farmers etc. is not half enough for them therefore we have a right to believe they must be plundering.[15]

[Signed] John Verniew.[16]

The editorial commented:

> We believe that there is no exaggeration in his [Verniew's] statement that [his] side of the county, which is not too well supplied as it regards a police force, is completely overrun with hordes of these fellows which swarm about the country at this time of the year. Besides, police officers cannot – any more than other men – be in more than one place at once.[17]

Verniew's gently sarcastic comment about promotion may well be because one of the policemen stationed in the north-west was Constable John Ashton of Meifod, who had been promoted to first class the previous year. Just three weeks before Verniew's letter, Ashton had been viciously attacked by a tramp. The attack on him, and his response to the tramps named Kelly and Cooke, was reported in detail in the newspaper:

> On Sunday night, the officer took the prisoners into custody upon a charge of vagrancy, whereupon Kelly, contrary to all precedent in the neighbourhood in regards to tramps, began kicking him furiously and called upon Cooke to strangle him. The policeman threw Kelly down with the object of securing him. Cooke thereupon commenced kicking the officer and wrested the handcuffs from him and struck him a severe blow on the head with them. The policeman then, in self-defence, drew his truncheon which he made good use of as to break it in halves. After a great amount of struggling he managed to secure both and bring them to Pool. [18]

The officer might have been responding to public or government pressure, a directive from the Bench, the chief constable, his own motivation or a combination of these. The strategy of being proactive towards tramps was effective, for Her Majesty's Inspector's report for Montgomeryshire (1871) announced that 'Vagrancy is represented to have decreased considerably',[19] although there could have been other contributing factors including strategies that were exercised by other counties.[20] The account of Ashton's securing of Kelly and Cooke is a type of active service that resulted in truncheons and staves becoming unserviceable, but highlights the degree of violence used by Ashton to overcome the two men. There are questions regarding the relationship between the police and different sections of society,[21] and there will be a return to this later in the chapter.

It was not only towards tramps that pressure came from those sections of the community able and motivated enough to write letters to the newspaper. For example, in April 1878 a person using the name 'Cat o' Nine Tails' wrote regarding youths throwing stones at passers-by at a location on the edge of Newtown:

> ... if this state of things is allowed to continue, persons will undoubtedly have to suffer injuries more severe than have hitherto been the case, and if some steps are not taken, or punishment inflicted, that would deter them from a repetition of this offence, pedestrians will be in constant danger. If the 'limbs of the law' would take a stroll in this direction they would no doubt find the air embracing, and their appearance would add to the general comfort and safety of the public, would be a great annoyance to these roughs and in the end would result in dispersing them or bringing them to their deserts – a thorough whipping – which would teach them how to conduct themselves in future.[22]

The gently sarcastic comment about strolling and finding the air embracing indicates a degree of dissatisfaction at the police's beats being normally at the centre of town, but the phrase following it shows a veiled acknowledgement of the force's peace-keeping effect. The same acknowledgement is present and similarly veiled in a letter of complaint sent a few years earlier:

> I refer to an act of vigilance on the part of the police officials of this town [Newtown] which I think should not be allowed to pass unnoticed. [Describes listening to Christmas street music in the centre of town.] When behold! A body of individuals who are paid for looking after thieves, rioters, drunkards, etc. and so enhancing our social comfort and enjoyment, appear on the scene and with an air that seemed

to say, 'I am the law of England embodied' the largest of these
gentlemen walked straight up to our musicians and – will it be
credited – actually ordered them to play no more! Of course
the musicians submitted as arguing with a policeman is as
dangerous as was jesting with a priest in days of yore. I say they
submitted, whether willingly or not I do not know, but I do
know there was a strong feeling of indignation on the part of
the listeners. One gentleman had the presumption to enquire
of the large individual before alluded to if he was quite sure
he was acting in accordance with the established law; he was
politely advised to go home and go to bed. For myself I must
say I never felt more indignant at any act of tyranny than I feel
at this ... I say that for the police to display such vigilance in
putting down a time-honoured practice ... in manifest opposition to the wishes of the public, is a monstrous abuse of the
power invested in them by virtue of the office they hold as
public servants.

Signed

One of Six Thousand [23]

'One of Six Thousand' clearly considered that the police
were their servants, and were meant to be controlling the
sort of disorder associated with the downtown, rougher sorts,
not respectable pastimes enjoyed by the more refined. The
violence meted out by policemen in some circumstances was
mentioned in the letter, and there is a suggestion that locals
experienced officers acting in a heavy-handed fashion. The
correspondence did continue, however, with further letters
explaining that the music was going on late into the night.[24]
Thus, the officers were validly acting on a genuine public
grievance. The same acknowledgement of the useful part
played by policemen in maintaining a level of order considered respectable by many is seen in the tributes paid to a
constable about to leave a station in the north-eastern part of
the county to take up a position as sergeant in Welshpool:

> Police officers in their difficult and arduous calling can not
> only do their duty well, but also by kindness and courtesy gain
> the sympathy and goodwill of the people who are not slow to
> recognise worth. [Constable Breese] has at all times

performed his duty well and courteously, gaining friends year by year ... Mr Breese has been here amongst us for the last thirteen years and I think you will all agree with me that he has not made an enemy during that time. He has been a vigilant officer, having no mercy on thieves and men of that class, but he has never overstrained the law in the least, being fair and just to all. He has been a peaceman in every sense of the word.[25]

Here again is a partly hidden suggestion that police officers were known to step outside the boundaries of legal behaviour at times, and that they could make enemies by their actions. Some of the attendees at the presentation have been traced, and they were all middle class, mainly farmers. The comment 'has not made an enemy' is likely to mean 'has not made an enemy of anyone considered respectable' and does not tell us anything about the sentiments of 'rougher' sorts. This speech also tells us that defence of property was of major importance to those celebrating the role of this particular policeman, whereas in Newtown, according to 'One of Six Thousand' rioting and drunkenness were of concern. In a presentation to Constable Poole, who had been stationed for four years in Tregynon, estate village of Lord Sudeley, but had recently moved to Berriew, the same reference to courtesy was made. This gives the impression that a degree of deference shown by a policeman to those who paid the rates was likely to be appreciated. In the known cases brought to court by Constables Breese and Poole, all were thefts by working-class people, with one case of drunkenness brought by Poole when he was serving for a time in Newtown.[26]

Occasions such as the presentations made to Constables Breese and Poole reinforced the idea in the minds of lower-class people that the police were in place for the good of those higher up the social scale. A prominent event was the bi-annual parade of magistrates at the assizes, where a contingent of police marched behind the justices, giving the impression that the officers were the servants of the ruling classes or, indeed, the Bench.[27] These were among the types of occasions that led to some people thinking: 'They [the police] go strutting about, well clothed and shod' and 'Who sent for the police? The middle class.'[28]

Some historians consider that the function of the new police was to suppress or destroy working-class culture and to impose alien values on the poor.[29] However, the middle classes were not exempt from police control, as a case from 1873 shows.[30] Here, a group of retailers and skilled workers was involved in the type of activity the police commonly monitored and controlled among the working classes. The case involved drunkenness and the assault of a constable in execution of his duty, which in this instance involved surveillance of a public house. During the afternoon of 26 March 1873, Sergeant Hudson, stationed in Newtown, heard 'a great noise' emanating from the Eagles Inn. In his testimony before the magistrates he said, 'I went in and looked in the smoke room where I found six or seven persons. [These included the future Sir Pryce Pryce-Jones]. The noise I heard proceeded from Mr Bryan and [the landlord]. I saw Mr Bryan was drunk.'[31] A few hours later, Hudson sent Constables Jerman and Edwards to look in at the inn whereupon the landlord, Edward Jones, shoved PC Jerman out of the building. The landlord objected to his business and his clientele being watched by the officers.[32] Two members of the group inside the pub appeared in court to give evidence that there was no drunkenness, and the charge was dismissed. However, the landlord's assault of the constable was deemed proved and he was fined £1. Here we see a policeman acting to quell disorder, yet Hudson nevertheless referred to the drunken man as 'Mr'. Police officers in court always referred to working-class defendants and witnesses either by their forenames and surnames, surnames only or as 'the defendant', 'the prisoner' or 'the witness'. In the Eagles case, there was a distinction being made between the forms of address used by the police for the usual, working-class court attendees, and middle-class men. Hence, deference of a sort was shown even when a middle-class man was the accused.[33]

POLICE ACTIVITY IN PARTICULAR AREAS, AND INFLUENCE ON ATTITUDES

Many of the cases seen at court took place in the centre of towns. Analysis of newspaper reports from the sample years

1869–70 illustrates that police work was concentrated on the centre of town, with a few incidents on the periphery towards the north, east and south, and no police activity at all in the leafy and desirable suburb of Milford described in Chapter 1. Most of the activity corresponds with the points at which alcohol was sold, but these were also areas of commerce, where householders were among those who part-financed the police force.[34] Thus policing the activities that caused public disturbances also made constabulary actions visible to many influential persons. In a description of the comparable English town of Horncastle in Lincolnshire, this sort of resident necessarily had an interest in the work of the force and would expect to see the policemen in action:

> The 'leading inhabitants', as they preferred to be called, were merchants, corn dealers, clergymen, shopkeepers, attorneys, doctors and schoolmasters ... They not only worked in it [Horncastle] and depended on its economic success but they lived in it, most of them in the central area, and thus were very much concerned with the quality of life there.[35]

Indeed, in Newtown in February 1874, the future Sir Pryce Pryce-Jones, who at that time lived in the centre of Newtown and could observe the two main roads from his rooms above his shop, testified during the trial of a man accused of assaulting a constable, and gave evidence that supported the police:

> I heard a row and threw up my window, and saw the officers engaged in a tussle with a man. I put on my shoes and went out and there saw the defendant very excited and busy. But he was not busy in assisting the police. – rather to the contrary. The officers were very much abused that night. I never saw men acting better than they did.[36]

When the evidence of a man such as Pryce-Jones was crucial, the police felt pressurised in the methods they used to deal with an incident, or indeed, whether to deal with an incident or not. It probably influenced the routes of beats, and police pursuance of prosecutions, as shown by an occasion when Sergeant Ross found a riot going on outside Pryce-Jones's dwellings on a spring evening in 1869.[37] He told the magistrates: 'I noticed a great number of people drunk about Severn Street.' Ross managed to clear the crowd and found that they were emanating from beer shops, one in particular that was alongside Pryce-Jones's building. The landlords were later charged with permitting drunkenness, and the police were probably motivated by a perceived need to please Pryce-Jones and neighbouring residents. This engendered a certain level of resentment as will be shown in a later section.

POLICE ACTIVITY AROUND TOWN

The most active of the policemen were Sergeant Ross and Constables Brown and Richards. Before becoming sergeant at Newtown, John Hudson was a constable stationed at nearby Kerry, but came into town on occasions. The men sometimes worked in groups during the evening and when trying to control disorder at or near public houses. The police were in a group of three when they attended a fight at The Unicorn in August 1870,[38] and generally patrolled difficult or potentially dangerous areas in groups of at least two.[39] Constable Richards was with Hudson at the railway station when an 'elated' man attacked him in November 1869. Richards and Sergeant Ross brought charges against a militiaman found drunk in Ladywell Street in June 1870, and a few weeks later Richards and Brown were in Ladywell Street when a drunk attacked Richards with a knife.[40] Richards could defend himself with his police-issue stave, a weapon that was proving to be a great asset to him in quelling disorder. He had testified at the trial of the man who baited him about his plough boy background: 'when I pulled my stave out, the assailant ran away.'[41] The man in the knife attack was a butcher, and Richards disarmed him by knocking the knife out of his hand with his stave. No injury is mentioned but it likely that the blow caused damage to the offender. There is evidence for this in the dialogue from a murder trial at the Montgomeryshire assizes in 1906 when the arresting policeman was cross-examined: Lawyer: 'You gave him a terrific blow?' Constable: 'I hit him hard.' Lawyer: 'You would hit a man hard who was coming at you with a knife wouldn't you?' Constable: 'Yes.' The policemen sometimes went further than the edge of town in pursuit of crime, when they were on the trail of a suspect who had made off from town,[42] sometimes in response to information received,[43] and sometimes on a scheduled journey out to inspect public houses.[44]

In Welshpool, known locations of incidents involving the police were concentrated around the town centre, very close to the central crossroads, the same as in Newtown. In both towns, the most common type of offence with which the police were involved was that involving working-class drunkenness, being more than seven times the figure of offences involving theft. Not only did these locations of police activity correspond with areas of commerce and therefore habitation of ratepayers as in Newtown, but also the residence of several magistrates. Census information shows that all the borough magistrates lived in one of the main streets that ran through the centre of town. Thus, these men had first-hand knowledge of the sorts of disorder that occurred in their neighbourhood, and of police responses. It seems that they were satisfied with the men's work, for the officers were rewarded with official recognition by the borough corporation, the mayor of which was the chairman of the Bench.[45] This again would give the impression to many that the police were working for the higher classes rather than the whole of the community.

POLICE WORK IN RURAL AND URBAN AREAS

In the village of Berriew, drunkenness and theft were present, but highway offences and offences relating to farm work were more prominent. In five of the cases, victims reported the offence to the policeman,[46] and in the others the constable himself observed the offenders and apprehended them. The manner of prosecutions before the inception of the county constabulary – where prosecutions depended on private initiative – was still apparent during the period under study.[47] For example, in May 1869 Edward Gwalchmae was charged by William Waring with assault; Gwalchmae was convicted and fined. He was then charged by Constable Sibbold of Berriew with being drunk and disorderly. At the same court, Henry Woodcock summoned John Griffiths for assault, and

Griffiths, too, was convicted and fined.[48] It is understandable that the system of private prosecution continued to take place in rural areas when one considers the letter from 'John Verniew' quoted earlier, in which he says that the nearest police station to his parish was six miles away and a policeman visited from there once a week. Even in urban Newtown, the old way of private initiative is illustrated in a case of theft in October 1869 when a tramp stole a pair of trousers from a shop. The shopkeeper chased the man, caught him and gave him 'a thrashing'. He later told magistrates that he intended to let the man go but some witnesses reported the matter to the police.[49] In this case the victim of the theft would have preferred the police to be less conveniently placed than they were. In a case of indecent assault, the victim did not go to the police but went herself to the magistrate to lay information and obtain a warrant.[50] That assault took place in notorious Ladywell Street, location of thieves, prostitutes and thugs who often appeared in court, and the victim may well have considered that her complaint would not be dealt with properly by the police. Nevertheless there were many examples to show that thirty years after the establishment of the county force, people were calling on the policemen to be peacekeepers, for example the landlord of the Unicorn in Broad Street, Newtown, who summoned the police to deal with a fight in the case described earlier. There was also an expectation among some – those who had the ability to write letters to the newspaper, probably ratepayers – that policemen should be dealing with crime, as the following letter illustrates, in which the original punctuation is retained. The document also illustrates the resentment that arose when policemen favoured certain residents:

> It is almost a pity to find fault with a staff of policemen of fine muscular appearance and official deportment such as ours are. But I believe a policeman is required to be something more than a monument of strength! On Sunday evening, as respectable families were passing through the Cross to church or to the different chapels, a group of young fellows were congregated opposite to Mr David Thomas's shop, chatting together with very unseemly clamour, blocking up the pathway and causing passengers to make a disagreeable detour into

the roadway in order to pass them. This, I am sorry to say, is of frequent occurrence on a Sunday evening. But the most strange circumstance was that two of our constabulary were 'vigilantly (?) looking out for squalls' opposite to Mr Pryce Jones's establishment, and allowing this great annoyance entirely to escape their notice. If policemen cannot detect the great nuisance in broad daylight, what inferences may not be drawn as to the condition of things when the shades of night have set in – especially when our public guardians seem to labour under the unfortunate infirmity of 'having eyes' but 'see not?'

Yours respectfully, Z.[51]

The 'Mr Pryce Jones' referred to in the letter was the future Sir Pryce Pryce-Jones, present during the incident with Mr Bryan at the Eagles Inn, who became Newtown's second most famous inhabitant after Robert Owen.[52] The letter had the effect of changing the force's approach to policing the centre of town, for the following edition of the newspaper contained a subsequent letter:

As one who has been frequently incommoded and driven to the middle street by groups of men and boys who made the Cross their trysting place upon a Sunday afternoon, I must confess my deep obligations to your correspondent, Z, for the mighty reform which he has been the means of accomplishing. It was the simplest yet the most effectual application I have ever witnessed. That part of the public thoroughfare on Sunday last and during the preceding week was as little inconvenienced as any other part of the town. The 'monuments of strength' as the police were facetiously called by your correspondent have to be complimented upon the good-natured manner in which they took the hint and the very zealous way in which they set about rectifying the evil. A few more of these truly homeopathic doses, if as judiciously applied in other directions, would work wonders in our little town.

Yours truly, One Deeply Obliged.[53]

The police thus responded to the concerns of those members of the public who had the ability to voice or pen their thoughts. Clearly, newspaper publicity had a role and influenced the police. Indeed, the following extract illustrates that the Press were manipulating the police and public opinion, and suggests that the police were giving stories to the newspaper:

> [Regarding gypsies keeping their horses overnight on other people's grassland in Welshpool] Police officer Edward Tanner and another were on duty at the Cross, these said gipsy fraternity drove their five old long-teethed screw horses down Severn Street, when Police Constable Tanner observed to the other policeman, 'Those chaps are going to put their horses into a nice bit of grass of somebody's,' and said he would see about it … Next day they were 'brought to book' and had to pay Mr Lloyd 12 shillings for the damage done and 10 shillings police fees. The occupiers of fields round the outskirts are glad of the vigilance of the police in this case.[54]

The use of the Press by all concerned, as a medium of communication and as a way of changing policing behaviour, deserves more investigation by historians. It suggests interesting links between reporters, editors and the police.[55]

RESPONSES FROM THE LOWER ORDERS

The discussion thus far has been largely on middle-class experience and attitudes towards police activity, but there is evidence in reports of court proceedings that enable an investigation of the police and wider public relationship. The working classes sometimes requested assistance from officers, which indicates a degree of acceptance and cooperation. For example, in December 1874 a woman was found dead in the rough working-class area of Astley's Yard in Newtown. This was the location of known prostitutes and pimps, and the site of a serious assault a few years earlier.[56] One of the witnesses at the dead woman's inquest said:

> I last saw her alive on Wednesday at about twelve o'clock at noon. I did not notice whether she had any fire on Wednesday but saw no fire or anything stirring on Thursday. I then became afraid that something was the matter with her … I went and gave information to Police Constable Pryce, and he came and burst the door open and went in.[57]

The following year, a travelling draper named Charles Miller described finding a corpse:

> When I went to the reservoir, one of the boys who accompanied me went to the end and called to me and said there was a man in the water. I looked and could see an object in the water. It was a man. His one hand was above the water. I came to town and informed the police. Two police officers returned with me to the reservoir, and with assistance got the body out.[58]

Constable Crowden testified to being called to the scene of a disturbance: 'On the day in question [I was] on duty at the Cross and I was sent for to go to the Market Hall Vaults, that a woman was drunk there and refused to leave.' The landlord said:

> The defendant came into the vaults with her husband, evidently the worse for liquor, and began to keep a noise, and [I] ordered her out but she would not go. [We] sent for the police and Crowden came and she left with him.[59]

This shows that methods had been established by which the public dealt with disorder and suspicious or out-of-the ordinary events, and these methods often involved calling the police.[60] Refusing to cooperate with the police has been defined as a form of hostility to the force,[61] but some people in Newtown at least were routinely bringing in the constabulary rather than handling situations themselves. This demonstrates a degree of cooperation that helped to maintain order. However, it is true that resentment of the police was noted in Newtown. Detail can be teased out of reports, giving valuable information about a mixture of attitudes within the general lower-class population, allowing social status analysis to be applied. This theory, used by psychologists, suggests that in a capitalist society, people whose status is high or rising are less likely to be prejudiced towards the police than those whose status is low or declining. Low status and income *per se* do not lead to prejudice provided they are rising. Thus, the worried neighbour, travelling draper and landlord were likely to have had rising status.[62]

TRUNCHEONS, HANDCUFFS AND POLICE TACTICS

Much of the policemen's time was taken up with street offences, usually involving alcohol and often accompanied by violence. In February 1874, three Newtown policemen dealt with an affray in the centre of town. Constable Crowden deposed to the magistrates:

> At about a quarter past eleven I was on duty at the Cross and saw the defendant who was drunk. I requested him to go home but he refused and went deliberately to a man named Alfred Francis and struck him in the mouth. I went towards him to take him into custody. He pulled off his coat to fight. I closed with him and threw him down, and police constable Jones came to my assistance and so did sergeant Hudson. He resisted very much and I had several kicks about the legs from him.[63]

Sergeant Hudson's evidence included details of an assault on himself: 'He [the defendant] was resisting them [Crowden and Constable Edward Jones] very much. I went to their assistance and in doing so, he commenced kicking me with all his might, making deliberate kicks. He kicked me about the legs and also about the face'. Hudson's recorded reply to cross-examination by the accused man – 'You were not hand-cuffed at the time' – intimates that handcuffs were used later, but no reference to use of stave or truncheon was made. Constable Jones noted that bad language had been used, although the exact words are recorded by blank spaces: 'I was on duty at the Cross and saw Thomas Edwards there drunk. Crowden went up to him and told him to go home. He said he would go home when the — he liked'.

Thomas Edwards resented being moved on by Crowden – moving-on being a method of crowd control described as being 'perhaps the most obnoxious to [those being policed]'.[64] But why did Edwards deliberately strike factory labourer Alfred Francis? From the wording of Crowden's testimony, it seems that the assault on Francis was in response to being moved on. Francis may have been assisting the police, which might not be as unlikely as it sounds, for during the same incident bricklayer Edward Turner certainly did respond to a request for help from Sergeant Hudson and was assaulted by a co-accused for doing so. Hudson said:

> On Saturday night last I was present when Thomas Edwards was being taken to the lock up, and called on Edward Turner to assist. He was doing so, and holding Edwards' legs. The defendant John P. Jones pushed through the crowd and ran at him [Turner] and struck him with all his might.

Thus, we have identified three groups: those who would physically resist the police, those who would assist the police, and those who would neither resist nor assist but would exact retribution on those who did assist. It is useful here to note that psychologists consider that aggression coming from prejudice requires a target that is already disliked. Psychologists also use the so-called 'scapegoat' theory, the basic proposition of which is that when the legitimate target of the aggression cannot be attacked, the aggression will be diverted onto targets where it is condoned or even encouraged. Thus, Turner, in the case above, was being used as a scapegoat.[65]

Examination of this case reveals another group – those who would not commit themselves in any way, these perhaps being the largest group. Various witnesses testified to a great row and a crowd, and Edwards was also charged with inciting this crowd to resist the police. Hudson testified that Edwards's words were, 'Kick him, don't let them take [the accused] away.' However, although Edwards was convicted of this offence, and John P. Jones of assaulting Turner, no one else from the crowd was charged with any offence, so Edwards's exhortations to the mass of people to resist the police were unproductive. Constable Crowden, too, made fruitless exhortations. He said:

> We were nearly exhausted and required more assistance. Unless we had had assistance, we should have had to leave him go. I called on Thomas Palmer to assist. I said, 'Thomas Palmer [a tin-plate worker], I call on you in the Queen's name to assist me in taking this man to the lock up.' We were all in uniform at the time. He replied, 'I cannot, I have left my shop door open.' He went away then and did not assist.[66]

In a situation such as this, it seems hardly credible that staves were not used, and yet the newspaper report does not mention any weapons. Nor did defence questioning during the trial produce any details about police physicality. A report of a similar incident in 1871 gives evidence of a truncheon, again following from an officer's attempts to move people on:

> It appears from the evidence of the police officer that a crowd of about thirty or forty persons had assembled outside the doctor's door on the night in question. The officer went and endeavoured to disperse them. The defendant [a militiaman] was there standing against the door and when the officer was persuading the crowd to disperse, the defendant said, 'What the h—l are you looking at me for?' The officer replied, 'You ought to have been in your billet at this time of night.' Defendant retorted, 'What has that to do with you?' and then struck complainant two or three times with his fist. The officer then in self-defence struck him with his stick. Defendant rushed towards him, took hold of the stick, and cried out to his comrades: 'Go into them chaps,' meaning the complainant and his brother officer, Tanner ... The officer was cross-examined by Mr Stanier-Jones for the defence but his evidence was not at all shaken.[67]

As in the earlier case, no other person from the crowd was charged with any offence, so the defendant's attempts to incite the crowd were ignored. The pugnacious nature of the militiaman was apparent in his reaction to the charge being brought against him – he himself brought a counter-charge of assault against Constable Ellis, claiming that the policeman had struck him first. The magistrates, however, threw this out and fined the militiaman £5. In both town centre incidents, the police used their staves and truncheons in a less ferocious manner than with the tramps at the bottom of society, most commonly apprehended in out-of-the way locations.[68]

The militiaman was not the only defendant who turned the law onto a policeman who had arrested him. John Pilot appeared at the spring assizes of 1871 charged with rape.[69] The charge was dropped owing to the non-appearance of the alleged victim, and Pilot subsequently took out a summons against Sergeant Ross, accusing him of perjury. This case came to nothing as Ross hired a solicitor and fought the charge successfully, but it is interesting that the sergeant then left the Montgomeryshire force and moved to the Midlands where he joined the Coventry constabulary.[70] The charge brought by Pilot prompted the move. Both these men who countered police charges with charges of their own were of the middle classes, although they were among proletarian companions at the time of their arrests. The militiaman could hire a lawyer and initiate proceedings, and pay his fine immediately. Moreover, lodging with a doctor suggests that he was of a higher order. John Pilot was a member of the extended Pilot family, notable merchants in Newtown, and so both men had fairly high status. In the light of status theory, it is likely that the militiaman's and Pilot's aggression was generated by affront at their standing being challenged by policemen.

The use of handcuffs has been mentioned. They, like the truncheons, were likely to have become worn out with use. They were used on the militiaman and on the tramps arrested by Constable Ashton in 1871, and on Thomas Edwards in January 1874. Six new pairs were ordered by the chief constable in October 1874.[71] Their use was causing concern in some quarters, for in December 1872 the local newspaper published an account of the trial of two detectives in Lancashire who were accused of inappropriate use of them. It is unlikely that *The Newtown and Welshpool Express* would have highlighted this case unless it had been pertinent at the time.[72] The piece read:

> The judge summed up. He said the case was important in this way and in this only: that in all the large towns in Lancashire, the number of the police bore a trifling comparison with the number of inhabitants. In some towns there were such a small number of police that if they were not protected by very important powers entrusted to them, and by the support of their fellow citizens in the jury box when they acted rightly, their lives would not be worth a day's purchase among the population with which they had to deal ... The jury would, however, be well aware that in the profession of the police, as in every other profession, unworthy men were sometimes

entrusted with great powers; and even worthy men, by the habits of their lives might be tempted into the commission of acts which neither law nor good sense could for a moment tolerate.[73]

Response to police action could take the form of support for the accused. In the summer of 1875, Thomas Jones went into the garden of Constable John Pearson in Caersws, in search of a rabbit belonging to the vicar's daughters. Pearson saw him and had him charged with trespass. The magistrates fined Jones one shilling. The convicted man was motivated to write to the newspaper, describing the events and the actions of the local community:

> Being on the ground at the time and seeing Mr Owen's children in pursuit, I assisted and went over the fencing and into the policeman's property, when he came up saying he would summons me, which he did. Such was the paltry charge laid against me that great sympathy was manifested on my behalf, for in a very short time I received a sum of money considerably more than was required to meet the demands of justice. In conclusion, I beg to tender my sincere thanks to my kind friends for the very timely assistance.[74]

INVISIBLE POLICING

Visibility was normally an essential part of the police. It was not enough for them to do their job; they had to be seen to do it well; hence the stress laid upon their visible presence and the importance of the uniforms they wore.[75] Originally, the police were formed in an attempt to prevent crime, and the wearing of a conspicuous uniform 'epitomized the preventative principle upon which it was grounded',[76] as well as 'being the essence of the policeman's authority'.[77] This is reflected in Constable Crowden's words when he testified about requesting assistance in the Queen's name from Thomas Palmer: 'We were all in police uniform at the time.' Later, in 1906, when a policeman was giving evidence about his apprehension of a murder suspect near Welshpool, he said, 'I was in my police trousers.'[78] It was as if officers expected – or were accustomed to receiving – respect, deference or obedience when wearing uniform. However, a method of pre-empting offences and of gaining information was by dressing in plain clothes and mingling with the crowds.[79] Constable Sibbald described his actions leading to the apprehension of a prostitute:

> Yesterday I was on duty in this town in plain clothes. Just about 11 o'clock I saw the prisoner, and suspecting her to have come to town for an improper purpose, I watched from about that time to about 6 o'clock. She went from place to place, and eventually into the back premises of the Angel Vaults. She was looking into the stables and lurking about.[80]

This sort of disguised policing was sometimes treated with scorn or deep concern because of its resemblance to spying.[81] Sibbald's seven hours of observation indicate the class of police work that led to charges of 'lounging about our streets' or 'men who do not really work for a living ... while the labourer toils from morning to night for ten shillings'.[82] Nevertheless it was used as a crime-fighting tool from the earliest days of the police force, as it was thought that a man in uniform would hardly ever catch a thief.[83] Undercover men would be sent outside their usual areas to divisions where they were not known, as illustrated in the case above – Sibbald was stationed in Berriew but was working in plain clothes in Newtown. Thus, when Constable Poole, normally stationed in Tregynon, arrested a drunk in Newtown, he was probably working undercover. Although in this study of the 1870s no specific community response to undercover policing could be found, in the 1906 case referred to earlier, the suspect caused a row in a pub when he suspected a sewing machine agent of being a detective.[84]

FORENSIC TECHNIQUES

In 1842, the Metropolitan Police founded a detective force at Scotland Yard, and it is said that Dickens based a character on one of the Yard's detective inspectors.[85] In Montgomeryshire simple detective techniques were being used in the early days of the force, for example when Constable Thomas Jones tracked sheep thieves in 1843 by following footprints.[86]

Techniques had developed by the 1870s as the journals of Constable Edward Jones of Llanfyllin show, although much of his detective work was the simple tracking as seen earlier. Jones's original spellings and grammar are retained in the extract that folllows:

> 26 May 1869 9p.m.: Eagles Inn: Received information from John Edwards Eagles Inn that a drake had been Stolen from his yard since 6p.m. ellis Evans Potter and Wm Humphreys (alias cythrel) were seen in the yard are Suspected Searched their Lodgings and Bull beer shop where they frequent and i found no clue.

> 20 May 1869 6p.m.: Town: Received information from Emma Hughes Williams that a Bonnet had been stolen from her shop in the cours of the Evening. She suspected two women that had left the shop about 5P.M. from my enquiries found that they were the Daughters of william Ellis of faenog Boncyn celyn llanfihangel went in pursuit found them near Llanfihangel with a Bonnet answering the description given in their posession took them into custod conveyed them to llanfyllin Lock-up. Gave their names Margaret Jones and Sarah Ellis both of Fawnog Rhiwlas.[87]

Back in 1843, Constable Thomas Jones investigated a rape case simply by 'making enquiries'.[88] By 1869, forensic science had moved on and chemical tests were being used; for example, in 1851 a professor of chemistry in Belgium identified poisons in body tissue and a German chemist had developed a chemical test for the presence of blood in 1863.[89] In the spring of 1869, Constable Edward Jones received information of an alleged rape, and although simple investigative methods were used at the start of the proceedings, new techniques were involved later. There was a suspect and he was taken into custody to be held there while further investigations were made. The complainant's undergarments were received by Jones and given to the local physician. The prisoner had three months to wait until his trial at the midsummer assizes, and it was while he was waiting that the more modern forensics emerged. First, Welshpool medical practitioner Dr Harrison examined the undergarments.

Blood stains were found and, although details from the first appearance before the magistrate are not known, it must have been suggested that the stains had come from menstruation.[90] This is clear because Constable Jones's wife examined the complainant, one month after the attack, for evidence of bleeding. The timeline can be continued, this time using Jones's own written words from his journal to describe events:

22 April: By orders Conveyed the Shift mentioned the 10th inst to Docr Harrison for inspection who recommended the same to be taken to Doctor Johnson an abilival [chemical?] Profesor Shrewsbury by order of Supt Delivered the said shift to Doctor Johnson together with a letter received from Doctor Harrison Returned to Station.

23 April: By orders from Spt Conveyd my Wife in a Trap for the purpose of Inspecting the Linen etc and monthly course of nature of the Prosecutrix Ellin Jones mentioned 10th inst.

This forensic work would have become public knowledge at a subsequent trial. However, in due course the grand jury at the summer assizes decided to ignore the charge, or throw it out, and so this important development in the application of forensic techniques remained largely invisible, known to only the police officers involved, Jones's wife and the medical men. This case is remarkable, for even nearly forty years later, the bloodstains on the murder suspect in 1906 were not subjected to any tests but were assumed to be those of the two victims. The degree of complexity in twenty-first-century analysis of body fluids makes it seem very unlikely that the professor could have reached any firm conclusions about the stains on the underwear in the rape case.[91] Nevertheless, the fact that it was investigated as far as possible makes this incident and enquiry noteworthy.[92] During the seventeen days between receiving the information and his wife examining the complainant, Jones travelled about 135 miles in the course of his investigations, and a further 52 miles investigating a robbery. He spent all of 6 April going to a magistrate for a warrant and walking to the home of the suspect in the rape case to serve the warrant upon him.[93] This was another reason why individuals still investigated and prosecuted many offences themselves.

CONCLUSION

The county police force that existed in Montgomeryshire in the 1870s had been growing and developing since 1840. Constables were positioned strategically around the county, and were organised by a system of chief constable, superintendents, inspectors and sergeants. Local people had grown accustomed to the presence of the force, and some members of the population used them to pursue their claims for justice and recompense. These members included many from the lower orders, indicating a degree of acceptance that contradicts certain studies of working-class and lower middle-class attitudes to the police, and can be explained by analysis of their statuses.[94] The lower orders were also seen to call out the police readily when an out-of-the-ordinary event occurred. There was hostility from some members of the public, and occasionally the police were attacked verbally and physically. They readily defended themselves with their staves, which were used as instruments of aggression at times. Many ratepayers expected the police to do more in response to disorder, and yet these expectations were selective, and hostility was seen to come from the middle classes when the police interfered with their enjoyment of activities. The police were active, particularly in town centres, where people of influence commonly observed them and the disorderly behaviour against which they acted. Undercover policing was carried out in attempts to pre-empt offences, and a remarkable, very early forensic investigation, shows that a sexual offence was taken seriously and that primitive detective techniques were followed.

The following chapter begins a study of the courts, looking first at the work of administrators of justice in the petty sessions, the offences with which they dealt and the people who appeared before them. Later chapters will consider the work of the higher courts of quarter sessions and assizes.

4

PETTY SESSIONS

ATTITUDES, DISCRETION AND DECISIONS

When magistrates attended petty sessions (or summary courts) they were confronted by a range of cases brought to them by members of the public or by the police. These cases could include low-value thefts or minor assaults, criminal damage or drunkenness, and a number of other offences deemed suitable for this lower court.[1] This chapter examines the work of petty sessions in Montgomeryshire, how people used the court, the value of this part of the justice system to those groups, and whether there was an 'upper-class conspiracy' against the largely working-class people who appeared there.[2]

THE WORK OF THE COURTS

The sessions saw a great deal of criminal work of various types. By far the most prevalent offence was that of drunkenness, being approximately equal to the next four most common offences put together (Figure 4.1). Powers of the magistracy were extended during the nineteenth century and resulted in increased work of the petty sessions,[3] but the contribution of the police also led to busier courts as it was they who brought the drunks to court.[4] In the eighteenth century the largest single category of offence was assault,[5] so by prosecuting drunkenness, the police had made a great change to the nature of the courts by the middle of the second half of the nineteenth century. When a comparison is made of Welshpool and Newtown to the less populated areas, it shows that anyone attending court in the urban centres would see an array of cases composed overwhelmingly of drunkenness, street disorder and assault, giving the impression of a 'wild west'.[6] Highway offences, school

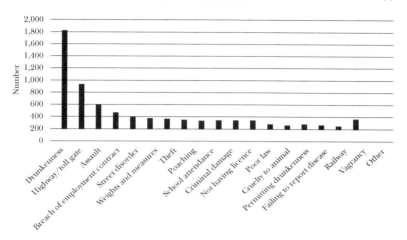

Figure 4.1 Types of offences dealt with by petty sessions. 1869–1878 (5108 cases)

non-attendance and theft, however, were also notable.[7] In other parts of the county, the 'wild' offences also dominated, but poaching, weights and measures, theft and poor law offences such as failing to maintain family members, were present too.

DRUNKENNESS AS A TARGET FOR POLICE ACTIVITY

Drunkenness constituted about a third of the offences prosecuted at petty sessions in Montgomeryshire, and drunkenness with its associated crimes formed a large proportion of cases heard at the lower courts throughout the country.[8] From the seventeenth century drunkenness was seen by some as a sin leading to crime, but during the eighteenth century, people started to see use of alcohol among the labouring classes as a danger to gender roles and to family life, as well as increasing crime.[9] The main role of constabularies was controlling public order and street crime, and it was largely victimless offences that the police tended to target – drunkenness, prostitution, street gaming and street selling.[10] Their involvement with thefts after victims reported their losses was a less prominent characteristic.[11]

The public order function was in response to the demands of those who ultimately paid their wages, viz. the ratepayers. It was also likely that there was pressure from the Bench, but how effective this pressure was, is unclear. Chief constables were answerable to magistrates' police committees, although often the committees would find themselves ignored. Indeed, the chief constables had the support of the Home Office, members of which objected to any attempts to interfere with police independence.[12]

By the mid-Victorian period, drunkenness was seen not only as a cause of wider social ills but as a pathological condition inflicting physical and moral degeneracy.[13] There were calls from the Church, particularly Nonconformists, for temperance with a view to addressing crime, prostitution and poverty.[14] The medical profession also contributed to the debate, as they saw that drunkenness was as much a product of social evils as a cause, and could be a result of an unhealthy environment. Here one is reminded of the correspondence and reports regarding unsanitary conditions. Whereas those promoting temperance campaigned that only by restricting alcohol to all would the danger of drunkenness be avoided, some physicians regarded alcoholism as a disease that required medical intervention.[15] There were branches of the Good Templars Temperance Association in towns around Montgomeryshire, and Sergeant Hudson was a member of the Newtown Temperance Association lodge.[16] There was pressure too from Freemasons, who were known for a preoccupation with moral uprightness,[17] and it was pertinent that Chief Constable Danily was a member of the Newtown lodge of Freemasons, having been instrumental in its foundation.[18]

CONSTABULARY ATTITUDES TOWARDS DRUNKENNESS

There were constant police efforts to clamp down on heavy drinking, and prostitution with its associated offences of petty theft and disorder. Chief Constable Danily appeared before Newtown magistrates in April 1869 to report his dismay at the scenes of disorder his officers faced near brothels. It was reported that he planned to 'exterminate' the women concerned, and that he and his force had been waging a war against the trouble caused inside and near licensed premises.[19] Extant copies of *The Newtown and Welshpool Express* begin with 1869, and thus reports of police activity are available only from that year onwards. However, John Danily became chief constable in 1868,[20] so the high level of arrests for drunkenness and vice may well have been at his instigation, following on quickly from his appointment. Indeed, the wording of newspaper reports suggests that his offensive against such disorder was revolutionary in the county, and yet it is also true that a sharp increase in prosecutions for drunkenness occurred nationwide during the 1870s.[21] Shortly after Danily's diatribe against prostitutes, Sergeant Ross attempted to sort out a disorderly public house.[22] In his evidence to the magistrates, he mentions women. It cannot be certain that these were prostitutes, but it seems likely that at least some of them were, as the house was across the road from Astley's Court, home of Ann Lloyd and Stephen Higgs, later convicted of a serious assault on one of Lloyd's clients.[23] Ross deposed:

> She [the landlady] asked me to clear the house. I told her she must regulate her own house ... There was a great noise in the bar. The bar I should think from its dimensions will hold six to eight persons. I cannot say who they were, there were two women there. I saw Esther Thomas there, drinking a glass of ale. She was quite drunk.[24] I will swear I did not tell Mrs Nock I would go after the men to the Queen's Head when she told me she had turned them out.[25]

The following year, the continued efforts of the police to reduce such disorder, directed by their determined chief constable, were seen when the officers staked out and then stormed the Waggon and Horses, near the canal basin. The landlord had already been warned by Sergeant Hudson about harbouring prostitutes, but the officer described what he found upon raiding the premises on the night of 19 January 1870:

> I visited the house again, in the company of Constable Richards, and found the house to be full of people, especially in the parlour. In the parlour there were no fewer than seven prostitutes, all from Newtown, one of whom had a jug of ale

before her. Another prostitute I saw with a man in a secluded place near the house went afterwards into the house. I stopped about there for some time and saw several of the prostitutes leaving the house with men, some of whom returned into the house again.

There is a similarity between these accounts and that of Constable James James of Merthyr Tydfil, who raided a public house in that south Wales town and recorded in his note-book: '[I found it] full of thieves and prostitutes drinking.'[26] There was a value to the police in knowing the resorts of prostitutes and criminals because as long as they existed, the authorities had a good idea of who the criminals were, where they were and with whom they associated. Chief Constable Danily's campaign against these places, therefore, in some ways played into the hands of the very people he was trying to suppress. He clearly took some effort to achieve his aims in the courts. In January 1872, he attended sessions in Caersws where seven men were charged with being drunk and riotous on Christmas Day. Danily appealed to the Bench, and the newspaper reported:

> He said that young men like the defendants were a great deal of trouble to the police when they [the defendants] were not at work. He pressed the Bench to make an example to others by punishing the offenders now before them.[27]

The justices gave Danily the result he wanted: relatively large financial penalties ranging from 10 shillings to £2, or four-teen days' imprisonment in default. This was the vigour against disorder that led to some of the local populace begin-ning to fear or despise him within a few years of becoming the chief. For example, Benjamin Blythe, a local man with a history of convictions for drunkenness, appeared at sessions in January 1875, charged with assaulting Inspector Davies. The report in *The Newtown and Welshpool Express* reads:

> The inspector stated that on the day in question the defendant was 'mad drunk' at the Oak Inn, and as the inspector and Sergeant Hudson were struggling with him, the defendant mistook the officer for Mr Danily, called him by his name and shouted, 'Damn thee, I'll ruin thee!', at the same time taking deliberate kicks at the inspector.[28]

Danily's obituary shows that he was an Anglican,[29] and showed clearly the zeal against alcohol and other vices often associated with religions and the Freemasons. His nature was expressed openly by one who knew him in a description written after his death. In it, the writer refers to him as 'The Major':

> Lacking the lustre of youth, yet those eyes retained something of that sternness which in other days must have been a terror to all evil doers. They flashed something of their old fire whenever The Major was provoked to expression of righteous indignation.

A picture thus emerges of the chief constable actively pursuing drunks and prostitutes, disorder and vice, within a short time of his appointment, resulting in increased work at the petty sessions. An analysis of the number of prosecutions for drunkenness in the county each year suggests that build-ups of offending were regularly suppressed.

DISCRETION IN THE WORK OF THE PETTY MAGISTRATES

The chief constable appears to have followed a personal agenda in his efforts against crime and disorder. What sort of discretion did the magistrates use? These men sat singly, in pairs or often in a group of three. Opportunities for discretion were numerous as they were the sole judges. There were advantages for the defendant because the cases were dealt with quickly and the penalties handed out were likely to be lower than in a higher court. However, there were concerns about the absence of 'the great safeguard of liberty', namely trial by jury,[30] but there were still many opportunities for negotiation and choices that could lead to a trial in a higher court. For example, at Berriew sessions in 1872 justices John Robinson Jones and John Bayard fined drunken blacksmith John Owen £1. The previous year, Bayard and Major Corbett had fined drunken miller David Williams a mere five shillings because his employer had pleaded for a lenient sentence.[31] These are examples of the magistrates using their discretion when sentencing, and sometimes their discretion frustrated the aims of the chief constable. For example, in January

1870, Constable Ellis of Welshpool charged prostitute Mary Griffiths with wandering about the streets with men in the early hours of a Sunday morning. The magistrates released her with a caution.[32] In May 1871 Constable Tanner charged William Rowlands of the Coach Inn, Welshpool, of permitting drunkenness but the Bench rejected the charge.[33]

There were other cases in which justices used their discretion in a way that the police considered too generous. Prostitute Mary Ann Richards had a long history of offending, and her first appearance in court, in March 1869, resulted in her receiving fourteen days imprisonment for disorderly conduct. Later in the year she received a two-month sentence for an assault on the wife of a hawker. Her next offence received leniency when drunkenness landed her in court again. The justices noted that she had kept out of trouble for several months and gave her a fine of five shillings.[34] Furthermore, when prostitutes Catherine Matthews and Sarah Wilson appeared before Major Drew at his home, Milford Hall, in the salubrious west end of Newtown, both were charged with drunkenness and disorderly behaviour. However, Drew accepted Wilson's plea in mitigation – that she had been assaulted by her client – and fined her one shilling, which was four shillings less than Matthews who had no mitigation.[35] At the same appearance, prostitute Ann Jones was charged with being in town for an unlawful purpose, a charge which she denied. Sergeant Ross and Constable Daniel Richards testified that she was well known to the police, and were confident that they had arrested the right person, but Major Drew acceded to Jones's tearful requests to give her a remand so that she could prove her story at a later date.[36] This leniency is worthy of further investigation, and a newspaper comment published shortly after his death confirms Drew's nature:

> With respect to the deceased it may be said that although, like all mankind, having his failings, yet the late Major Drew had many excellencies, prominent amongst which may be considered his kindness and almost fatherly care of the aged and infirm of the town... Many poor and aged persons will miss his benevolent ministrations to their necessities... It is said, and we have no reason to dismiss its correctness, that many acts of

real charity, of which the world will never be the wiser, were dispensed quietly and unostentatiously at Milford House... For a great number of years the deceased occupied a seat on the Magisterial Bench of his native district, and it is only right to say that those who knew him best will give him the credit of being actuated by a desire to do justly, at the same time to love mercy.[37]

Not all of the magistrates were so open to appeals from defendants, but on the whole, as other historians have found, magistrates' willingness to make concessions to the poor had an important impact on the texture of local social relations, and may have provided some important checks on the power of the 'middling sorts'.[38]

Landowners could use their discretion when perhaps it was politic to do so, as when Canon Herbert, who usually sat at petty sessions in Berriew, allowed a case of poaching on his land in the parish to be discontinued upon the defendant paying costs.[39] Similarly, in November 1870, the Earl of Powis's solicitor dropped the charges against three men who had cooperated with his gamekeeper, although he did, however, proceed against the one man who would not give his name.[40] It has been said that the ideology of paternalism and deference in the countryside both permitted and demanded a certain generosity on the part of landowners.[41] This was particularly the case when the land involved had previously been common or shared. In the case of Canon Herbert, there was another motivation for leniency. The reverend gentleman had been elected honorary canon of Bangor Cathedral in 1855,[42] an establishment that had a history of receiving Montgomeryshire tithes.[43] The payment of tithes was an issue that was to contribute to riots in the early 1880s,[44] and awareness of local sensibilities may have influenced the Canon's judgments. The idea of community was said to imply harmony, and helped to legitimise the position of the middle classes.[45] The magisterial playing-down of the impact of poaching offences also helped to minimise opposition to the landowning classes.

Poaching offences often appeared in court during the winter months. This was the crime closest to the justices, as many of them, such as Canon Herbert and the Earl of Powis, were landowners and probably had sympathy for other land-owners who suffered trespass and losses. In 1870, the chairman of Berriew petty sessions explained grudgingly that they had 'no alternative but to dismiss the case' against a farmer, charged with killing a pigeon, because of a judge's ruling.[46] This is an example of magistrates having to endorse behaviour that was at odds with their own sensibilities. Some-times magistrates felt it was necessary to do this to continue the courts' popularity with the lower classes.[47] Their judge-ments may also have been influenced by political thinking if the persons involved were enfranchised; by 1872 voting had become secret, and a disgruntled man could object with his vote.

When three young men claimed to have permission from a tenant farmer to catch rabbits on his land, which he rented from Lord Sudeley, the clerk gave his opinion that the farmer could not give such permission.[48] This was essentially a crime against Lord Sudeley, and the prosecutor was Sudeley's gamekeeper. The justices were both landowners but there was no suggestion here of favour towards His Lordship. In fact, the Bench openly overruled the clerk, and the defend-ants were discharged. The two magistrates in this case could just as easily have found the men guilty, so the defendants were lucky in the Bench before which they found themselves. In southern England, legal proceedings against trespassers and thieves of wood from a Sussex forest created a defiant feeling and seemed to encourage further offences in attempts to 'test the system'.[49] Some Montgomeryshire magis-trates may have tried to pre-empt this sort of behaviour by handing out lenient sentences or dismissals. The same could not be said of other cases, where the justices did not even adhere to the sentencing descriptors in *Stone's Justices' Manual*.[50] For example, labourer John Thomas was fined £1 for poaching; in default, he received one month in gaol. Poacher Thomas Smout was fined £2 on two separate occa-sions, and both times received a one-month gaol sentence in default of payment.[51] In all three of these cases, fourteen days was the maximum according to *Stone's*, and the excessive sentences reflected the seriousness with which those particular magistrates viewed the crime, or possibly ignorance. There is a question over why their clerk did not advise them that they were stepping outside the law, but it is not clear from the newspaper report whether a clerk was present, and if he was present, who he was. According to trade directories, all the local magistrates' clerks listed in Worrall's *Directory* (1874) were qualified and practising solicitors, but often clerks varied enormously in their industry and competence.[52] Quite possibly, as with the Sudeley case, the magistrates were simply choosing not to accept the clerk's advice. A remarkable demonstration of discretion was shown by Llanidloes magistrates in 1872. Since the sixteenth century, English was the sole language of public administration and of the criminal law courts.[53] However, when Welsh-monoglot hill farmer Thomas Jervis faced his neighbour Lewis Jerman, over a charge of criminal damage, the proceedings were conducted entirely in Welsh, with the required translation into English not provided.[54] *The Newtown and Welshpool Express* reported:

> The hearing of this case caused considerable amusement in court, but being conducted in Welsh, we are not able to give more than a summary of what was so fluently stated by the complainant and defendant ... Several witnesses were examined on both sides, the defendant, in a long, energetic and gesticulatory speech, which for fluency would not have done discredit to an assembly of bards, denying the charge. At first it appeared problematic as to whether their worships had any jurisdiction in the case, but after a long hearing the Bench came to the conclusion that the offence had been committed and inflicted the penalty of 2 shillings and sixpence.[55]

This means that the justices and the clerk must have been Welsh-speakers. The 1891 census, in which the languages of all individuals in Wales were recorded in the form 'Welsh', 'English' or 'Both', shows that the clerk, locally born John Jenkins, was bilingual. None of the justices was present in the census, but earlier censuses show that they were all locally born.[56] As well as this, the justices were a physician, a vicar, and a factory owner employing 200 people. Thus, it is possible that all the men, or at least some of them, knew the participants in the case personally. Time again, the magistrates showed discretion in petty sessions, and here is an example of magistrates using their discretion to suit local language needs. In *History of the Justices of the Peace*, Thomas Skyrme says:

> Some of those on the commissions were unable to stand the strain [of having to deal with Welsh-language issues in court] but much credit is due to the many Welsh justices who stead-fastly did their best to apply the law in what were sometimes intolerable circumstances.[57]

However, the magistrates here were clearly pro-Welsh. Indeed, as they made no effort to provide a translation, they were perfectly happy that the proceedings went ahead solely in Welsh and were therefore unintelligible to some of the people in court. It was noted in an earlier chapter that members of the Llanidloes Bench rarely attended the higher court of quarter sessions, possibly because of logistical reasons. However, it may have been because at quarter sessions there was no chance at all that a trial would go ahead in Welsh only.[58]

FAVOUR SHOWN TOWARDS SOME DEFENDANTS

There were two curious and seemingly inexplicable shows of discretion by Welshpool magistrates in June 1869 when Owen Jones, a blacksmith from Newtown, appeared before them charged with assaulting Superintendent Strefford. The officer had been attacked, both verbally and physically, during two separate incidents on the same day.[59] In front of the justices, Strefford gave unequivocal descriptions of the events following the end of the annual militia training, which began on 22 April and ended with an inspection on 17 May.[60] The men, including Jones, were paid off on 18 May and were in high spirits. 'High spirits' had not led to discretion favour-able to the defendants in other cases, but here the magistrates were willing to be generous, and the case was dismissed. At the same court, Sarah Coles appeared charged with stealing a petticoat from a house in Welshpool at which she and her militiaman husband had been staying during the training. Coles admitted the theft but, according to the newspaper report, the magistrates gave her the benefit of doubt surrounding the case, and the charge was dismissed. An explanation for these shows of discretion lies in the fact that connects the two cases – that both cases involved members of the militia. The control of the militia was in the hands of the lord lieutenant. His role as such included recommending men for places on magisterial Benches, and recommending men to be appointed deputy lieutenants to assist with the running of the county militia. In 1846, the Earl of Powis wrote to a government official recommending twenty-five men as deputy lieutenants. Four of these were men who also became magistrates in due course and were still sitting during the period of the present study.[61] One of them was John Davies Corrie – who was on the Welshpool Bench with borough magistrate Thomas Bowen the day that Jones's and Coles's cases were heard.[62] Thus, at times some magistrates 'looked after their own'.[63]

Most complainants and their accused had to air their cases in open court. Victims of sexual assault had to describe their experiences in front of their alleged attackers and the press, and mothers and putative fathers had to discuss their bastardy cases similarly in front of newspaper men.[64] However, petty sessions – where the justices were in sole control of events – provided a forum at which magistrates could, again, 'look after their own' and give them privacy in which to describe their disputes. This was seen in January 1870, when the justices' clerk at Llanidloes accused one of the Bench of putting him in fear of personal injury. This was the same court that conducted a trial in Welsh with no translation. The newspaper reported:

> After a short consultation between the Rev. J. Evans and Mr Cleaton on the Bench, they, in company with Capt. Crewe-Reade, retired to a private room where, after a short time, the advocates of the respected parties were requested to join them. In a few minutes the magistrates, acting clerk, suitors and solicitors returned to the court where it was stated that the case had been disposed of privately, and the terms of the settlement were not stated in court.[65]

The justices thus had a forum in which they could exercise personal discretion at will. There did not appear to be any person present who queried their actions, except the newspaper reporter whose article could be construed as a veiled criticism.[66]

CONSISTENCY OF SENTENCING

It has been shown how the police, directed by the chief constable, were focused in their aims, while the magistracy appeared unpredictable both in their judgements and the way in which they conducted their courts. There was also a degree of inconsistency in their sentencing in that they sometimes did not abide by the law or showed undue leniency. Sentencing patterns therefore will now be explored, with analyses enabling statistics to be compared in order to look for patterns and anomalies, and to see if anything can be deduced about the nature of the county from the level of fines handed out. Drunkenness was by far the most notable single offence, comprising a third of the total number of offences, and statistics were calculated for all the petty sessional divisions, including the range of the fines imposed, the average fine and the modal, or most common, fine. It should be borne in mind, however, that out of a total of 1,756 drunkenness cases found in the sample studied, the value of the fine imposed is known for only 892 (51 per cent). This is because often the newspaper report gave the fine including costs. It was found that none of the courts imposed a fine that was above the maximum permitted, namely £2, and in most divisions the modal value was 5 shillings. However, the mean and mode showed considerable divergence for Benches dealing with small numbers of known cases, therefore the analysis takes the four Benches in which the data are most internally consistent and dependable. For Newtown, Welshpool, Montgomery and Llanidloes, the measures of central tendency are very similar, and these Benches also show similarity between the range of fines levied. An obvious difference is the high value of fines imposed in Welshpool, where 72 per cent of convicted individuals received a fine of more than ten shillings compared to Newtown, where 20 per cent received

this high level of financial penalty. Conversely, Welshpool
magistrates gave small fines of less than five shillings to only
21 per cent of persons, compared to 72 per cent in Newtown.
Can a factor be found to explain higher fines being given in
Welshpool? Study of the details of the crimes shows that it
was the same range of people offending in the different
areas. Often they were labourers, women with no given occupation, tinkers and vagrants. However, many of the middle
classes, including farmers and shopkeepers, were also
charged with drunkenness. Thus, the higher penalties
imposed in Welshpool may have been based not so much on
the circumstances of the offence, which could be very similar,
but on some other class-based criterion. This could be ability
to pay, and would indicate a generally higher income in
Welshpool.[67] If Welshpool justices also gave long prison
sentences this would point to a strict Bench in that town.
However, analysis of prison terms imposed indicates that
Welshpool magistrates were giving below the county average
for length of sentence. The Montgomery Bench was giving
slightly above. It must be said that the number of sentences
involving prison was small, and thus definite conclusions
cannot be drawn, but this investigation supports the suggestion that magistrates were basing their fine levels on ability to
pay and that the income in Welshpool was generally higher
than elsewhere in the county.

ANALYSIS OF FINES IMPOSED

Most of the people convicted at petty sessions received fines.
Calculations involving known fines give a mean county fine
of 19s. 8d. Examples of cases that resulted in fines well over
the county average were that of a publican who served beer
to an intoxicated person, resulting in a £20 penalty,[68] and
indeed publicans generally received higher fines than the
drunks they served. Other examples are a veterinary surgeon
who left his horse to suffer on a road,[69] and a farmer who
kept a horse and groom without a licence.[70] The penalties
imposed for breach of employment contract appear high,
but were usually the amount of pay owing, not a fine *per se*.[71]
In a similar way, poor-rate penalties tended to be the amount

of financial support owing. Another offence receiving a high penalty was the prosecution of the Cambrian Railway Company on four counts of failing to ensure clean pens for the transportation of animals. Upon conviction, the company received a penalty of £10 for each count.[72] It is clear from this analysis that in Montgomeryshire fines were well below the maximum allowed, which reflects the relatively low prosperity of the county. New laws also created criminals. Prior to the 1870 Education Act, families did not have to send children to school, and it was usual for offspring to join parents at work.[73] Now the new legislation was changing common working practices and was causing real hardship.[74] The justices seem to have recognised this and were sympathetic as in some cases they would not enforce payment of fines if the children started to attend, or while very poor families sought assistance from the poor-law guardians.[75] It was recognised that these parents were not criminals in the accepted sense, and this explains why justices were sometimes willing to be accommodating.[76]

BIND-OVER ORDERS

Most of the sentences, about 90 per cent, handed out by Montgomeryshire magistrates were fines. A small proportion of assault and disorder offences received bind-overs, and on two occasions petitioners applied for bind-over orders to be imposed on alleged troublemakers. In modern terms, such a restriction is defined as 'not a punishment but is to prevent apprehended danger of a breach of the peace'. The order must be for a specified fixed period and involves a financial bond. Furthermore, there has to be sufficient information before the court to justify the conclusion that there is a real risk of a breach of the peace unless action is taken to prevent it, and the alleged aggressor has to agree to the order.[77] No such definition existed in nineteenth-century terms, but magistrates were very ready to impose a bind-over because of apparent 'magic effects' of the scrutiny of the community.[78] An investigation now follows in order to discern the nature of the bind-over order in nineteenth-century Montgomeryshire. Looking first at those assaults which received financial or custodial penalties, sometimes the offence took place in the presence of witnesses, and occasionally resulted in a visible injury. Typically, the details of the assaults that received bind-overs were very similar to those receiving other penalties, but whereas a fine or prison sentence was given to only one of the parties, the bind-over was often given to both. The impression given by this is that the justices regarded the pattern of behaviour deserving a bind-over to be more of a quarrel, with each side being as culpable as the other.[79]

THE BIND-OVER ORDER USED IN CASES OF DOMESTIC ASSAULTS

During the nineteenth century, domestic violence against women became increasingly unacceptable, and in 1878 the Matrimonial Causes Act gave magistrates the power to order the separation of an abused wife from the abuser, and order him to pay maintenance. Later, the Summary Jurisdiction Act of 1895 allowed the wife to obtain a separation order.[80] Analysis of a murder case in England in 1864 shows that the court was already demonstrating attempts to 'place violence against wives beyond the pale of respectability'.[81] In December 1870 in Newtown, John Jenkins, a journeyman tailor living with his family in Albion Yard in Newtown, was charged by his wife with abusing her. The man asked the Bench if they would order him to pay a medium amount of maintenance to let him be free of her.[82] The magistrates were unable to accede to this, but it was appeals to the Bench such as this that led to the 1878 Matrimonial Causes Act being passed eventually. Mrs Jenkins was not in court, and the Bench chairman, Canon Herbert, ordered that both parties should appear at a later date so that the situation could be addressed. The reappearance took place two weeks later, but Mrs Jenkins was not disposed to prosecute. Consequently the case was dismissed, but Canon Herbert did give Jenkins a caution. It was common for applicants to overrate the magistrates' legal powers to intervene in domestic disputes, and they often showed a mistaken belief that the justices could make protection orders or grant a divorce or separation.[83] Often a wife did not want to proceed because if a husband was imprisoned or fined it would mean financial difficulty for the family.[84] A bind-over order was often at the request of the wife, and mentions fear of retribution upon release as a woman's motivation for not wanting her husband to be imprisoned. Sometimes the woman hoped that merely the appearance in court would have a deterrent effect on the man.[85] John Morgan, a Welshpool tailor, received a bind-over order for assaulting his wife and was not punished by the court by any fine or term of imprisonment.[86] The Bench may have taken into account this man's promise to be of good behaviour in the future.[87] However, the penalty for common assault in the late nineteenth century was a fine of up to £5, or up to two months' imprisonment without a fine.[88] There was also the charge of aggravated assault against a female available to the Bench, and this was punishable by a fine of up to £20 or six months' imprisonment. The sentences imposed in this case show that the sentencing directions in Stone's for assault were not used,[89] but the magistrates may have considered that the restraining effect of the bind-over was a better protection for the woman than a one-off fine or period of custody. It also is clear that sometimes the justices considered a domestic assault to be something removed from other types of violence, something that needed to be dealt with differently. This is seen in the judgement of the Berriew Bench when they allowed such an assault prosecution to be discontinued on the defendant's paying costs 'as it was a family affair'.[90] The following year, the same phrase was used in a different petty sessional division, when a man's assault on his sister-in-law was given a low fine.[91] The chairman in both cases was John Robinson Jones, and in a later section there will be an analysis of judgements in court being a reflection of a justice's personal opinion.

Women were about ten times less likely as men to receive bind-over orders for assault.[92] This is likely to reflect the women's inability to find the money for the bond required, which was considerably higher than the level of a fine, and here again is an illustration of the justices using their local knowledge and discretion. Historians accept that a woman's economic situation was a gender-associated factor contributing to sentencing outcomes.[93] An illustration of this that is pertinent to the present discussion is the case of Mary Horley, charged with using threatening language towards her sister. Horley was unemployed and living on her married sister's charity. She was unable to pay the bond required for a bind-over, so in default was removed to custody for three months.[94] By giving the bind-over, which they knew she could not pay, the magistrates were in effect giving custody as the sentence. As far as disorder was concerned, the impression of an ad hoc approach to the handing out of sentences appears. For example, four men fighting at a railway station were fined by Caersws magistrates, but two men fighting in Llanfyllin were both bound over.[95] A Montgomery woman who threatened to dash her neighbour's brains out was bound over for six months, but a Welshpool woman who used obscene language towards another was fined.[96] The nature of petty sessions as a forum where the justices had sole discretion and ability to bring in their own sensibilities and experiences when making judgements is apparent. It is possible now to give a definition of a bind-over order in nineteenth-century, Montgomeryshire terms: that such orders were imposed in cases where a continuing pattern of violent offending was occurring, with contributing factors coming from both parties, or when the supervisory nature of the order may have had a helpful restraining effect. They were sometimes imposed for one-off incidents of street disorder, and often replaced a financial or custodial sentence, particularly for assaults involving family members. They were occasionally used as an indirect way of imposing custody.

CONSISTENCY WHEN SENTENCING TO IMPRISONMENT

Periods of incarceration were often imposed when a convicted person defaulted on payment of a fine, and Mary Horley received imprisonment when she was unable to find a bond. Prison as an initial sentence was less common, with 152 persons receiving custody for a range of offences including drunkenness, assaulting a police officer, pickpocketing and vagrancy. What was it about these cases that made them deserving of custody? Richard Hughes was already a well-known face when he appeared in court in Montgomery in January 1869.[97] He received seven days for his

drunkenness on this occasion, and was to see the interior of
Montgomery gaol again for the same offence in 1871 and
1872.[98] His repeat offending made his crime worse in the
eyes of the justices, as five drunkenness charges against other
people at the same hearing resulted in minimum fines.
Hughes was described as having the alias 'Dick Luney', inti-
mating that his pattern of behaviour was recognised locally as
being particularly eccentric, with his noticeable behaviour
making him a special case.[99] The seven-day period he
received was the length allowed for default of a small fine,
which gives an indication of how serious the Bench considered his offending to be.[100] Alfred Owen had already received
several convictions for drunkenness when he was charged at
Welshpool sessions in 1875. He did not appear to answer this
time, and in his absence was given twenty-one days, presum-
ably to be arrested on a warrant.[101] Richard Jones appeared
in court on a drunkenness charge for the forty-ninth time,
and received one month in gaol.[102] Thus, as far as drunkenness was concerned, prison was being used almost as a last
resort for repeat offenders, suggesting that the magistrates
considered custody to be the most onerous of penalties. This
is seen in their use of prison as a threat when they gave
Charles Benbow a five-shilling fine and told him that if he
defaulted, he would be sent inside for fourteen days. They
were speaking outside the law here, however, as the maximum
term of incarceration permitted for default of this amount
was seven days.[103] The same magistrates had given the correct
sentence a year previously, when they threatened Sarah
Beedles with fourteen days in default of the higher fine of
twenty shillings and when they threatened to send Ann
Jenkins to gaol if she appeared before them again charged
with being drunk and disorderly.[104]

   The Newtown Bench expressed their desire to protect the
police when they sentenced Samuel Davies to a month in
gaol for an assault on Constable Rees, although at the same
sessions they sentenced Benjamin Blythe to a forty-shilling
fine for an assault on Inspector Davies.[105] There were differences in the nature of the offences in that Davies had
launched a deliberate attack, bitten the officer, inflicted a
serious wound and subsequently absconded, whereas Blythe

had mistaken the inspector for Chief Constable Danily and was now very contrite. William Pryce was given two months with hard labour for a knife attack on Constable Richards in Newtown. Thus, a pattern is appearing of heavy sentences for attacks on policemen, and indeed out of 14 incidents of such assaults, 13 received gaol sentences or fines of at least ten shillings. The one exception was a miner who attacked and beat up Sergeant Owen in Llanidloes and received a five-shilling fine, equivalent to a first-time drunk's fine for disorder.[106] It is unclear from the newspaper report why such a low-level fine was imposed.

By the 1850s, petty sessions were dealing with many larcenies, or thefts.[107] Table 4.1 summarizes the lengths of custody given for different types of offences.[108] Overall, items that were more valuable received longer periods of custody but there are a few anomalies. It seems unreasonable that the theft of coal worth ten pence should receive the same sentence as stealing £22, but on studying the facts of the cases, the coal theft involved a degree of subterfuge and betrayal of an employer's trust.[109] The man who took the £22 stole it from his grandfather and left a letter telling of his

Offence	Length of sentence
Theft of £11 12s.	
Stealing equipment worth £4	3 months
Stealing coal worth 10d	
Stealing organ grinder's monkey	1–2 months
Stealing pieces of cloth	
Stealing £22	
Theft of trowel	
Theft of seven rose bushes	
Theft by finding of donkey	7 days
Theft of plasterer's tool	
Theft of half a pound of butter	

Table 4.1 Range of stolen items and the gaol sentences received at petty sessions

plans, but the old man did not see it until after the matter was in police hands. The magistrates described it as a 'very peculiar case' and wanted to inflict the smallest penalty.[110] The magistrates thus showed a great deal of discretion in their judgements. They did not generally show the same determination as the police in pursuing prosecutions, and there are instances where both consistent and inconsistent approaches to judgements and sentencing were apparent.

LOCALS' USE OF THE COURTS IN PURSUANCE OF PARTICULAR CAUSES

It has been shown how the police used petty sessions to pursue their campaign against disorder, and that the Bench had sole discretion in judgements and sentencing. Those members of the public who appeared in court in the various roles of prosecutor, defendant, witness or spectator were not, however, simply bit-players in the action around them. Vivid pictures can be painted of the working classes obtaining justice and advice, and not having to face the 'ruling class conspiracy' against them that some historians argue existed.[111] When Ann Griffiths was threatened by her neighbour over use of a shared bread oven, she firstly went to their landlord to try to resolve the situation. Later, when the neighbour physically assaulted Griffiths, and thus when the dispute involved criminal actions, Griffiths sought the protection of the law.[112] She obtained a summons for the arrest of the neighbour and the pair appeared before Canon Herbert and Captain Crewe-Reade. Griffiths was granted compensation, and the neighbour was given a fine but went to gaol in default. This is an example of local people using the easily accessible local courts to achieve satisfaction and recompense. The lower orders also had the confidence to use the system for their own ends, and this was recognised by the justices themselves. After labourer's wife Sarah George failed to appear to prosecute her case of alleged assault by a neighbour, magistrate Charles Thruston observed that it was a common practice for people to take out summonses in order to bully or frighten, with no intention of appearing in court to pursue the claim.[113] It is clear that often prosecutors were using the courts to sort out their disputes, and disagreements were frequently aired before the Bench. Charge and counter-charge were commonly seen, and often involved neighbours. For example, in September 1870 the Machynlleth Bench heard the case of Hannah Jones *v.* Elizabeth Gittins, followed by Elizabeth Gittins *v.* Hannah Jones. The newspaper reported that 'after a patient hearing, the magistrates dismissed the summonses, each side to pay its own costs'.[114] Many examples of this sort are seen, with both sides often being bound over to keep the peace, or the cases being dismissed. Evan Ashton may well have been taken aback when both he and the person he charged with assaulting him were required to pay £5 to be bound over.[115] Although Charles Thruston made his comment about people using the justice system to intimidate others, he made no mention of those landowners who used the criminal courts to establish rights for themselves. Edward Morris's lawyer stated at Llanidloes sessions that Morris had brought a case of illegal fishing 'not for vindictive reasons but simply for the assertion and maintenance of his rights',[116] and farmer James Powell admitted to Welshpool magistrates that he had brought a charge against a youth (of criminal damage to a boat) in order to stop people from using his vessel to cross the Severn.[117] The summary courts were often used by individuals for resolving their disputes, and the magistrates were fully aware of their mission to help resolve those problems and disputes that arose from miscellaneous rather than class-based social relations.[118]

The magistrates did not necessarily support people in authority. County court bailiff Nathaniel Hawkins was shocked when the Welshpool Bench convicted him of 'annoying' twenty-year old basket maker William Morgan.[119] River bailiff John Dickens charged three men with throwing stones at him and had a witness to support his claims. Nevertheless, the case was dismissed because of lack of identifying evidence, especially since five witnesses came forward to say the defendant was elsewhere at the time.[120] As well as enabling local people to have their say in support of others, court appearances enabled a woman, who might not be able to defend herself physically against a man, to fight against perceived injustice. When tollgate lessee James Pryce tried to throw his gatekeeper out and assaulted her in the process, she took him to court. Even though Pryce had legal representation, the magistrates found in favour of his unrepresented female former employee, and she received compensation.[121] Even when a defendant had indeed committed the crime of which he or she was accused, the formalised arena overseen by dispassionate parties with set rules, allowed detail to be introduced which could provide mitigation. William Williams took Jane Gough to petty sessions, accusing her of hitting him. After hearing various witness give testimony, the justices deemed the assault proved, but as Williams had used the words 'thou art nothing but a prostitute', deemed by the Bench to be 'very provocative', they told him he was very much to blame, and inflicted a minimum fine on Gough.[122] However, as seen with some assaults on wives, the records of sessions indicate that various magistrates allowed a family dispute to be treated differently from others. After Edward Bebb struck his sister-in-law three times in the presence of her husband, it was deemed a 'family affair' and a minimal fine of sixpence was imposed.

CONCLUSION

Members of the public were not intimidated by the local courts. They used the sessions readily to sort out disputes and to establish rights, although the situation was often different when it came to domestic assaults. The petty sessions could almost be described as a court of appeal. Residents commonly brought their disputes to be heard by the justices, who were local men of standing and property who judged the cases using local knowledge, their own sensibilities, and guidance from *Stone's* and their clerk. They were not averse to ignoring the latter two sources of advice, however. There was one remarkable case in which the proceedings were conducted entirely in Welsh without a translation into English. The cases show that the justice system was not closed to the lower orders, and they used it readily at times to pursue their own agendas. The impression given by these sessions is of a flexible and highly selective system.

The police brought many offending members of the public to petty sessions where Chief Constable Danily saw his efforts rewarded or frustrated. He and his officers could not rely on the magistrates to support the constabulary's pursuit of disorder, as the justices used their discretion when deciding on penalties. This meant a rather ad hoc approach to the sentences imposed. However, the officers could generally be confident that if they were assaulted while on duty, the courts would come down heavily on the aggressors. Study of the financial penalties imposed across the full range of offences shows that the justices took ability to pay into account, revealing that Welshpool was more prosperous than other towns, but that the county as a whole was poor. Bind-over orders were given as a method of controlling behaviour but involved a financial component that was beyond the means of many, particularly women.

The next chapter investigates the court of quarter sessions, where the magistrates were not the sole arbiters, but where local men played a part in the judicial decision-making process.

5

QUARTER SESSIONS

FARMERS, FELONS AND JURIES

Attention here is on a higher court where cases deemed more serious were heard. The magistrates will be seen again, but with other justices from around Montgomeryshire, sitting on the combined county Bench. The chapter will explore the process by which cases appeared in the court, and examine the contributions made by the public and the police. The input of magistrates will be examined to look at whether the discretion seen previously – at times generous and lenient or inexplicably stern and harsh – appeared again, and sentencing patterns will be pursued. The overall investigation will be to discover if quarter sessions favoured the middle classes, how the influence of that social group was seen in court, and to what extent it diminished or enhanced the magistrates' discretion.

DID STATUS OR INCOME HAVE A BEARING ON THE ROUTE TO COURT?

During the seventeenth and eighteenth centuries, virtually all detection of crime was a matter of private initiative, with the state intervening only in matters concerning the role of government, for example in forgery or coining offences.[1] In the nineteenth century an individual's decision to proceed with court action was supposedly a merit of the British legal system, and it has been calculated from Monmouthshire quarter sessions data that during the first half of the century, at least 66 per cent of prosecutors were the victims.[2] Court proceedings often 'nourished ill feeling' within a community but nevertheless complainants frequently brought to the courts charges of violence and assault, which arose frequently from disputes between family members or near neighbours.[3]

The new, professional police of the nineteenth century usually prosecuted only when they themselves had been injured, or in cases of larceny from the person, or in street crime. In quarter sessions about 21 per cent of the cases studied were prosecuted by the police, and these were mainly crimes of theft.[4] Study of the details of the cases reveals no apparent reason why the police took charge of some of the cases and not others. They often prosecuted when the victims were women, but not always, or when the accused person pleaded guilty and the victim did not appear. It is said that:

> ... the new police were sucked into acting as prosecutors from their early years because of the poverty of some of the victims of theft. [A police superintendent] explained to the constabulary commissioners that on one occasion, arresting police constables had been obliged to pay for a bill of indictment since the two prosecutors in the case were too poor. It may be significant that in several cases in mid-nineteenth century Bedfordshire, in which the police had acted as prosecutor, or joint prosecutor, the victim or joint prosecutor was a woman ... In 1866 there were ninety-five indictments at quarter sessions of which 47 were preferred by Nottinghamshire constabulary ... These Nottinghamshire cases do not readily reveal much in the way of common characteristics suggesting why some rather than others were taken on by the police.[5]

When considering quarter sessions, there is another change brought about by the police as they made the higher court accessible to people who might otherwise not have pursued their losses. There were some cases in which the police went to extraordinary lengths to apprehend the suspect. For example, the jury at Hilary quarter sessions in 1870 heard the facts of a case involving the theft of fowls and potatoes from a farm a few miles from Newtown.[6] Not only did Inspector Davies visit the scene of the crime, but Constable Hudson went in pursuit of a suspect gang of gypsies described by the farmer, travelling about twenty-five miles until he caught the gang in Shropshire. In another theft case heard at the same sessions, Inspector Davies testified that he trailed a suspect from Llandinam to Berriew, a distance of about sixteen miles. At the Easter sessions of 1869, the jury heard how a man suspected of obtaining money by false pretences was found in police custody in Maentwrog which is about forty miles away by road.[7] Although in earlier times victims themselves would chase suspects for long distances, by the mid-nineteenth century those with money sometimes paid the police to do the chasing. There is no record that the victims in the cases mentioned earlier did so, but they were a farmer, a butcher and a timber merchant – men who could pay a fee. They were also the sort of men who would be called for jury service, so the police might have wanted to be careful not to antagonise them. In fact, the butcher mentioned was on the jury list at the midsummer sessions six months earlier.[8] It is also possible that these men were members of so-called felons associations, as was James Eddowes of Welshpool, who became a felons association committee member in March 1870 and prosecuted two labourers at the Michaelmas sessions later in the same year. John Hickman, John Morris and John Sayce were also association members, and each brought charges to quarter sessions during the decade.[9] Such societies were groups of men who banded together and were prepared to pay the costs of apprehending suspects and bringing them to justice, including offering rewards for information.[10] There were at least 450 such associations created in England and Wales between 1744 and 1856, and newspaper descriptions of events in Welshpool show that there was one in that town during the period studied here.[11] Study of the names of members shows that they were retailers and skilled workers, living around the centre of town and included the sort of men who could be found on the local board, possibly become magistrates or be called for jury service. They were the kind of men already identified as those who were influenced by observable police activity. At a time when accused persons were increasingly using lawyers to defend themselves, and complainants were more and more reluctant to take on the prosecutions themselves,[12] membership of a felons association eased the way to hiring an advocate to do this for them. The joining fee, however, effectively excluded the poor from their number. Notable in the list of names are Edward Harrison and William Withy who were chairmen of the Welshpool Bench at times during the 1870s, and members of the local board. One wonders how they could possibly have been considered impartial in their judgements in court. Sometimes there was a 'preoccupation with law and order at a broader level' by members of the Bench who were also involved in community politics, as was the case with Harrison and Withy.[13] Appointments to the board of the local infirmary could create political debate,[14] and although no such discussion is recorded regarding appointments to the Bench, it is likely that there was disquiet in some quarters regarding political motivations.

In 1904, local solicitor Charles Edward Howells wrote an article for *The Montgomeryshire Collections* in which he described the foundation of the Welshpool felons association in 1836.[15] He listed the rules of the newly formed society, and one of them was:

> That the treasurer, secretary or either of the committee upon notice given them of any such offence as aforesaid are empowered immediately to cause proper advertisements to be printed, published and dispersed, and to dispatch such persons as they shall think proper in pursuit of such lost property and suspected person or persons. And that the treasurer pay all costs, charges and expenses attending the pursuit, apprehending and prosecuting all such offenders out of the funds of the society.

Thus, the pursuit of the gypsies across the hills near Newtown to Shropshire may well have been a result of membership of such a group, although no record of a Newtown association has been found. The limiting effect of costs was a contributing factor in the foundation of the Welshpool group. The preamble to the rules and regulations read:

> … whereas several horses, sheep and other cattle have been stolen and frequent burglaries, felonies and larcenies of various kinds committed in the parish of Pool and its neighbourhood, and the offenders have often escaped justice for want of immediate pursuit and effectual prosecution … we do agree … to raise and maintain a fund for the prosecution of all such offences.[16]

It should be noted that the Welshpool association was founded at the same time as Welshpool Borough police, and it has been found in studies of other counties that there was a correlation between foundation of felons associations and early establishment of police forces. Often men of influence in those areas required more than the protection of just one type of force, or encouraged the police by giving rewards.[17] A similar association was founded in Llanfair Caereinion, a farming area ten miles west of Welshpool, in 1875. This was a relatively late foundation and supports the local feeling that country areas were poorly patrolled by the county police who had been in place for thirty-five years. No doubt the main purpose behind this association was the same as in Welshpool, but the local vicar, the Revd E. Jones, was broader when he made an address at the first annual meeting, touching on Christian teaching in his reference to revenge:

> We have met here for the first time to inaugurate the establishment of a society for the prosecution of felons. I hope there are not many in this parish who correspond with the definition of felon. This society will naturally not be popular with the class of people who are in the habit of committing petty thefts, and I take it that the mere fact of such a society being established amongst us will be the means of preventing acts of this description. The law is rigorous but does not contemplate revenge; but punishment is necessary to ensure respect for the laws of our country.[18] It is not so much for the positive good that our society has done that we rejoice. We all know that 'prevention is better than cure' and I am glad to hear that the members have already felt the benefits of having such an association amongst them, and are congratulating themselves upon the good already done. It is not so much to catch the mice that we have a cat but to scare them, and it is gratifying to hear that the society has been the means of scaring the offenders. Another good effect of the association is that it brings us together, and I am convinced that the more we are brought together the more we shall esteem each other. I have great pleasure, gentlemen, in giving you success to the Llanfair Association for the Prosecution of Felons. (Loud applause).[19]

In a later address by one of the members, a toast was made to
the farmers of the area, the speaker claiming that Llanfair
farmers were among the best in the county. This gives a sense
that farmers were the most vigorous and successful complainants, and possibly most of the membership. A motivation for
prosecution of cases was a victim's desire to protect his or her
reputation,[20] and there was an element of this among the
farmers, especially those who were prominent in the local
community, those perhaps who appeared on the superior
grand juries which will be discussed in a subsequent section.
During the vicar's speech, plaudits were made to the magistrates of the Llanfair Bench, described as being 'noted for
their wisdom', giving the impression that petty sessions
judgements were usually made in favour of the prosecutor.
As well as this, the justices were landowners and employers,
the sort of men the felons association members wanted to
keep on their side.[21] During the first year of its life, the Llanfair association employed solicitor Charles Spencer Thorne
to prosecute its cases, revealed by the censuses to be in his
early twenties and not likely to be very experienced.[22]
However, when Thorne left the area in February 1875, his
successor was Welshpool heavyweight, George D. Harrison,
solicitor to local major landowners and magistrates Capt.
Mytton and John Naylor. The engagement of this prominent
lawyer shows that the association had proved popular and
worthwhile, and that subscriptions were of such a level as to
enable payment of Mr Harrison's fees.

THE CASES

Quarter sessions, although with its pomp and ceremony a
more visible event in the community than petty sessions, was
a situation in which a much smaller number of cases was
heard. Over the course of the ten-year period 1869–78,
almost ten times fewer cases were heard there than at petty
sessions.[23] The percentages of different types of crime were
also very different at the lower and higher sessions. In
summary courts, offences involving drunkenness, poaching
and highways were the major feature, whereas at quarter
sessions theft cases dominated (Figure 5.1).[24]

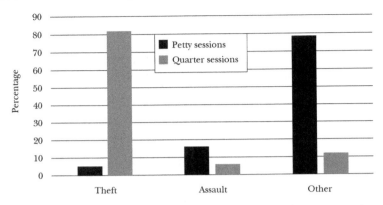

Figure 5.1 Percentages of cases appearing at petty and quarter sessions, 1869–78.

At petty sessions, the few theft cases that were heard included food and crops, livestock and money, but were mainly tools and equipment or clothes and footwear. At quarter sessions, the biggest single type of theft was that of clothing or footwear, reflecting their value and the gravity with which this category of theft was generally regarded.[25] The criteria which determined whether the accused was sent to the higher court were seriousness and whether or not there was a guilty plea.[26] Money thefts prosecuted before petty sessions involved small amounts of a few pence or shillings, whereas all the money thefts at the higher court were of relatively large sums, the largest amount claimed to have been lost being £40. The average amount was £5 8s. although most losses were less than £4.[27]

In an agricultural area, such as mid-Wales, the theft of livestock might be expected to be prevalent, with animals left out in fields liable to be taken by locals and suspect outsiders such as tramps and hawkers.[28] But this sort of case constituted only 9 per cent of thefts prosecuted during 1869–78. Studies of horse and sheep stealing in Wales at the end of the eighteenth century and into the first three decades of the nineteenth century have found that Montgomeryshire was a major source of stolen horses with its proximity to the English border, particularly to Shropshire, being fundamental to the thefts as it meant that disposal was relatively easy. These thefts have been identified as an indication of the pre-industrialised nature of the county at that time, with few other criminal opportunities available.[29] One of the objects of the various felons associations was to pursue the loss of livestock, and as three cases originated in Llanfair Caereinion after the date of foundation of that town's association, it will be useful to see the progress of them through the legal system.[30]

John Jones lived with his family on a farm near Llanfair Caereinion. In early March 1878, a police officer came to him with two hens that had been seized from a tramp found wandering locally. Jones had not reported the loss; in fact, he was not even aware that any stock was missing. He said at the trial of the tramp, 'I counted them at the end of February and there were forty-two. I counted them again on 16 March [when the officer brought the hens to him] and there were thirty-five. They are my hens to the best of my knowledge.' Here is an example of a farmer simply not noticing a 17 per cent reduction in numbers. The tramp in this case was tracked down and arrested following a tip-off from a poultry dealer in the town of Meifod. At the trial the dealer said,

> The prisoner came to me with couple of fowls and asked me to buy them. I said, 'They are old ones,' and he said, 'One was a two-year-old but the other was quite a young one'. He asked me 5 shillings for them but I said they weren't worth it. I then sent for Constable Richards.

The poultry dealer also said that he had come across the prisoner previously. His eagerness to send for the constable could have been from suspicion and from a concern for law and order, or it could have been from a desire not to be implicated in any dishonest dealings. Traders were regularly associated with receiving stolen goods, and dealers and retailers made profits from receiving. There were butchers and poulterers who received game from poachers and who sometimes even organised poaching gangs.[31] In a second case from Llanfair Caereinion, farmer John Emberton lost three fowls, stolen by a tramp known as Australian Jack. The same tramp also stole two fowls from Emberton's neighbour Margaret Edwards.[32] It is not clear if Emberton was a member of the felons association, and as the suspect pleaded guilty, there was no trial and few details are available. What is clear, however, is that whereas Emberton was a prosperous farmer of 205 acres, Mrs Edwards was a widow with relatively meagre nine acres. In a show of cooperation, or a desire to see the thief suitably punished, Emberton assisted the less able widow with the expenses, thereby enabling a prosecution that otherwise would not have taken place. This also shows that the better-off members of the community were at an advantage when it came to pursuing losses.

THE INPUT OF WOMEN IN PROSECUTIONS

Widow Margaret Edwards of Llanfair Caereinion could only pursue her loss of fowls with the support of her neighbour. In 1871, widow Elizabeth Parry lost a horse from a field on her sixty-eight-acre farm in north Montgomeryshire.[33] From the depositions it is clear that Mrs Parry was proactive in organising her servants in tracking hoof prints and sending word to the nearest policeman, some five miles away.[34] Leaflets advertising the theft were also printed and distributed, and here is evidence that a better-off farmer, because of more available resources, could help herself.[35] This supports the previous assertion that the better-off members of the community were at an advantage. The list of members of the Welshpool association showed two female members who were represented by men at the inaugural meeting.[36] By the 1870s more women members were likely, and these could be some, perhaps most, of those women who were represented by police at sessions. The charges they brought were solely those of theft. Some of these cases seem unusual in that the items stolen were of low value and a summary hearing would have been appropriate. Examination of the details shows that the victim in one of the cases was the headmistress of a private Welshpool school who lost a pair of stockings from a washing line. The other was the housemaid of a lady described in court as 'Mrs Hughes of Cemmaes', shown on the census as living on independent means and having three live-in servants.[37] The policeman in this case, also a stockings theft, trailed the suspect for four miles and arrested him, at which point the man exclaimed: 'You will not take me up for stealing a pair of stockings I should think!' It is not clear why the theft of these stockings resulted in a quarter sessions trial, but it meant that the respectable woman was given the benefit of not having to share the court with the prostitutes and tramps at petty sessions. Her complaint was also seen to be treated more seriously. Perhaps Mrs Hughes was on good terms with the local magistrates who sent the case up to the higher court. Any prosecutor could opt for taking the case to the higher court instead of petty sessions if he or she particularly wanted to make an example of the offender,[38] but details studied here suggest that in the case of a woman victim, her respectability had something to do with the decisions made. There are cases known where details of an offence have been deliberately manipulated, often to spare the accused person from a severe penalty.[39] The stockings case here also shows a manipulation, but this time to spare the prosecutrix having to attend petty sessions.

DISCRETION OF THE WIDER COMMUNITY: THE GRAND JURY

The general public made little contribution to discretion in the lower court as they had no say in the judgement or sentencing. At quarter sessions, there was a difference because a selected group of men – the grand jury – could determine a case's continued journey through the legal procedure. They could even throw it out (find 'no true bill', or 'ignore it') at the very beginning of the court's criminal business.[40] Grand jurors were selected from a pool of men who were wholly unrepresentative because the selection was restricted to men of between twenty-one and sixty years of age who owned or rented property of a at least a certain minimum value.[41] These men were of higher social standing than those selected for the jury at the trial itself, the so-called 'petty jury'. The men understood that a seat in the grand jury implied higher status, but instances were found when a particular man sat in the grand jury in one session, and the petty jury in another, showing an implied change of status or 'downgrading'.[42] An investigation was carried out to determine the characteristics of these men. The analysis shows that the largest single type of occupation represented was that of farmer, with about forty providing grand jury service in any one year during the period studied. Retailers, including men such as drapers, but also those who might have used artisan skills such as shoemakers and tailors, were the next most prolific group at around twenty sittings per year. Merchants were also included in the retail group. Skilled manual workers, for example plumbers and blacksmiths, served between two and sixteen times per year. Professional men such as schoolmasters and land agents, and those who classified themselves as gentlemen, served between one and eight times per year. These occupational sets were the sort of men who constituted a group gaining greater recognition during the nineteenth century as, for example, in the campaign for parliamentary reform in 1830–2. The term 'middle classes' recognised the considerable range of status and wealth denoted by the term, from prosperous merchants and manufacturers to shopkeepers and master craftsmen.[43] Middle-class formation has been defined as being not only those with middle-status occupations but also a self-aware social group that could act collectively. This is perfectly illustrated in quarter sessions where the middle classes acted in concert in the form of the felons associations and juries.[44]

Analysis of grand juries in the industrialised English Midlands found that members were mainly farmers, tradesmen, professionals and gentlemen, and that very few were artisans or skilled manual workers.[45] This is different to Montgomeryshire, where gentlemen and professionals were few. Eighteenth-century Essex juries were dominated by farmers, artisans and tradesmen, which is similar to the situation found here. This suggests that the social mix in mid-Victorian Montgomeryshire resembled south-east England a century earlier and that in economic-development terms, the mid-Wales county had fallen behind the booming Midlands.[46] Figure 5.2 interprets occupational representation at quarter sessions held at Newtown and Welshpool. This shows detail that reflects Welshpool's borough status, with its slight swing towards a more commercial nature. The home locations of grand jurors were mainly in the more prosperous

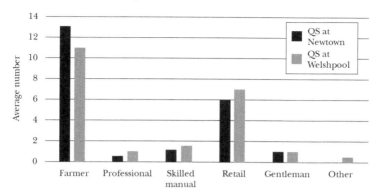

Figure 5.2 Occupational representation on Newtown and Welshpool grand juries, 1869–78.

regions of the north and east. The western side of the county sent few men to the grand jury, which supports the earlier analysis that less prosperous farms were in the west. Those from the west who did serve on the grand jury were from the pockets of commercial enterprise at Llanbrynmair and Machynlleth.

The grand jurymen referred to the bills of indictment and depositions, and could call on prosecution witnesses and question them.[47] All this went on behind closed doors, and with such secrecy it would be unwise to speculate on their deliberations, although some historians consider that a high level of 'not found' decisions might indicate a tendency of grand jurors to give defendants the benefit of the doubt.[48] Among the present findings, the thirty-nine ignored bills (13 pe cent of the total number of cases) included sexual assaults, malicious wounding and house- breaking, but by far the largest type was that of theft, with a total of twenty-three of the thirty-nine ignored. It was at the grand jury stage that the rape case against John Pilot was thrown out, followed by proceedings by Pilot against Sergeant Ross for perjury.[49] The secrecy of the grand jury, however, made perjury difficult to detect and impossible to prosecute, which could explain why Pilot did not pursue the charge.[50] As Pilot and his co-accused were discharged when the case was thrown out, the judge stated that it could be reopened at a later date if the woman decided to cooperate. This illustrates how the ignoring of a bill was not the same as an acquittal, and thus a discharged defendant was still tainted. Pilot was likely to have charged Sergeant Ross with perjury to make himself look the victim.[51] It was earlier noted that there may have been a conflict of interest when magistrates Edward Harrison and William Withy took their seats on the Bench, as they were also felons association members. A similar conflict can be seen in the sphere of the grand jury, as association members were the very type of men who were selected for service. Ten members of Welshpool felons association appeared in the grand jury at least once during the 1870s and could hardly be considered impartial, indeed one of them was William Withy, and the others included the influential vice-president of the felons association. Conflicts of interest of this kind, which would worry us today, seem not to have been of concern to people of that time.

THE PETTY JURY

The cases deemed *prima facie* by the grand jury proceeded to trial. Like the grand jury, the petty jury was selected by the high sheriff from those able to sit because of the value of their landed property. When the jury was selected from lists of qualified men from rural parishes, many of them were farmers.[52] As the 'higher class' of man was selected for grand jury service, it is expected that petty-jury analysis will show predominance of men from a somewhat lower class. It was found that gentlemen were not represented at all and professionals had all but disappeared, although the general findings were the same as seen for grand juries.[53] This similarity was inevitable, given the local social structure, one in which farmers in the east predominated as men of standing, and in which retail categories of employment were the next most numerous and socially significant group. 'Retail', of course, can cover a wide span of wealth. The property requirement meant that most of the working classes and landless poor were excluded, and some wealthy, non-landowning groups such as large tenant farmers and commercial men, whose main assets were in stock, were sometimes also excluded.[54] It has been said that a jury's composition was more clearly marked by those it excluded than those it included.[55] The largest single group here was farmers, outnumbering retailers and skilled workers combined. It was surprising that one farm labourer featured in the lists, but this will be because he owned a small amount of land sufficient to meet the minimum requirement.[56] Many of these jurors were newly enfranchised following the 1867 Reform Act, and were growing in political self-confidence and awareness of their new role in decision-making. Just as different levels or hierarchies were seen among the magistrates and police, so here was another such layering. As before, the hierarchy was determined by financial situation, and a man knew his place by the particular role he was able to play. However, opportunity to sit as a juryman was a matter of chance, or even design, because of the part played by the high sheriff and the way he organised the lists of potential jurors and his subsequent selection process.[57]

MANIPULATION OF THE JURY LISTS

The lists of names show noticeable features. Sometimes the men were arranged in alphabetical order of surname, and at other times the arrangement seems random. The alphabetical method was somewhat inefficient or even mistaken, with Benbows and Breezes etc. selected time and time again. Moreover, the alphabetical method meant that very often a jury box was dominated by farmers who often constituted a majority in the lists of potential jurymen. These flaws appear to have been identified by the magistrates themselves, for spreadsheet analysis reveals that the alphabetical method, which was used consistently for at least nine sessions, was discontinued after the beginning of 1871. The new method that was used subsequently may have been a directive from the lord lieutenant, or a decision taken by the wider Bench. The usefulness and significance of the change becomes apparent when consideration is made of the pools of potential jurors supplied from parishes where there was a preponderance of farmers. For example, at the Hilary sessions of 1875, if the list had been put into alphabetical order, nine farmers would have appeared in the jury box along with three retailers. However, the new arrangement with non-farmers placed at the top of the list, resulted in a selection of three farmers, seven retailers and two skilled manual workers. List after list from 1871 onwards shows retailers and manual workers placed at the top, resulting in more of them being represented in the box. The situation where the percentage of non-farmers taking a seat in the jury surpassed their percentage in the list of potential jurors as a direct result of this new method, is illustrated Figure 5.3. These sessions were chosen to illustrate the point because they were ones at which large numbers of farmers featured in the lists of men from which the high sheriff selected the juries. The change becomes more apparent when the same analysis is done for sessions prior to 1871, shown in Figure 5.4. Here, apart from Hilary 1869, the percentage of non-farmers in the jury was below the percentage in the lists. This analysis makes it clear that although the wider general public, in the form of the juries, had a say in judgements made at quarter sessions, they nevertheless were controlled by manipulation of the jury lists by the high sheriff. This management allowed a greater range of backgrounds to take

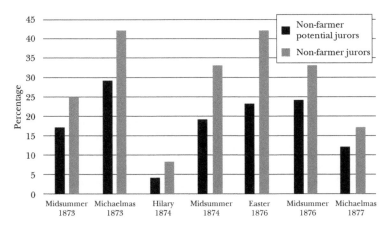

Figure 5.3 Comparison of non-farmers in the list of potential jurors and in the jury, after 1871

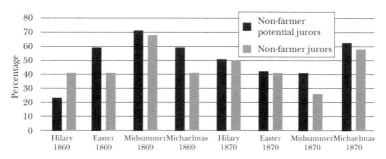

Figure 5.4   Comparison of non-farmers in the list of potential jurors and in the jury, prior to 1871

part than might otherwise have appeared, although it was still men of the middling sort only who formed the jury and therefore still were unrepresentative of the general community. The inappropriateness of the alphabetical method is shown at the Hilary sessions of 1873 held in Shrewsbury, when the grand jury consisted of twenty-one farmers and one gentleman.[58] This demonstrates that the change was not due to a nationwide directive from the Lord Chancellor, and was not likely to have been from the chairman of the Montgomeryshire Bench, the Earl of Powis, as he also regularly sat on the Shropshire Bench.

<h2 style="text-align:center">MAGISTRATES' DISCRETION</h2>

Clothing theft formed about 40 per cent of larceny cases at both petty and quarter sessions, and at both types of court the item stolen was often a pair of boots. The cases of clothing or footwear theft heard at petty sessions were clearly suitable for summary appearances as the defendant was either a juvenile or pleaded guilty, and in one of the cases there was a suspicion that the man had been 'set up'. The indicted cases that arrived at quarter sessions mostly showed features that made them more serious. For example, the theft might have involved the loss of other items which made the total value higher, or the accused person pleaded not guilty or had previous convictions. One of the boot thefts was remarkable, however. This case involved twelve-year-old Walter Ruscoe who, as a juvenile, should not have appeared at quarter sessions.[59] Moreover, he was sentenced to a term of imprisonment, albeit just one day, and twelve strokes with a birch rod.[60] This was an unusually harsh sentence, as analysis of offences committed by children and dealt with at summary courts shows that they were treated in a non-severe way in all but one case. This one case resulted in a short prison sentence followed by reform school. Generally, the children would be discharged, or receive six strokes. It is perhaps significant that the child who was sent to reform school stole from a farmer who appeared on jury lists,[61] and Walter Ruscoe stole from a skilled craftsman who had been on the Hilary sessions grand jury six months earlier.[62] There were five magistrates on the Bench on the day that Walter Ruscoe appeared namely Sir Watkin Williams-Wynn, who was deputy chairman of the Bench; John Robinson Jones, Major Drew, the Revd Canon Herbert and Richard Jones. It appears that Ruscoe's heavy sentence was formulated by the first two magistrates in the list, as it has been shown how Major Drew was well known for his leniency, and he, the Revd Herbert and Richard Jones had sat on similar cases at petty sessions where discharges or six strokes were given to children. In the one summary case where the prison and reform school sentence was given to a child, it was Robinson Jones who was in the chair. The Walter Ruscoe case, therefore, is important because it shows how analysis of court reports can indicate certain characteristics of the justices involved. It also illustrates how the magistrates on the Bench worked together, and how discretion came into play, for after the sentence was announced to Ruscoe, the Bench adjourned and on their return, the sentence was revised. The boy would now receive just the one day in prison and no beating. One can picture these men in the retiring room, with Drew, Herbert and Jones arguing the point, trying to convince the other two that a less severe sentence should be imposed.

OFFENCES INVOLVING VIOLENCE

After thefts, assaults formed the next most common charges, although they constituted only 6 per cent of the cases at quarter sessions. In all the assault cases, the attack was made worse by involving indecency, biting or the use of a weapon, most commonly a knife. Several assault cases of this type, and others just as serious, had been dealt with at petty sessions. and it is unclear why the justices in petty sessions did not send them to the higher court. Indeed, a case involving the assault of Constable Daniel Richards with a knife in Newtown seems more serious than the assault of Constable Lewis with a stick in Welshpool a few weeks earlier, and yet the Newtown petty magistrates did not send the knife case to the higher court but dealt with it themselves. The Welshpool magistrates sent Constable Lewis's stick case to quarter sessions.[63] Major Drew and Richard Jones, both involved in reducing Walter Ruscoe's sentence, were the magistrates who dealt with Constable Richard's knife assault in petty sessions and were often among the justices who kept serious assaults in the lower courts. Capt. Crewe-Read shed light on such decision-making when delivering the sentences of himself and Major Drew on an assault case in October 1869:

> [We] consider that a brutal and cruel assault had been committed on an old man. It appeared [the accused men] had been at militia practice and were returning, and with the weapon that they were allowed to use had inflicted the injuries from which the complainant suffered. The crime committed was a serious one, one which – if they were convicted at the [quarter] sessions may render them liable to penal servitude or a long term of imprisonment. [We have] decided to deal with the case summarily.[64]

Their leniency went on. The initial sentence given to one of the accused in this case was imprisonment for one month. The man begged for a fine instead, and Crewe-Read and Drew agreed to revoke the imprisonment and sentenced him instead to a fine of £5. This illustrates how magistrates could be mindful of the wider implications of sentences, and although at quarter sessions their opportunities for discretion were reduced owing to the role of juries, they could still be circumspect when sentences were decided.

ATTITUDES TOWARDS ASSAULTS

When Elizabeth Hughes's house was broken into and a knife taken, she could identify the recovered item because the handle had some nicks on it.[65] 'The knife now produced by the officer is the one', she said. 'There are three marks on the handle, made by my boy, for which I beat him.' Next, the son – young David Hughes – took the stand to describe the man he saw near the house, and to identify the knife. The newspaper reported that 'He said in an undertone to the Bench, "My mother beat me for making the nicks in it."'[66] The ordering of corporal punishment of children has already been seen occurring regularly in Montgomeryshire. These beatings, when sanctioned by authority figures, were generally acceptable,[67] and domestic assaults were judged at petty sessions and often considered to be worthy of a bind-over order. Violence between women was regarded as dispute, and dealt with at petty sessions. Some violence, however, could be treated more seriously and sent to the higher courts. Twenty such offences in the present study were tried at quarter sessions.[68] They were all committed by men, with the majority being committed against other men, although all those classified as indecent assaults were against females, including three children.[69]

There was a notable difference in statements or depositions made when it came to interpersonal offences, with attention being paid to the minutiae of the assault. This contrasts with the depositions of victims of theft, where identification of the lost items was a key detail included, as well as identification of the accused person and his or her opportunity for taking the goods. However, the length of theft depositions was usually less than one page. Small detail did not seem to be required. It is almost as if guilt was assumed, and might have been related to the fact that in most cases heard at quarter sessions, the accused person was of a lower class than the complainant. Of the 146 people accused of theft, 64 per cent were convicted. Assault depositions, however, were commonly two pages or more in length and included verbatim details of words spoken.[70] For example, in Evan James's two-and-a-half-page testimony, part of a nine-page bundle, he described the moment in a fight between himself and Thomas Evans that turned a brawl into a more serious crime in the Queen's Head public house in Newtown: 'I was wounded in the head. Blood was flowing freely down my face.'[71] He and his brother-in-law went to wash the wound, and he went on: 'I was bleeding very much at that time. Mr Hall's assistant was sent for and he came and dressed my head. I felt very weak next day.' The brother-in-law's testimony provided more detail:

> They were going to commence another round when I observed by the light of a lamp a knife shining in the prisoner's uplifted hand. I shouted to the prosecutor, 'Mind, Evan, he will kill you, he has got a knife'. Prosecutor however knocked him down and fell upon prisoner and shouted out, 'Here's the knife, he has got it in his hand.'

There were many instances when a police officer was called to a fight in a pub, resulting in charges of drunkenness or disorder being preferred against the protagonists at petty sessions. In the Queen's Head case, however, prosecuted at quarter sessions, the landlady did not call the police to break up the fight, leaving the men to sort it out themselves outside the building. It was only later that Sergeant Ross was called and told about the knife incident. The officer deposed: 'I went and apprehended prisoner on a charge of stabbing Evan James.' With the testimonies of the victim, his brother-in-law and the doctor, along with the defendant's admission that he had a knife in his pocket at the time, he received a six-month gaol sentence for his guilty plea to a charge of common assault. He would not admit a charge of inflicting grievous bodily harm, but his admission of the lesser charge was accepted. The prosecutor magnanimously asked for a lenient sentence to be given.

At the same sessions at which the Queen's Head case was heard, Edward George was accused of inflicting grievous bodily harm on Thomas Parry. The general details of the George case were very similar to the previous instance, except the weapon was a poker. A surgeon confirmed two severe wounds on Parry's head and a police officer described finding the metal bar. In this case, however, the defendant was acquitted. The difference here was that a defence witness,

Parry's landlady, who initially did not come forward and did not make a statement to the committing magistrates, stated that she overheard the prosecution witnesses agreeing to embellish their recollections of the events.[72] She said in court:

> I heard Parry say to Mary Barrett, 'Poll, you must not say that I took the poker out, you must say that I came out first without my boots and that I turned back to put them on. You must keep your counsel or I will be done.' He afterwards said that he would pay her well.

Several prosecution witnesses testified to seeing the accused man strike the victim, and the surgeon's testimony confirmed deep lacerations that Parry was unlikely to have inflicted himself or let someone inflict upon him. Yet, in the eyes of the jury, the embellishing of his and others' testimonies seems to have overridden the commission of the assault by George. This might be considered a perverse jury decision.[73] Alternatively, this might be an example of a jury taking all the circumstances of a case into account, arriving at – in their minds – a fair resolution which took into account embellished or fabricated prosecution evidence. Magistrates at petty sessions have been shown to take circumstances into account, and to be receptive to appeals by defendants, thus there would seem to be no reason why juries could not be so minded.

SENTENCING

As quarter sessions dealt with offences deemed more serious, it is expected that the sentences imposed upon conviction would be more onerous. Every sentence handed down on the 352 cases during the period 1869–78 was imprisonment, even though many of the cases seemed no worse than those heard at the lower court where a fine was the normal sentence. A survey of the sentences gives an impression of randomness at times. For example, Edward Hampson, with no previous convictions, received twelve months' hard labour for stealing fowls, but John Mills, with a similarly clean record, received six months for the same offence at a different court. Both had pleaded not guilty.[74] Certain classes of crime received sentences that seem fair when compared to each other, as in the case of Elizabeth Williams who stole £10 and received three months, and Frances Jones who stole £15 and received six months.[75] Consistency was usually seen in the sentencing of young people, who normally received two or three weeks in gaol followed by three or five years in a reformatory.[76] Penal servitude was given in twenty-two of the cases, whereas ordinary custody with hard labour, was given in 203 cases. Penal servitude was meant as a replacement for transportation, although at the time that the first Penal Servitude Act was passed in 1853, transportation still existed and penal servitude ran alongside.[77] Table 5.1 shows the lengths of penal servitude and their corresponding transportation sentences, indicating that the former was considered more onerous than transportation.[78] Penal servitude for men meant imprisonment with hard labour. There would be an initial few months of solitary confinement at Millbank or Pentonville, followed by transfer to another gaol for the hard labour element which might be road building or stone breaking.[79] For women, it meant being sent to Millbank for two months of coir picking followed by cooking, cleaning and laundry at one of the convict prisons.[80] However, there was much contemporary confusion about the meaning of the term 'penal servitude', and even the Lord Chief Justice in 1856 claimed not to understand it.[81]

Montgomeryshire magistrates gave penal servitude to repeat offenders. For example, at the Easter sessions of 1870 John Williams received an extraordinary twelve years of penal servitude because of his three previous convictions, whereas

Length of penal servitude sentence (years)	Equivalent length of transportation (years)
4	7
4–6	7–10
6–8	10–14

Table 5.1 Length of penal servitude and corresponding length of transportation as set out by the first Penal Servitude Act of 1853

his co-accused were given ten to twelve months of ordinary imprisonment with hard labour.[82] At the midsummer sessions of 1870, hardened criminal Stephen Higgs was given seven years' penal servitude but his accomplice, first-time offender Ann Lloyd, received twelve months of ordinary custody with hard labour.[83] In all the cases but two, a repeat offender received penal servitude. The two exceptions, who received ordinary custody with hard labour, were firstly a sixty-two-year-old man, and he was spared by his age.[84] The second was a twenty-year-old woman for whom the jury asked for mercy. The most common length of penal servitude given was seven years, given in eighteen of the twenty-two sentences. This, according to Table 5.1, would correspond to ten to fourteen years of transportation. An investigation of transportation lengths given by Montgomeryshire quarter sessions between 1850 and 1868 duly showed that ten years was the most common length.[85] Thus the sentencing involving penal servitude was following a pattern of transportation set years previously. By giving the distinctive punishment of penal servitude to repeat offenders, the Montgomeryshire magistrates were adding to the creation of a 'discrete being, the habitual offender'.[86] The magistrates similarly adopted the surveillance terms of the Habitual Offenders Act enthusiastically. The Act came into use in August 1869 and the Bench implemented it at the next session. From then on, most of the convicts who received penal servitude followed by surveillance were given the maximum period of surveillance allowed (seven years). Even prisoners who received a short term of ordinary custody sometimes received the maximum surveillance. For example, Thomas Thomas, who had committed an offence in 1859, upon being convicted of stealing hay in 1870 was given three months' hard labour followed by seven years of police supervision.[87] Habitual criminals had first been defined in 1833, and a Select Committee of 1838 further described them as those who made their livelihood by the repetition of offences. Seven months before the justices started implementing surveillance, a *Times* editorial stated that habitual criminals were 'the enemies of society of which we wish to rid ourselves'.[88] Perhaps the Bench was making a determined effort to 'save' the county.[89] They were, too, taking into account the fate of the convicts' families, as a man at home could provide for his family whereas a man inside could not. By giving Thomas Thomas a long period of surveillance the justices were effectively saving ratepayers from several years of poor relief,[90] and one remembers Thomas Barrett's speech when he became mayor, and thereby chairman of the Welshpool Bench:

> I assure you I feel very proud of the position you have placed me in this morning … I shall make it my study to do all that I possibly can for the interest of the ratepayers, unbiased in every form, and if I do make a mistake, it shall be an error of judgement and nothing else … I thank you very much for the confidence you have placed in me today and I hope that this day 12 months you will be pleased with what I have done. It will be a pleasure to me to carry out everything for the interest of the ratepayers (applause).[91]

Thus it can be seen that the magistrates were demonstrating the same sort of discretion seen at petty sessions, although this could take place only when it came to sentencing, as their options for judgements were now in the hands of the jurymen. But juries could even influence sentencing as in the case of William Lewis, convicted of unlawfully knowing and abusing a child.[92] The chairman of the Bench 'dwelt with great severity on the heinousness of the crime' and yet felt restricted in the gaol term he and his colleagues could give because the jury had requested mercy to be shown. The man received eighteen months with hard labour.

THE INFLUENCE OF QUARTER SESSIONS ON THE LOWER COURTS

While the jury system restricted the magistrates' discretion in some respects, there was a way in which it provided the justices in the lower court with an extra option. This is illustrated in a case from 1869, when a serving girl accused her employer's husband of assault.[93] The case was heard by Major Drew and Richard Jones in the clerk's office in Newtown. After hearing all the evidence from both sides, and a lengthy period in the retiring room, Major Drew announced:

We have gone into this case more fully than is usual in such cases, from a desire to discharge our duty properly towards both parties. There is great discrepancy in the evidence given; on the girl's part there is a positive assertion of acts that go far to support the charge made by her. This, on the other hand, is contradicted by positive testimony on the part of the defendant. Under these circumstances, we think that it is a case for a jury, and not for us to say whether the complainant is, or is not, to be believed.

Each side was probably frustrated that his or her story was not given preference, but from the magistrates' point of view, whichever side they believed, there could be dissatisfaction from parts of the community. By deciding to send the case to quarter sessions and hence to the juries, the decision was now out of their hands and eventually this case was dismissed by the grand jury at the Easter sessions.[94] It is interesting to note that by explaining the reasons for the Bench's decision, Major Drew was following the modern practice of giving reasons,[95] and not the usual nineteenth-century practice of 'putting together of heads' and the sentence being given without explanation.

CONCLUSION

Although petty and quarter sessions were both courts dealing with local matters, and included magistrates sitting on the Bench in both, the tone of the justice delivered was different in the two arenas. The ability to dispense discretion in the lower court was useful to many, and all manner of disputes were brought by people to the forum. At quarter sessions, many opportunities for discretion were removed from the justices and placed in the hands of the juries. The jurymen's presence in court was determined by their financial and social status, and reflected the growing influence of the middle classes. The secrecy of the grand jury mirrored that of the Bench's retiring room and gave an advantage to the complainant, who could present his or her case in private. It was at this stage that the case against John Pilot was quashed, and while the circumstances of that decision will never be known, it was after this hearing that Pilot pursued Sergeant Ross for perjury.

A complainant often went to considerable effort to pursue the offender. Many could be helped in this via membership of a felons association which assisted with the payment of costs. An association could also pay a police officer to track down the suspect. Even without membership of such a group, available funds made prosecution a more accessible option. Being part of the set of men who paid rates meant inclusion on jury lists, which gave instant access to court decision-making. Time and time again, overlaps were seen between complainants, jurymen and felons association members. Such court users probably expected the justice system to be on their side, especially when people such as the chairman of the Welshpool Bench, Thomas Barrett, spoke of doing everything he could in their favour albeit speaking at that time in his role as mayor. Although the administration of justice was controlled by men, women of the middling sort could also have expectations from the system. They were unlikely to have to share the waiting room with the lower sorts at petty sessions, and could rely on being represented in sessions by a policeman if desired, although this might have involved a fee. Although much of the discretion available to the magistrates at petty session was missing in the higher court, two avenues were open to them. First, the jury lists were found to have been manipulated by the high sheriff, a magistrate acting in a superior role, and secondly, in the handing out of sentences. The same sort of discretion observed in the lower court, sometimes giving the appearance of randomness, was seen again. Magistrates, however, did not have complete control over this area, as petty jurors could influence levels of sentencing from their box by asking for mercy. There is some evidence that sentencing could have been for the benefit of ratepayers.

The following chapter will examine the proceedings of the highest court, namely the assizes, and the roles of the various participants.

6

ASSIZES

CLASS, REPUTATIONS AND STEREOTYPES

The highest court in the county was the assizes. Here a visiting judge directed the flow of proceedings and gave out the sentences, but the public still played a major part in decision-making since men from the middle classes formed the petty jury, as they did in quarter sessions. The grand jury, however, was composed of magistrates and other members of the gentry. Aspects of the wider culture were reflected in court, including relations between the different classes from which the various players in the court were drawn.[1] It is the aim of this chapter, therefore, to identify whether the lower classes were subjugated by the assizes or if there were ways in which they could make their sensibilities known and obtain satisfaction. It will examine the roles played by defendants, complainants and witnesses, and consider the roles of visiting barristers and judges, and their effect on locals' access to justice. The way evidence was presented, and by whom, is explored, and the contribution of expert witnesses is investigated. The chapter also scrutinises whether the legal process reinforced stereotypes and reputations, and if professional competency constituted any part of the decision to remove solicitors' right of attendance at quarter sessions.[2]

THE CHARACTER OF THE ASSIZES

Like quarter sessions, the assizes formed a social occasion for the upper classes as much as an assembly that could determine the future lives of members of the community. The scene was set even before the formal proceedings began, with the judge's parade. This involved his lordship in a coach drawn by horses, accompanied by marching magistrates, police and trumpeters, and a service according to the rites of the established Church of England. There was an exclusion of the majority of the local populace due to their likely Nonconformist allegiances and possibly their language.[3] *The Newtown and Welshpool Express* always carried reports of the judge's parade, for example, at the spring assizes of 1869:

> The commissions of Oyez and Terminer and general gaol delivery were opened in Welshpool on Monday last before the Rt. Hon. Sir William Fry Channel, one of the Barons of the Exchequer, who arrived by the 2.50 p.m. train. His Lordship was met at the station by the high sheriff, J. P. Davies Esq. of Fronfelin; A. Howell Esq., under sheriff; the other county officials, a detachment of county constabulary with trumpeters and javelin men, and proceeded to the court where the commissions were read. The court adjourned until ten o'clock on Tuesday morning. At 4.30 His Lordship proceeded to attend divine service at St Mary's Church where ... the assize sermon was preached by the Rev. William Lutener.[4]

Comments made by judges in their opening remarks to the grand jury could bolster the idea of 'two nations',[5] and set an agenda for the forthcoming sessions. For example, in 1870 Baron William Fry Channell said that he 'exhorted the grand jury to assist, by all the means which lay in their power, all institutions having for their aim and object the promotion of sobriety and good order amongst the lower classes'.[6] At the maiden assizes in March 1874, Baron Gillery Piggott praised 'the gentlemen of the county' for the 'good example set by the higher orders',[7] and in 1876 Baron Sir Fitzroy Kelly, Chief Baron of the Exchequer, said:

> Considering the amount of the population and that a great many of the working classes and of the lower order of society were to be found amongst them, it was certainly a matter of great and sincere satisfaction to him, and it must be to them, that there were only three cases in the calendar ... It was to be hoped that this was partly due to the care and attention they [members of the grand jury] bestowed in the discharge of their social duties to those around them, and partly, he hoped, to the late legislation with reference to the education of the masses.[8]

Thus, there was an understanding among the gentry that they had a specific role in controlling the greater part of the population, instilling within the wider community an idea of 'knowing their place'.[9]

THE CASES

During the decade 1869–78, a total of eighty cases appeared at the assizes.[10] These included assault, manslaughter, attempted murder, rape and a range of other offences, but the most prolific was theft, with a total of twenty-eight cases. Together with twelve burglaries, offences related to the misappropriation of property accounted for nearly half of the crimes.[11] Although the range of stolen items included furniture, watches and farm stock, the most common item was money. The amount stolen ranged from a few shillings to £21, and offenders and victims included people from all levels of society although most of the offenders were unskilled workers. Perhaps surprisingly, hawkers and low-skilled labourers were victims of these higher-value thefts almost as much as skilled workers. A sixty-three-year-old labourer kept £21 in a drawer in his house, and it was stolen by his lodger, a skilled craftsman.[12] Another such victim was John Davies, who had spent several hours in a public house in Newtown, during which time an independent witness observed a weaver picking Davies's pocket. The weaver was subsequently convicted after a lengthy trial at the summer assizes of 1871.[13] The main points of this case are very similar to Red Mary's theft of George Russell's gold ring two years earlier, but the amount stolen from Davies was the relatively small sum of 3s. 3d. This was surely suitable for a hearing before magistrates at quarter or even petty sessions, and did not merit its appearance at assizes. The explanation could be that the committing magistrates considered a theft from a drunken labourer by a skilled worker, one who could afford a solicitor to instruct a London barrister,[14] to be too serious for a lower court. An alternative explanation is that the victim in this case, Davies, had bypassed the magistrates and gone straight to the grand jury at assizes and asked for a bill of indictment, which was permissible.[15] Burglaries took place in different locations all over the county, and were more likely to occur in a small settlement or isolated farmhouses. Only one such offence occurred in a town.[16] The items stolen included money but were as likely to be food, clothes and household articles such as candlesticks and linen. Boots were proving to be a very common target for thieves, as were keys. Boot thefts appeared at both petty and quarter sessions, and although circumstances of the offences and details of the perpetrators varied, the way in which the cases were handled seems random. For example, an ironmonger who stole boots and other items from several farmers was sent to quarter sessions by a Newtown Bench, but two labourers whose offence was very similar but in the far north of the county, were sent by a different Bench to assizes.[17] As has already been noted in earlier chapters, the justice that defendants received depended upon the magistrates before whom they first appeared, with Newtown defendants probably hoping to appear before lenient Major Drew. These cases exemplify how local people's route to justice, whether they were victim or accused, was determined by the upper classes. The gentry's position was reinforced, and the same control they had over their servants and other employees was seen again in court.

THE ROLE OF LAWYERS IN THE ASSIZE COURT

By the 1870s, although the police brought public disorder cases to petty sessions and were involved in some others, notably those in which the victim was a respectable woman, there were still many cases in which the victim was the prosecutor. The position of Director of Public Prosecutions (DPP) was not created until 1879, after years of debate about the advantages for society of having such a figure.[18] There was nevertheless a degree of professionalisation seen in assize courts prior to this, and from the mid-eighteenth century, prosecutions were increasingly undertaken by solicitors on behalf of private individuals. Judges also allowed barristers to stand in for defendants, thereby evening up the balance of justice and enabling a more rigorous testing of evidence brought by the prosecution. When lawyers handled a case, the ordinary person was distanced from the administration of justice, with law and government being done in people's names rather than with their direct participation.[19] Accompanying the increased role of lawyers was the introduction of rules about the admissibility of evidence and modes of expression. For example, the term 'beyond reasonable doubt' began to be used in the middle of the eighteenth century, and medical testimony, even if it was only quasi-professional, was preferred to vernacular observations.[20] Lawyers controlled the jury's access to evidence, and whereas in earlier centuries juries had been active participants in criminal trials, they became increasingly silenced, although they still had the power to decide a trial's outcome, even, at times, going against indisputable evidence.[21] Lawyers, thus, were of major importance in higher-court proceedings but there was a significant limiting factor: their cost to the individual victim or defendant. Many prosecutors could afford only the least able solicitor, the sort who would accept the one guinea that the court would award as expenses,[22] and thus the presence of legal representation could indicate ability, or willingness, to pay and therefore label or marginalise a group. It indicated a person's position in the social hierarchy in the same way as clothing, house or seat in the jury box did.

In the present study, none of those pleading guilty had a solicitor or barrister to plead on their behalf, but on two occasions, the judge himself helped to establish the facts of the case. In one of these cases, a young man was accused of stealing ten gold sovereigns from his grandfather, a miller, who decided to go forward with a prosecution. After stating the facts of the case, prosecuting counsel applied to the judge for a lenient sentence, explaining that the youth had been waiting in gaol for four months. The judge asked the grandfather to take the stand and questioned him as to the nature of his grandson's character. After hearing the evidence, his judgement was to give one month with hard labour.[23] In the second of the two cases, the judge asked for the prisoner's father to step into the box, and then asked him questions to establish the details. He explained his judgement to the father very carefully, and obtained a promise from him to be more responsible.[24] The youth was then discharged. Here is evidence that the judge would assist an undefended party to gain a fair hearing, and although it was further control by the upper classes, such defendants may have been very grateful.

Of the twenty individuals pleading not guilty, seventeen did not have representation. The defendant had the right to cross-examine the prosecution witnesses,[25] but only six of them did so. Notable was twenty-six-year-old Elizabeth Gough, accused of stealing money from a house in Llanidloes. Not only did Gough cross-examine, she also produced witnesses to support her side of the story. The judge directed the jury to acquit, and they did so. Thus she had cleverly defended herself against an experienced barrister.[26] Gough showed a knowledge of the legal system possibly acquired through previous appearances in court, or she may have sought advice in this case. Whatever it was, she used the established rules of evidence to her advantage, and she was not overawed by the proceedings. It has been said that it was barristers who 'enabled a more rigorous testing of evidence', but here was a local woman doing it herself.[27] Two of the cases were burglary by small gangs of tramps, and cross-examination by the defendants themselves in the absence of a defending barrister sheds light on some important details about contemporary police procedure, and again shows lower-class people being knowledgeable about legal proceedings.[28] In the first case, the gang members were apprehended in Chester and the stolen items retrieved from a pawnbroker. At the trial, one of the men asked the arresting police officer, a Chester detective, how he knew they were in the city and which pawnbroker to go to. The detective admitted to obtaining his information from a man named Morris who, he claimed, was with the others at the time of the burglary. Under questioning, witness Constable Edward Jones of Llanfyllin inconsistently claimed to have followed Morris along a road at the same time as following the others along a different road. The witness named Morris was not arrested in Chester and was not present at the trial. It is possible that Morris was an undercover detective or an informer, and as he did not appear in court, his evidence could not be tested. Undercover techniques were certainly used to target vagrancy in 1870s Warwickshire, where the chief constable said, '... more will be done by one in plain clothes [than a policeman in uniform]'.[29] Support for the informer theory comes from examination of the second case of tramp burglary. Again, three men appeared in the dock and questioned the two police witnesses. Two of the three had been arrested in Flintshire but the third was apprehended in an unnamed place by an unidentified officer, and the judge decided that there was no evidence against him. During this trial, the judge intervened, making some comments that helped the defence. According to *The Newtown and Welshpool Express,* Baron Sir William Fry Channell

> subjected the witness [Sergeant Breeze] to a very severe examination and his lordship made several remarks that were not very complimentary. [Later] His Lordship said that the [prosecution] witnesses had given their evidence in a most disgraceful way.

Channell's intervention uncovers a feature of his personality confirmed by known facts. His entry in *The Dictionary of National Biography* states that he was severe with regard to criminals,[30] and the account of the tramps' trial suggests that his severity could be shown to anyone in the witness box.[31] This will have given the local populace a degree of reassurance that the law could be fair, and it is likely that they enjoyed hearing about a policeman being berated. Communities often resented the police, particularly their heavy-handedness to which locals could not respond except through letters to the newspapers.[32] Now here was his lordship demonstrating heavy-handedness to an officer. The community knew, however, that only a member of the upper classes could speak in such a way to a police sergeant and get away with it.

STEREOTYPES

The absence of defence counsel indicated the social class of a defendant, and stereotypes were also promulgated in the court. The judges' words to the grand juries at the start of proceedings, such as those of Chief Baron of the Exchequer Kelly quoted earlier in this chapter, showed their belief that criminals and those of low moral standards were from the working-class majority. Domestic servant Mary Jane Grey, appearing at the spring assizes of 1869 on a charge of burglary, fitted this pattern.[33] There was another stereotype that figured largely in nineteenth-century sensibilities, and this was the 'fallen woman'. Seduction narratives in fiction, drama, poetry or song commonly concluded with misfortune for the women who had 'fallen', and further misfortune was to be her lot.[34] The ideal of innocence and modesty was not restricted to the upper and middle classes but was impressed upon working-class girls at school and within the wider community. Community condemnation of neighbours' bad behaviour 'operated as powerful constraints against deviance', and a woman needed to be seen to be morally superior to men.[35] Mary Jane Grey had failed in this, as she appeared in court on the burglary charge in an advanced stage of pregnancy. She tried to provide mitigation for herself by producing documents that she claimed proved great provocation, showing that she thought this might help her. Although the judge would not let Miss Grey take the stand to verbalise her argument, he permitted her to write it down. This he studied, and then read the documents, which were letters from a lover who had let her down. Miss Grey had pleaded guilty to this charge of burglary but was facing a second charge of attempted arson, to which she pleaded not guilty. She had no defence counsel and there were no prosecution witnesses for her to examine. However, the judge decided that she had not intended arson but had done what she did 'just to let the prosecutor know that she had been in the house'. This seems a rather surprising comment for the judge to make. It appears that he was treating her claims of great provocation as a submission for 'no case to answer'. The defendant could make such a submission if there was no prosecution evidence on which a jury could properly convict.[36] This was clearly not the case here, as the judge accepted that fire lighting had taken place, and in any case, it was for the jury to decide, although the judge could make a direction. The clerk of assize made no observation, and the judge sentenced Miss Grey solely for the burglary, without the jury making any judgement on the arson charge. Her punishment was six months' imprisonment with hard labour. He added that the labour should be such that she could manage in her condition, and with *The Newtown and Welshpool Express* reporting that Miss Grey 'appeared to feel very acutely the degradation of her position', the judge looked with sympathy on circumstances of the failed romantic liaison. This sort of benevolence towards unfortunate women has been seen already at petty and quarter sessions, and agrees with two other nineteenth-century stereotypes – that of the 'wronged woman', and that women, being innately good, would not ordinarily be drawn to crime.[37] There is also a clue in the language used in the newspaper report: the piece begins with her described as of a 'respectable appearance'. A discussion of a similar case states:

> Like this woman, many working-class women in these stories were clearly regarded as 'respectable' even though they were unmarried mothers. Pregnancy and illegitimate children were treated not as grounds for moral outrage against the mother, but rather as interesting and often melodramatic details in the 'crime of passion' stories, since pregnancy frequently proved to be the motive.[38]

Class, too, was an issue in the Grey case. The man involved was upper-middle class, being the son of a man of independent means. He had attended a prestigious grammar school in Wrexham, and his brother went on to become a Conservative party agent in the early 1900s.[39] This sort of story was highlighted in Chartist newspapers as they emphised the difference between the classes, and it also makes this case a 'narrative of a particular genre', involving stereotypes.[40]

THE CONTRIBUTION MADE BY COUNSEL

Investigation now turns to the scenario when a defence barrister was present. Just as the tramp's questioning opened a window on details that he hoped would help his case, so could counsel's examinations reveal details that might make a difference to accused persons who did not have the ability to defend themselves. A male type-cast, often mentioned in contemporary popular culture, now appears. This was the country squire, a single man of fortune, marrying to produce a legitimate heir. Such a squire appeared in court in 1876, not as a defendant but as the complainant, charging one of his tenants, Anne Jane Jones, with theft.[41] As with Mary Jane Grey, this also illustrates the divide between the lower-class woman and the higher-class man. Capt. Devereux Mytton might have thought that his position in the county – magistrate, one-time high sheriff and relative of Viscount Hereford – the sort of man charged with keeping the lower classes in order, would enable him to use the assizes to his advantage. However, as Mary Jane Grey had used evidence of a failed liaison as a defence, so did Anne Jane Jones's barrister use his professional skills to demolish the reputation of the Captain.[42] Now the evidence was used not so much to show provocation as a form of mitigation, but to show the complainant in a poor light. Miss Jones was charged with the theft of items from a house on his estate. The items were furnishings that bailiffs siezed upon Miss Jones's non-payment of rent as a commercial tenant. However, these furnishings were part of the fittings of the house, belonged to Mytton and should not have been taken. It seems unreasonable for Miss Jones to have been charged when it was the bailiff's mistake, and her counsel's approach was to raise the issue of an illicit affair that had turned sour, to account for the charge being brought against her. In the witness box, Mytton was required to answer questions of an intimate nature and was obliged to admit that he had been a regular visitor to Miss Jones's living quarters, even after his marriage, and that he decided to evict her when rumours of her being his mistress first broke.[43] The judge summed up with the following words:

> Gentlemen of the jury: I do not think there is evidence sufficient to bring the charge under the definition of the criminal

law. I do not think there is act of stealing on the part of [Miss Jones]. The woman simply said nothing. She did not do any act to get rid of them, she simply said nothing when she saw goods belonging to her landlord seized. That was very wrong but not criminal. I must therefore direct you to acquit [Miss Jones].

The jury did acquit, but it had been a long and complex hearing, involving the questioning of Mytton's agent and lawyer, and various other witnesses. This is the sort of scenario where the administration of justice was taken out of the ordinary person's hands, unlike those cases discussed in earlier chapters where the accused persons were able to defend themselves. The rental agreement was scrutinised and the difference between criminal and civil liability discussed. This may have been too far beyond the ability of Miss Jones for her to cope with herself, and before the advent of legal representation she would have found herself in gaol or hanged.[44] Thus having the proceedings taken out of her hands was to prove a good move. There is a question over Mytton's motivation for bringing the lawsuit, which served to keep the scandal in the public eye. Mytton must have been very determined to keep on and try to change a private wrong between himself and another party into a public wrong committed against the state.[45] It is possible that Mytton chose the option that was less costly for him, as he would have had to pay for a civil suit himself. Sometimes the criminal law was used by unscrupulous people to pursue a civil claim, and private prosecutions were deployed in the services of malice, harassment and blackmail.[46] Here there is a suggestion that Mytton thought his position in the county might give him an advantage,[47] and there are questions about how this case ever managed to get as far as assizes, let alone to a trial. The courts generally took care in the rules of evidence and conduct of cases to ensure that everyone was subject to the law to the same degree.[48] Here, however, the grand jury who heard the prosecution evidence was composed of Mytton's colleagues from the county Bench and included two of his near neighbours, the best man at his wedding three years earlier, and a distant cousin. These personal connections were all public knowledge and served to give the local population the idea that the magistracy and court personnel were, to use modern parlance, all in bed together, reinforcing the *status quo*.[49] This case exemplifies several important points. First, Miss Jones might easily have 'gone quietly' when faced with a lawsuit against her, but she did not. She took on the challenge, recruited the services of a legal team and provided them with information to enable a winning defence.[50] Second, the case undermined Mytton's gentry position, with his behaviour itself undermining the words of the judges about the higher orders' role in society. Third, the court system gave the majority in the community the means by which to make their feelings clear: as Miss Jones left the court, she was cheered and congratulated while Mytton himself was jeered and barracked, further serving to undermine his position as a respected member of the upper orders.[51]

There was a case in which a member of the gentry class appeared in the dock. This was William Napoleon Nolan, a property dealer attending a land sale in Newtown in December 1868.[52] A tradesman made an insulting remark about the size of his nose, and Nolan reacted by attacking him with an umbrella, inflicting a wound that required medical attention.[53] Certain facts can be ascertained from newspaper reports. Firstly, and possibly most importantly, Nolan was Irish, and it seems very likely that it was his accent that led to the insults. The *Liverpool Mercury* described him as 'a hot-blooded Irishman'.[54] He was in Newtown only temporarily and could easily have absconded from justice, and might readily have done so, especially as the victim wanted compensation. The magistrates therefore did not grant him bail but held him in custody until the spring assizes, an incarceration of three months. However, similar woundings had been dealt with at quarter sessions, and Constable Lewis's knife attack had been dealt with at petty sessions. Hilary quarter sessions were just three weeks away from the date of the incident, and yet his status as a gentleman resulted in his appearance before a judge at the highest court. Time and again, the higher the class of the person involved, the higher was the court that dealt with the offence. Mr Nolan must have been dismayed that his trip to Montgomeryshire with his wife to view land finished with a three-month stay in Montgomery gaol.

As the professionalisation of courts proceeded from the middle of the eighteenth century, so the idea began that parties could produce their own proof to show from the witness box. Rules about hearsay evidence developed, and thereby the so-called expert witness came about – a person who could give evidence about a case, using knowledge and training, without actually having been present at the time of the offence.[55] Thus, a further level of bureaucracy was introduced, although in this area, and for once, a woman could have a role – in the form of a midwife. Nineteenth-century expert witnesses often included men of science, such as geologists and chemists, or professional men, such as clerics and navigators, but perhaps the most familiar figure was the medical expert, who could be a physician, surgeon, apothecary or midwife, and who had a professional reputation that he or she would want to maintain or enhance.[56] Very often, the medical expert would be semi-official, brought in by a magistrate or coroner to provide non-partisan advice. This was a reason why the prosecution preferred to put this sort of witness in the stand at the end of its case, as he was unlikely to help their side much, whereas a medical expert hired by one or other side would be more partisan and therefore be heard at the head of that side's case.[57] These witnesses commonly appeared at infanticide and concealment of birth trials, where midwives, physicians and surgeons might all appear, because proof of birth and survival of the birth process both needed to be established. Juries often ignored expert witness testimony,[58] but not before details of a highly personal and intimate nature would be heard in open court. The whole process was taken out of the hands of the accused woman, and this was the second time of such a trial, because the same details would have been discussed at the inquest in a coroner's court earlier.[59]

A concealment case was heard at quarter sessions in March 1871,[60] when a single woman, Anne Jones, employed by Miss

Mary Yearsley, a lady of independent means, appeared in the dock. In October 1870, a servant discovered the body of a newborn baby wrapped in a bundle placed in a spare room. Initially, the coroner's inquest led to a charge of manslaughter, but this was dropped on the direction of the judge at the assizes, and now the prosecution was trying to prove that Anne Jones had concealed the birth of the infant.[61] The first witness was the servant, who gave an incriminating description of the accused woman's attempts to recruit her assistance in disposing of the body, attempts which the servant resisted. Throughout his cross-examination of this witness, the defence barrister continually tried to bring Miss Yearsley into the picture, but the servant steadfastly placed her out of the scene, and this higher-class, respectable lady was never called to the witness box. The 1861 Offences against the Person Act extended the offence to include any person involved in the concealment, and it is clear that the defence barrister was trying to show that Miss Yearsley must have been party to the concealment. It sounds unlikely that Miss Yearsley would not have been aware of events in her household, especially as the accused woman was Miss Yearsley's companion and normally slept in the same bedroom. The servant did testify that on the night in question, Miss Yearsley had gone to sleep in a different room. Thus it seems very likely that she knew exactly what was going on. Miss Yearsley, however, was the antithesis of the person identified by the legal system as the sort who should appear in the dock, and she never did.[62]

Next came the midwife.[63] She said that Miss Yearsley had summoned her on the night of the birth, but denied seeing the lady of the house or having any words with her at the time in question. She also denied knowing that the accused woman was pregnant or had given birth, and this seems extraordinary. Perhaps she was trying to distance herself from any culpability, given that the aforementioned 1861 Act could have made her guilty as an accomplice. Next in the witness box was Thomas Barrett, surgeon.[64] He described the events that he witnessed over the weekend in question, and the accused person's denials that she had given birth. He then gave details of the *post mortem*, listing his observations and responding to prosecution questioning that 'death may have been produced by a combination of causes', and that an injury to the tongue of the baby 'may have been caused by the prisoner in her efforts to deliver herself, or may have been wilful'. This candour, and the language, described by others as 'seeming to want the symptoms to speak for themselves', was emblematic of the non-partisan nature of medical testimony, even when it was specifically representing the prosecution.[65] Sometimes when there was evidence pointing in two directions, the court would call a bystander expert to testify.[66] In the Anne Jones case, after Barrett had made his non-committal comments about the tongue injury, the judge called Edward Harrison to the stand.[67] He, too, was non-committal: 'In my opinion, the injuries, if made at all, would have been made after death', and admitted that he did not examine the dead baby. So the medical men were both trying to be non-partisan, almost seeming to be helping the accused woman.

The decision was now left to the petty jury, and this introduces a group hitherto unstudied in this chapter. Although the names of the men are unknown, the extant jury books giving lists of eligible men show them to be farmers and skilled tradesmen such as butchers, carpenters and corn merchants.[68] Therefore, the men charged with the key decision in the proceedings were those nearer to the class of the defendant.[69] Petty juries were notorious for their perversity, sometimes being completely at odds with any direction from the judge. The poor quality of petty juries, as well as their lack of education and intelligence, has been identified by historians and the attorney-general tried unsuccessfully to introduce a clause to the Juries Bill of 1873 to try to improve matters.[70] Some juries, however, were seen as not simply passive auditors but inquisitors, asking pertinent questions that helped to get to the nub of the issue.[71] Welsh juries were particularly noted for giving contra-verdicts but here there is a suggestion that religion was playing a part: a writer in the *Cornhill Magazine* in 1877 said, 'If some of [the jurymen] happen to be also his fellow chapel-goers of the same denomination, the acquittal may, it is feared, be predicted with approximate certainty.'[72] The point here is that a petty jury, composed of ordinary, middle-class men, had important influence and could contradict the decisions made by upper-class men in the grand jury, as they did in the Captain Mytton case.[73] There was a division in thought between those who considered the woman committing infanticide or concealment as 'an object of peculiar compassion and sympathy' and those who felt she was 'callous' and concerned only with 'getting rid of an encumbrance'.[74] Very often, the petty jury would seem to be of the former opinion, for example in Carmarthenshire, where out of eleven cases where the woman in the dock pleaded not guilty, only one resulted in a conviction.[75] It has also been argued, however, that when magistrates made such dismissals, it was because of distaste that the case had ever been brought.[76] In the Anne Jones case, there may have been issues to do with Miss Yearsley's possible part in the events and her non-appearance in court. The jury may have considered that not all questions had been answered. After a lengthy discussion, including an hour in the retiring room, the jury returned a verdict of not guilty.[77] Baron Sir George Willshere Bramwell[78] was surprised: before sending them out to consider their judgement, he had directed them to find the prisoner guilty.[79] When they delivered the result of their deliberations he said, 'I hope you will be able to reconcile your consciences with the verdict you have given, for by no mental process can I discover the means by which you have been able to do so.' This was not the only controversial comment he made. As Miss Jones was released from the box, she was greeted with clapping and 'other outrageous demonstrations'. A woman who had been shouting was brought to the judge who said, 'Well, well. But considering her appearance and considering the character of the jury I think that if they can be forgiven for forgiving the prisoner, then she ought to be forgiven for applauding.' *The Exeter Flying Post* reported:

> The assizes have passed off in Exeter without anything particularly worthy of comment, and the learned judges, as far as I can learn, have not had much fault to find with the decisions of the juries. Not so at Welshpool where Mr Baron Bramwell has been forced into an expression of disgust at the impenetrable stupidity or the disgraceful dishonesty of juries.[80]

However, a journalist on *The Oswestry Advertiser* argued the point:

> In defence of Welsh juries: The daily papers which, English-like, seem to delight in poking fun at other peoples, have this week contained a paragraph headed 'Baron Bramwell and a Welsh jury' in which the case of concealment of birth at Welshpool and the strange verdict returned are recorded. The verdict was strange enough but the foreman of the jury was an Englishman. And what, after all, is the absurdity of this verdict compared to that which a London jury returned in the Tarpey case [in which a woman with a baby was found not guilty even though she admitted guilt]?[81]

The Newtown and Welshpool Express then added in a leader:

> Mr Baron Bramwell is again amongst us and has had occasion, perhaps rightly, not quite to express his satisfaction with a Welsh jury at Montgomeryshire assizes. A Welsh contemporary has taken up the cudgel and delivers a rebuke to the English dailies. Reference is made to the Tarpey case and the palpable miscarriage of justice when a ladylike appearance and a baby in arms did more in favour of the accused than the impression on the minds of the jurymen usually made by learned counsel.[82]

This debate may well have pleased Bramwell as he is known to have enjoyed controversy.[83]

REPUTATIONS OF EXPERTS

It has been shown how stereotypes could be perpetuated, and personal reputations brought down in court. As expert witnesses became a feature of the legal proceedings, there were now opportunities for professional reputations to be affected too. Medical experts tended not to contradict each other, and they avoided partisan and judicial contests wherever possible. This is because medics needed to inspire confidence in the public who paid their fees, and this is a reason why there is a paucity of recorded battles between experts.[84] However, a battle was seen at the Montgomeryshire spring assizes of 1873, when Jonathan Edwards appeared in

the dock accused of the manslaughter of William Jones.[85]
Edwards had followed Jones out of a public house and given
him a severe kicking and beating, particularly around his
private parts. Jones survived the assault and received attention in his house by his usual medical practitioner, a surgeon
by the name of Thomas Edwards. Jones lived for a further
nine days and then a post-mortem was performed by an independent local surgeon, with Thomas Edwards in attendance.
Both these experts appeared for the prosecution at assizes
and yet they gave conflicting evidence. Mr Justice Mellor
referred to this in his charge to the grand jury:

> There appears to be a great difference in opinion regarding
> the medical testimony. One gentleman, Dr Edwards, who has
> frequently attended the deceased during life and was with
> him in his last illness, most positively affirms that the cause of
> death in this case was congestion of the lungs, while on the
> other hand Dr Huddart, who made a *post mortem* examination
> of the body states that the deceased's death resulted from
> external injuries received. You will, therefore, in this case be
> guided in the manner in which the respective medical men
> gave their evidence *viva voce* as to whether you can reconcile
> the apparent great difference of opinions held by these
> gentlemen.

A detail that is not apparent in the coverage of the case but is
obvious from the censuses is that Dr Edwards was aged
sixty-one years and had worked in the locality since at least
1851; Dr Huddart was a newly qualified, twenty-three-year-old
surgeon.[86] Some of the techniques that the older man used
were old-fashioned. For example, he spoke of how he bled
the victim in order to reduce his fever. However, bloodletting
had gone out of favour years before. In fact, Edinburgh
doctors invented a theory in the 1850s to explain why they no
longer favoured the treatment, without losing face for having
used it in the past.[87] Mr Justice Mellor's direction to the grand
jury drew attention to Edwards's experience and knowledge
of the deceased, but tactfully does not dismiss Huddart's few
years in practice. The same judge bolstered the reputation of
a solicitor's clerk in 1878 when he directed a jury to believe
the clerk's evidence over five working-class witnesses in a case

of attempted murder.[88] Here, a gamekeeper had been shot by a poacher on an estate a few miles from Newtown. This was at a time when poaching has been linked to rural poverty, and a connection made between theft of estate game and reduced rates of poor relief during winter unemployment of agricultural workers.[89] Also, the sentences given for night poaching was so severe that often the poacher felt compelled to resist violently when confronted by a keeper.[90] However, here there was nothing to suggest that desperate need was a factor. The man's defence was that he had been at home with his mother at the time of the offence, then later in a pub. The clerk, however, claimed to have seen him on the road near the shooting, and the jury and judge considered that this professional person's evidence was by far the more reliable. The convicted man was a weaver – the very sort identified as the particular breed of man who would undertake night poaching.[91]

SEXUAL ASSAULTS

An area in which reputations of both prosecutor and defendant could be crucial was in cases of sexual assault. Study of Merionethshire police books shows that many crimes of a sexual nature did not proceed to higher courts.[92] Often, when rape cases did come before the quarter sessions and assizes, the magistrates or judge would instruct the grand jury to ignore bills where there was evidence to throw doubt on the victim's testimony. Sometimes juries might reduce a charge to common assault, and often the accused person would receive an acquittal.[93] During the period 1869–78 a total of four rape cases appeared at Montgomeryshire assizes, and in none of them was the accused man convicted.[94] One of these was the case explored earlier, where Constable Edward Jones of Llanfyllin obtained a report from a professor at Shrewsbury regarding blood stains. Although the contents of the report are unknown, the grand jury decided to ignore the case after hearing the prosecution evidence, so the report was likely to have helped the defendant by throwing doubt on the circumstances of the assault.[95] Two of the other bills were also ignored, and in the fourth case the man was acquitted mainly because the woman waited several days before bringing the charge.[96] Many victims gave up their attempts at obtaining justice because it was so difficult to get a conviction, and because of the trauma of the trial.[97] Judges were always looking for signs of enticement, or prevarication, and indeed Mr Justice Mellor, at the spring assizes of 1873, advised the grand jury that 'a woman of ordinary strength could have resisted an assault'.[98] In other counties such charges were considered by some to be used too freely,[99] but this could hardly be so in Montgomeryshire, with only four cases being pursued in ten years. The relative respectability of the parties was clearly of crucial importance, and army officers, other men in uniform and employers were rarely convicted of rape.[100] Critically, when decisions were made by victims on whether to pursue a case, a woman trying to prosecute a man for rape jeopardised her reliability as a witness because she was now making her respectability questionable.[101]

PROFESSIONALISATION OF THE COURTS AND IMPLICATIONS FOR LOCAL PEOPLE

John Langbein has explored how solicitors began to be involved in private criminal prosecutions from the eighteenth century, and how judges started allowing defence counsel to take part in trials from the 1730s. He describes this as a 'fateful step', beginning the path towards the adversarial criminal trial, but admits that documentary evidence of the reasons for the change in practice does not exist.[102] He argues that barristers began appearing in numbers at the Old Bailey following a series of scandals involving flaws in the operation of the trial process,[103] and their appearance at courts elsewhere soon followed.[104] By the 1870s barristers had been attending Montgomeryshire assizes for some years following the establishment of these assizes, upon the abolition of the court of great sessions where solicitors had previously held right of audience.[105] Barristers subsequently started looking for work at the lower courts too, and approached Montgomeryshire quarter sessions at the beginning of the 1870s.[106] Here the exact moment of the change in practice can be pinpointed, and, as was found at the Old Bailey in the eighteenth century, it was the result of a scandal, and in this case it involved the withholding of justice from a lower-class woman.

Before barristers made their way into quarter sessions, it was solicitors, when employed by prosecutors or defendants, who examined witnesses to elicit information. Things went badly wrong for the solicitors in midsummer 1871, and it was this debacle which allowed the barristers to find a way of obtaining right of audience at quarter sessions. John Thomas was charged with stealing a watch from David Jones, and Sarah Anne Jones was charged with receiving it from Thomas.[107] Local lawyer Charles Howells prosecuted the case, and Thomas and Sarah Anne Jones each had their own defence solicitors. The details were complicated, involving evidence from police officers in two towns, and various people handling the watch at different times. At the end of the trial, presiding magistrate and deputy chairman of the Bench, Charles Watkin Williams-Wynn, summed up favourably with respect to John Thomas and unfavourably to Sarah Anne Jones. The jury then acquitted the man of theft but convicted the woman of receiving the watch knowing it to be stolen. This contradiction was apparently unobserved by the clerk and Williams-Wynn who sentenced her to six months hard labour. The only people in the courtroom who noticed the contradiction were Sarah Ann Jones herself, who was led away 'strongly denouncing the injustice of her sentence', and the reporter from *The Newtown and Welshpool Express*. He wrote:

> From time to time we have heard much of the glorious uncertainty of the law and frequently we are obliged to be witnesses of its absurdities. Last week a case of the kind occurred which may in some respects be considered the climax. In referring to it we do not do so for the purpose of provoking a smile at the expense of the jury who tried the case, or to join in the remarks which were made by some who heard the verdict delivered.[108] Our opinion is that in the manner in which the case was delivered to them there appeared to be no alternative but to act in the manner they did ... We know it is practicable and is practised, to withdraw a major charge and

to prefer a minor, but whether the same rule applies to the abandonment of the minor charge and the substitution of the greater, we are not lawyers enough to say. The whole affair is not satisfactory.[109]

Williams-Wynn wrote to Jones's solicitor and advised him to submit a petition to the Home Secretary for a pardon for the woman. This was done, and the appeal was successful.[110] Williams-Wynn, and the Earl of Powis as chairman of the Bench, may have felt a degree of humiliation from this affair where the jury and Bench demonstrated absurd errors of judgement. Certainly the fiasco played into the hands of the barristers. Near the beginning of the same sessions at which this failure of procedure occurred, a contingent of five barristers had submitted a petition to Williams-Wynn. They asked for exclusive right of appearing and conducting cases at the Montgomeryshire quarter sessions which, they claimed, was the only court of quarter sessions in which that right had not already been conceded.[111] They promised that they would attend regularly and in such numbers as would be able to conduct the business of the court.[112] Williams-Wynn decided to bring up the matter for discussion at the following sessions. The barristers could not have predicted the furore that was to arise over the Thomas and Jones case, and could not have realised how opportune for them was their application. It was the first matter discussed at the Michaelmas sessions.[113] The Earl of Powis mentioned a possible saving of time by having cases argued by barristers, with only a 'trifling' increase in cost, but perhaps the most telling comment was from magistrate George Whalley who said, as reported in the newspaper:

> He thought it would be well to introduce the gentlemen of the bar to the quarter sessions as they would be fresh from Westminster Hall where legal business was conducted in the best possible manner, and their presence at quarter sessions would tend to improve and facilitate the conduct of public business and be a consequent advantage in the administration of the law.

The only dissenting voice to the adoption of the application was Capt. Mytton's. Perhaps he wanted to protect the interests of his relative, solicitor G. D. Harrison, who would lose business. He said he did not see why the court should grant an exclusive right to the barristers as long as there were local solicitors who had quite as much ability. One other magistrate seconded his move to reject the application, but the votes were cast in favour. This was a disaster for the solicitors, both in view of the fees they would lose and with regard to their loss of reputation. These men had power over others owing to their expertise, technical knowledge and accompanying mystery, all of which placed them above the common level of their fellow townsmen. Moreover, their fortunes partly depended on successful mediation of their relationship with the public.[114] Now the gentlemen of the Bench had demolished the solictiors' standing, aided by the jury and their colleagues' poor decision-making at the trial of Sarah Anne Jones

CONCLUSION

The assize court was a theatre in which Disraeli's concept of the 'two nations' of the upper and lower orders was established at the very start of proceedings by pageantry and by the words of the judges. This, and the general Anglican feel of proceedings, reinforced a perception held locally by some of being looked down upon by the English establishment. Further demarcation was made during proceedings, with his lordship controlling business and making unilateral decisions over process and sentence that reinforced his status as the highest person in the court. The aristocratic members of the Bench never appeared at the assizes to take their seats in the grand jury, rejecting the superior role of the Bench in this court. The judges often made comments that illuminated their opinion of the lower orders, to which those individuals could not coherently respond. Employment of legal representation served to define class, but defendants, nearly always from the lower orders, were not necessarily cowed by this arena and could put forward their own successful defences or at least make spirited attempts. Several suits involved women, who, although disadvantaged and totally removed from the administration of justice, were nevertheless able to help themselves, often with the aid of counsel. The court provided a unique situation for the lower orders to triumph lawfully over those sited further up the social scale, partly owing to the role of the petty jury, which was composed of men lower in social rank than the gentry class. The judge very often contributed to help the defence, notably in the case of a pregnant woman.

Stereotypes including the fallen woman, the pompous judge and the squire were seen and confirmed in court. The non-appearance in the dock of the gentry class reinforced the idea of the lower-class criminal. Events tended to perpetuate these stereotypes, although the figure of the lower-order woman taking on the legal system single-handedly is a useful addition to knowledge of women standing up for themselves.[115] Reputations could be reinforced, sometimes upon direction of the judge, as in the case of two conflicting surgeons. In one case, the reputation of a so-called 'gentleman of the county', supposedly setting a good example to the lower orders, was demolished by the very man himself, who had pursued his case solely to subjugate his tenant. The judge too could possess a reputation that preceded him, and any comment or sentence given out by him during the business of the assizes often increased it. The court could also help to bolster the careers of barristers, and during the course of 1871 their reputation for efficiency at assizes helped to oust local solicitors from having right of audience at quarter sessions.

The following chapter will look closely at the most prevalent crime, namely theft, and the perpetrators of these offences. The opportunities and the roles played by gender will be considered.

7

THEFT OFFENCES

MATERIAL CULTURE, GENDER AND OPPORTUNITY

The focus here is on the crime seen most often in the higher courts, namely theft. The offenders, as well as complainants, will be viewed, as well as both groups' engagement with the legal process. There will be an examination of the relative experiences of men and women, and an investigation into whether the location of crime had a gendered nature. The different rhythms and patterns of male and female daily lives may have influenced their motivations for theft and their *modi operandi*, and this will be explored.[1] An attempt will also be made to determine the attitudes and motivations of offenders and complainants through a study of their own comments made in depositions.[2]

A REVIEW OF THE CASES SEEN IN COURT

A total of 352 cases appeared before the county Bench between Hilary 1869 and Michaelmas 1878 (Figure 7.1). During this period, the amount of work dealt with by the courts showed a generally downward trend, similar to that for the whole of Wales and in England. The most prolific offence prosecuted in the Montgomeryshire quarter sessions was theft, but others included breaking and entering (which nearly always included theft of items) and assault. Receiving stolen items also featured, and the crimes categorised here as 'other' included passing counterfeit coins, animal maiming, attempted arson, being a rogue and vagabond, deserting a child and attempted suicide. Other studies have found that the crime rate was lower in rural areas, and there are clear differences between heavily industrialised areas such as Merthyr and less built-up areas such as Pwllheli.[3] Reasons given for the variance include the character of the peasantry

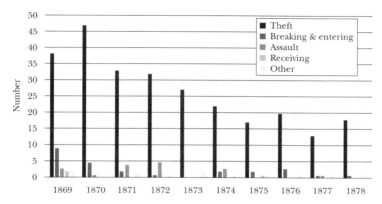

Figure 7.1   Offences seen in quarter sessions each year (352 in total)

and a cooperative mentality among members of the rural community. Deference or a 'feudal dependence' is also cited as a reason for a lower rate of crime in rural areas,[4] and lack of policing in rural areas may have resulted in a lower level of recorded crime. Court records reveal the familiar appearance of unskilled workers in the dock, and often multiple crimes committed by individual offenders.

CONTEMPORARY THOUGHTS ABOUT CRIME

It was acknowledged that crime was largely an urban problem. There was a focus on London in much public discussion, with many of the more alarming and best-publicised nineteenth-century offences being committed there. As the century progressed, crime was increasingly publicised in the other burgeoning urban environments, where a growing proportion of the public was located.[5] Thomas Plint declared:

> The pickpocket and the thief can find no nesting place amongst the statesmen of Cumberland and Westmorland, or the miners of Durham and Cornwall. They fly to Birmingham, London, Manchester, Liverpool, Leeds. They congregate where there is plenty of plunder, and verge [greenery] enough to hide in.[6]

James T. Hammick emphasised that the criminal classes were mainly found in towns and, generally, crime in rural society was not considered so serious. Charles Brereton said:

> The majority of thieves exist in gangs, practise fraud by profession, and live by a constant series of depredations ... criminals in the country only occasionally once or twice a year steal a sheep, pig, corn, hay, wood, turnips, poultry as the case may be.[7]

Journalist Angus Bethune Reach, however, like many others in the 1830s and 40s, identified a 'startling' amount of crime in rural areas, out of proportion to the number of people living there, and believed that this was the result of agricultural poverty.[8] Others have identified rural dwellers as more prone to violent crime, with urban dwellers being more likely to experience property crime.[9] Montgomeryshire was a county with town and country characteristics, and an investigation was carried out to discover if Montgomeryshire was a small-scale version of the nationwide picture described by Reach and others. Court reports and censuses were used to establish the precise geographical locations of crimes. The presence of a resident police officer was adopted as an indication of a settlement being of significant size, and the information shown in Table 7.1 was obtained. The proportions of crimes occurring in populated and isolated areas were 59 per cent and 41 per cent respectively. This gives an almost one-to-one correspondence between population and incidence of crime in both areas, which does not support Reach's assertions about rural crime being out of proportion to population but does add weight to Verniew's call for more police activity in less populated areas. However, a focus on Welshpool and Newtown gives the results shown in Table 7.2. This analysis shows that crime was disproportionately high in the two most populous towns and justifies the extra officers stationed there – eight in Newtown and seven in Welshpool. In comparison, Llanidloes had two officers and Montgomery had one. Brereton's comment about rural criminals stealing livestock and crops was certainly apparent, with thefts of these commodities being the most common, but almost non-existent in urban locations. Clothing and

		Percentage of county population	Percentage of quarter session crime
Population having resident policeman	38464	57	59
Population without resident policeman	29159	43	41

Table 7.1 Proportions of quarter session crimes related to population

	Percentage of county population	Percentage of quarter Session crime
Newtown and Welshpool	13	31
Remainder of county	87	69

Table 7.2 Proportion of quarter sessions crimes related to the population of Welshpool, Newtown and the remainder of the county

money were also widely stolen in isolated areas, but constituted only about half as many thefts as livestock and crops. Money was the biggest single target for theft in more populated areas and was approximately equal to livestock thefts in rural areas.

LOCATION OF OFFENCES

When considering crime committed by females, studies have found that a disproportionate amount of offending took place in industrial areas.[10] For example, during the middle years of the nineteenth century, 40 per cent of persons committed to the upper courts in Merthyr, Cardiff, Newport and Swansea were women, contrasting 'starkly' with Cardiganshire, where about 1 per cent of apprehended persons were women. The present study found that in Montgomeryshire 18 per cent of the persons appearing in the dock were female and that they were unlikely to commit offences in isolated areas. In general, offences took place in the woman's home area: in a house, which might be the employer's house, on the street or in a shop.[11] It is said that the boundaries of women's lives were circumscribed, with domestic responsibilities keeping them near the home,[12] but another reason for not venturing abroad could be that isolation increased the risk of sexual assault. For example, in June 1870 Elizabeth Morris was attacked on the canal towpath near Newtown while on her way home from the market.[13] Females were largely responsible for purchasing items for the home and family, a responsibility that took them out of the house and into shopping areas. Although this journey from the home left them vulnerable, there were also temptations and opportunities that could turn women into culprits rather than victims. Some shop thefts were clearly opportunistic, as in the case of Frances Jones who was convicted of stealing money from a woman who had momentarily left her handbag on a shop counter,[14] and two farm girls who picked up a bonnet from a shop counter while browsing.[15] But women could also show a degrée of devious behaviour. Elizabeth Hughes claimed that her employer sent her to a draper to order a shawl on approval. Little did the draper know that Hughes had recently left the employment and intended to appropriate the item herself.[16] Another woman engineered a distraction in a shop while waiting to be served, and purloined several waistcoats.[17] Theft of clothing by women has been regarded as an indication of 'petty' criminality and a reflection of lower-class women's desire to emulate women of a higher status,[18] and the wearing of good clothing could also contribute to increased self-esteem and respectability.[19] In nineteenth-century Montgomeryshire, the thieving of such items was found to be slightly higher by men than by women, with women showing a greater propensity for theft of money, so is there any indication that women's motivation for theft involve a desire for emulation? When Elizabeth Hughes was found 'on the street' in Newtown after she had deceived a draper into giving her a valuable shawl, she was wearing the garment. When market stallholder Elizabeth Pilot noticed a bolt of fabric and a silk dress missing, she suspected her employee, Mary Ann Braidsdell, and obtained a warrant for the woman's lodgings to be searched.[20] Found in Braidsdell's room were the silk dress as well as a garment, described as a tunic, that Braidsdell had made from the stolen fabric. Ann Williams stole a bonnet and a shawl from two different women in Newtown, put them on and was apprehended wearing them, and Mary Ann Nason was found in a pub wearing a silk dress stolen from her employer.[21] This could indicate envy on the part of the thief, and the dream of a different self-presentation.[22] Nason was not alone in her efforts to wear fine clothing: in the 1860s, the periodical *Punch* poked fun at working-class women who tried to follow fashion with cartoons picturing servants in ridiculous and indecent situations by insisting on wearing crinolines while cleaning.[23] In Hughes's case it might also have been a way of 'getting even', as her cross-examination of Mrs Pilot during the trial revealed that Pilot had made her a present of a wedding dress but had deducted the cost of it from Hughes's wages. Although the details of many of the offences are not known, there is at least some indication that the women were stealing for their own use, with little evidence that they stole for financial gain. It would have been much easier for Braidsdell simply to sell the cloth than go to the trouble of making the tunic, particularly considering the increased risk of being discovered. The fact that she did make it up into wearing apparel suggests that, for the time being at least, she intended to use it herself. It has been argued that people 'were moved by a desire for novel and popular fashions',[24] and the 1870s was a decade when Newtown entrepreneur Sir Pryce Pryce-Jones was becoming increasingly famous for his tweeds. He showed his products at exhibitions and won medals for his goods. He also supplied shawls to Florence Nightingale, Queen Victoria and her daughters.[25] Newspapers often carried advertisements that described the sorts of goods available at that time, and some contemporaries considered that promotions of this type encouraged shoplifting. Also at the time of Braidsdell's case, fashion magazines were becoming popular, having been available from the late 1860s. *The Month's Fashions* was first published in London in 1868, and paper patterns for gowns became very popular at this time, although they had been available earlier.[26] Fashion was associated firmly with elite modes of consumption emanating from London, and different meanings might be associated with particular items or certain colours, making clothing a medium that could be used for complex sartorial elaboration within social classes.[27] Fashion was also part of the 'social ritual' which served to maintain class boundaries.[28] The cloth stolen from Mrs Pilot was described as 'Parramatta', which was originally made in Australia but had started to be made in Britain and had received exceptional reviews.[29] Perhaps the temptation of the bolts of cloth on Mrs Pilot's market stall was too much to resist.[30]

Newspaper reports provided a further pressure to emulate, for example, the description of high sheriff Capt. Mytton's wedding in London:

> The bridal costume was of white satin, richly trimmed with lace, orange blossom and stephanotis, gold lockets, earrings and bracelets. [The bridesmaids' dresses] were of blue and white. The skirts, made long, were of blue silk and had two wide flounces, scalloped at the edge, under which were white muslin plaits. The bodices and tunics were of blue Japanese silk, richly trimmed with Valencienne lace.[31]

The ordinary, working woman did not have access to this sort of finery, and an advertisement placed by the Pilots showed that they supplied more accessible clothing, 'cast-off' from the higher classes, from their shop in the centre of town. Study of old photographs of rural Welsh communities shows that while the upper orders had discernible fashions that changed constantly, the costume of the lower orders was relatively static,[32] and any book on the history of fashion shows that the styles of expensive clothing changed on a year-to-year basis.[33] Thus, clothing was a means of communicating status and class, and the upper classes could communicate through their wearing apparel more effectively than the working classes. An advertisement from *Peterson's Magazine* describes the sort of appearance that Mary Ann Braidsdell may having been trying to achieve with the stolen Parramatta, as the description specifies the tunic: 'Costumes of this kind are, this season, trimmed with several rows of machine stitching, and are made as plainly as possible. The skirt is narrow and round. The tunic is buttoned down the front and the jacket is close fitting and double-breasted. This is really the prettiest costume of the season.'[34]

Regarding men's thefts of clothing, there is evidence of selling on. When market trader Thomas Swain helped himself to various items of clothing from Mrs Pilot's stall, he immediately hung them up on his own stall for resale.[35] Shoemaker Owen Davies stole twenty pairs of boots from his employer and took them straight to a Newtown pawnbroker who gave Davies the choice of pawning them or selling them. Davies chose to sell and then absconded to Shropshire.[36] When Thomas Burke stole a length of cloth and various pieces of apparel in Newtown, unlike Mary Ann Braidsdell, he made off to Shropshire where he sold some of the items to a lodging house keeper.[37] Most of the clothing thefts in this study were committed by tramps who were found wearing the articles. If tramp thefts are discounted, then a picture emerges of women stealing clothes for their own use, and men stealing for financial gain. In Phillips's analysis of Black Country clothing thefts, he makes the deduction that 'those who stole regularly while also being employed ... could hardly be called professional thieves since stealing clothing was not particularly lucrative. They were neither honest poor nor criminal class but an important third category – people in employment who supplemented their income with theft.'[38] But this statement is the sort of generalisation criticised by some historians for omitting women. It is a generalisation that does not identify an important fourth category – women who stole clothing for their own use.[39]

Street thefts committed by women were always those of money or small items of value such as a watch, whereas men's street offences were often thefts of livestock on market days, but rarely money or valuables. This does not seem readily explainable by differently gendered material aspirations, and so is most likely to be related to contrasting opportunities.[40] A man would not be out of place browsing around animal pens or taking away a sheep in a cart, and a woman on a street, looking into shop windows or mingling with buyers inside, would not necessarily be suspicious.[41] These locations would offer her the readiest opportunities. There was a type of location, however, where men did carry out the sort of theft normally associated with women, and this was an arena where their mingling would not look out of the ordinary – in public houses. The circumstances of most of the public house thefts were similar for both sexes, often opportunistic, picking the pocket of a drunk or some other person sitting nearby, or walking off with an item left carelessly.[42] Prostitutes created opportunities for such offences, as seen in the case of Sarah Lewis, who picked a client's pocket,[43] and men sometimes engineered thefts such as that committed by Thomas Fitzgerald when he tricked a bartender into giving him money.[44]

Opportunism thus facilitated thieving, and opportunities for stealing particular things have been said to be culturally disposed, often arising from gendered activities.[45] As the nineteenth century progressed, women were excluded from many forms of developing industry or work, and segregated into low-wage occupations, thereby reducing their opportunities for theft. This can be seen in Montgomeryshire. There were nine cases of women's theft from their place of employment, and in all but one, they were employed either as domestic servants or as charwomen in private homes or inns, and in one case, a tollhouse.[46] They stole a limited range of items including money, jewellery, beer and clothes. This contrasts with male offenders whose workplaces were farms, an office, a warehouse, railway station, the market place, mines, a canal wharf, coal depot, shop, hotel and boatyard.[47] The items stolen by men included materials such as lead piping, coal and wool, horse tack, money, farm produce and livestock. Men's wider work opportunities gave them access and opportunity for temptation and dishonest activities. Women's purloining, too, was within their everyday boundaries, and the role of family shopper could provide a defence. At the midsummer sessions of 1869, two farm women charged with stealing a bonnet from a shop successfully argued that they had picked it up by mistake while browsing, and in 1870 Jane Jones's solicitor successfully argued that standing near the prosecutrix and then walking away was no proof that she had picked the woman's pocket.[48] No woman among those charged here ever broke into a shop or stole large items involving a high degree of risk. This sort of theft from a shop was the preserve of the male. The women's shop thefts considered here contrast with William and Samuel Edwards, who burgled a shop and stole a side of pork that was in the process of being salted.[49] John McNamara pretended to be an agent for a Liverpool sewing machine company and swindled a shopkeeper out of six shillings, which involved taking a machine away for 'repair'.[50] Although male thefts were often on a larger scale, it could be argued that the men too were acting within normal male boundaries: travelling about, carrying large objects, mending things.[51]

Another generalisation sometimes made is that the getaway for thieves was easy, with emphasis on the ease of disappearing from a lodging house, shop or pub.[52] This generalisation, however, seems relevant only to men: in all but one of the cases involving solely women, the culprit was found in the location of the theft, or within easy reach of it. When charwoman Ann Goodall was suspected of stealing a jacket in Berriew on 23 August 1871, the local police officer knew where she lived and obtained a warrant to search her home, although this was not done until twelve days later. The officer also searched Goodall's mother's house and found the item.[53] Elizabeth Davies noticed an item of her underwear missing at Christmas 1872 but did not suspect her servant of taking it until three months later. Davies then fetched the local policeman who searched the servant's box and found the garment.[54] This kind of evidence suggests that women were bound more strongly to domestic situations and less likely to roam unaccompanied away from habitation.[55] Physiology and clothing were also relevant: a man's getaway would not be restricted by pregnancy, menstruation or long skirts,[56] although it is fair to say that the last of these certainly enabled concealment of stolen articles.[57] When a gang of tramps, including two females, were seen near a farm in the hills above Newtown, the farmer suspected them of stealing fowls that had gone missing. Constable Hudson tracked them down in Shropshire where one of the men was rueful. He said to the officer, 'If it had not been for these women, you would not have had us – we would have been well away.'[58]

MALE BOUNDARIES

When the focus is on isolated and populated areas, a difference appears between male and female patterns.[59] Although males offended nearly equally in both populated and isolated areas, females were much less likely to offend in areas where there were few people present. In four of the eight cases where women were charged with offences in isolated areas, they were in those locations with men, either gypsies or tramps crossing the countryside.[60] In the other four cases of women offending in isolated areas, they stole from places where they were employed.[61] In only 11 per cent of men's cases was rural workplace theft involved. Usually the men were opportunistically at the scene of the crime. For example, Evan Breeze claimed to have been in a drunken stupor and mistakenly went into a farmyard where he killed a hen by accident.[62] John Lewis stole leather from a lead mine in the hills near Llanidloes where he had called looking for work. Later the same day he stole wool from a field near the mine, then made his way to Newtown where he tried to sell it.[63] In general, male movement around the country enabled and facilitated criminality. For example, boatman John Watkin agreed to transport a load of ketchup between two stops on the canal, and during the journey consumed some of the sauce himself.[64] John Wilson, an American, claimed that the boots he stole from a cottage near Newtown were a pair he had brought with him from Cardiff.[65] In a case illustrating the enabling of crime by the advent of railways, John Bowker and Josiah Beech travelled home by train to Liverpool from Newtown, and opportunistically stole £59 from a farmer during the journey.[66] This case illustrates how criminality prompted the movement of another group of males – the police. Sergeant Hudson from Newtown located Bowker and Beech in custody in Liverpool and went there to interview them.[67] Success for the police was measured in convictions, so they were motivated to make arrests. In an agricultural region such as Montgomeryshire, where farmers' rates helped run the force, the officers needed to be seen making an effort on behalf of them.[68] Great trouble was taken to secure a conviction against the juvenile Mary Anne Nason, who had served time in a reformatory following criminal behaviour several years earlier. She was prosecuted for theft from a surgeon, and a sergeant from the Warwickshire force travelled to Welshpool to give evidence against her. Constable Edwards of Llanbrynmair travelled nearly fifty miles to apprehend Thomas Vaughan who had stolen fifteen shillings from his timber merchant employer.[69]

ATTITUDES TOWARDS CRIME

The quarter sessions Benches heard a wide variety of cases other than theft although the numbers of these other offences were small. Men committed the majority. Burglary and assault were the two that featured most significantly, and the patterns observed in the theft analysis are seen again. Women committed two cases deemed house breaking. By definition, house breaking took place during the day, and both of these cases occurred in populated areas. Wearing apparel was stolen in each case. In one instance it was underwear, and the woman was found wearing it, having been searched by the arresting officer's wife. In the other, the items included a silk scarf and an artificial flower. Significantly, neither case involved a violent or forceful entry into the premises.[70] Breaking and entering or burglary count as violent crimes as they include an element of power being used,[71] and on this basis, these two house breaking cases by women would have been excluded as there was no violence. Montgomeryshire's proximity to the border with England is said to have encouraged burglary, as goods could be disposed of easily, but this analysis is confined to men, as the evidence here for women shows that they retained the items.[72] Men's mobility is again reflected in these violent crimes. In 1874, four tramps broke windows and gained entry into a widow's house in the north of the county. They fled over the hills, first to Llanarmon and then on to Chirk. A police officer followed them and arrested the men in Wrexham.[73] Two sailors removed six panes of glass from the windows of a cottage in the south of the county, intending to commit a felony. They were noticed and, disturbed by shouting, jumped over fences and ran off up the hillside. They were stopped by field workers who held on to them until a policeman arrived.[74] Here is an example of a getaway that could hardly have been attempted by a woman in a long skirt. There is a clear difference here between this location and the route that the gang of fowl stealers, including two women, took along the flat Kerry Ridgeway.[75]

ATTITUDES TO THEFT REVEALED IN TESTIMONIES

Witnesses' comments in their depositions reveal attitudes and motivations. The words of the rightful owners of stolen property sometimes indicated an initial high level of trust in the people who later stole their goods.[76] Shoemaker Edward Jones described how he would leave his shop in the hands of his journeyman, Owen Davies, who later purloined twenty pairs of boots from him: '[I] occasionally left him in charge of my business when I went from home and he had access to the whole of my property in the shop and warehouse.'[77] Shop foreman Hugh Edwards allowed Elizabeth Hughes to take away five shawls on approval. He said: 'The prisoner came to our shop and said, "Mrs Pilot has sent me for a few woollen shawls to select some from". I wrapped up for her five shawls ... and she took them away. I knew the prisoner was a servant with Mrs Pilot.'[78] Mary Ann Braidsdell turned up at Mrs Pilot's market stall offering her services as a guard to watch over the stall. Mrs Pilot took her on but within a matter of weeks, Braidsdell had stolen fabric and a silk dress.[79] A remarkable degree of trust was shown by surgeon William Kortright Brock in the role he gave to former reformatory inmate Mary Ann Nason within his household.[80] 'I hired the prisoner as a nurse about five months ago and she remained in my employ up until last Sunday week. On [that day] she was left in charge of my house while I and my family were in church.' Brock's two infant children were left in Nason's care, and upon the Brocks' return, they found Nason gone, having pilfered clothes, jewellery and money. 'Our two children, the one aged about sixteen months and the other five weeks, we heard crying upstairs. We went upstairs and found the children in separate bedrooms, crying.' Mr Brock pursued Nason with vigour, alerting not only the

local policeman but Superintendent Strefford in Welshpool, and accompanied the local constable to Shrewsbury.

Related to the degree of trust shown by employers is the
fact that some did not notice items had been stolen until
alerted by others. Edward Jones, who lost twenty pairs of
boots, said, 'I happened to be at the shop of Mr Cornelius
Owens who keeps a grocer's and a pawnbroker's on Ladywell
Street. While there I noticed hanging up several pairs of
boots which I believed to be of the class of goods worked by
me.' Networks of acquaintances often helped in locating
items once their loss was noticed, although usually the
informants were unidentified. An exception was in the case
of the shawl theft. Hugh Edwards said, 'From information I
received from Mrs Pilot's son on Monday night, I went in
search of the prisoner and found her up New Road. I found
her going up the road with a young man on horseback.'
Usually the owner was vaguer about the sources of information. For example, Mrs Pilot said, 'I received information
and went to the house where the prisoner was staying.' Some
of the complainants realised that having definite evidence to
produce in court could bolster a case, especially if an independent witness could confirm it. Edward Jones described
how he and the Cornelius Owens set up a trap:

> He [Owens] put the boots I picked out of the stock under the
> counter and the prisoner came. Owens then said to the pris-
> oner, 'Where did you get those boots from I bought from
> you?' Prisoner said, 'I had them returned from a friend, they
> were boots I had lost.'

When Margaret Ellis suspected Jane Thomas of stealing
waistcoats, she searched the woman in the presence of a
witness: 'I sent for Jane Jenkins and she saw me take the waistcoats [from under Thomas's dress].' Jenkins confirmed this
in her statement: 'Miss Ellis beckoned to me to come in and I
saw her take the waistcoats from the prisoner.'[81]

All the cases that came to court included depositions from
police officers who had been called in by complainants.
Some victims appear to have been content to use the police
to carry out the function which, years before, they would
have had to do for themselves or with the help of parish

constables, namely tracking down and apprehending the suspect. Constable Breeze of Llanfair Caereinion described how Mr Ellis had come to him to tell him of the thefts of waistcoats: 'On the 14 August Mr Ellis told me of the robbery and that he would see me the following morning and on the next morning he showed me the waistcoats and afterwards on the 22 [August] he handed them to me. I apprehended the prisoner on the charge.' Hugh Edwards obtained the warrant for the arrest of Elizabeth Hughes for the theft of the shawl, but he expected Constable Crowden to serve it on her, which required a trip to Llandiloes. Constable Sibbald had to travel to Ellesmere in Shropshire to apprehend the man who had stolen the twenty pairs of boots from his employer.

Complainants did not necessarily bring in police officers immediately. Sometimes individuals could produce a confession by going to see the suspects and confronting them. It certainly worked in the case of the boot thief. After initially claiming that the boots were a consignment he had lost earlier and had been returned to him, Owen Davies changed his mind and said (in the testimony of the complainant): 'The boots are yours, Jones, and for God's sake forgive me, I am an old man.' Such intervention by the complainants themselves may explain why the police officers' statements nearly always contain little detail apart from finding the suspect, receiving the stolen items and taking the suspect to the lock-up. Complainants may well have used threats, perhaps of bringing in the police, a court case, withholding a character reference or even violence, in order to bring about the confession. Often the depositions show that the suspects initially denied the accusations but inexplicably changed their minds. Edward Jones said the suspect's mind change came after 'some conversation between me and the prisoner'. Mrs Pilot went to see May Ann Braidsdell who initially said that she had bought the Parramatta from someone in the Crown Inn, and that the silk dress had been given to her by her sister, but very quickly confessed. According to Mrs Pilot, 'She said, "I am very sorry and would not do such a thing again".'

Occasionally, however, the police did conduct interviews which are recorded in their depositions. An example is when

Constable Crowden found Elizabeth Hughes at her aunt's house in Llanidloes. Hugh Edwards had already described her actions in New Road:

> I told her I wanted her to go along with me. She had the shawl that she had from me in the morning on at the time. She refused to return with me but took the shawl off and threw it over my shoulder and said, 'You want nothing further with me so long as you have the shawl'.

Now, at the aunt's house, Hughes asked Constable Crowden, 'What can they do with me now that I have given the shawl back?' Mary Ann Nason also made her confession to a policeman after being tracked down to a public house in Coventry. The officer searched her himself and appears to have obtained the admission of guilt easily. Her words indicate that the constable had used a threat against some other, unknown person: '[I] charged her with stealing them and she said, "No one else has taken them but myself and no one else will have to suffer for it".' Prostitute Mary Morris confessed to Constable Richards in her lodgings after he had searched her himself. He also deposed that she produced the gold ring from a hole where she had hidden it. Without the missing item, the case was likely to fail,[82] so if he searched her and did not find the ring upon her person, why did she then produce it from the hiding place? She may have been telling the truth when she said that she never intended to keep the ring,[83] or it could indicate that Richards used verbal or physical force to produce a result. Notably, in both these cases where the woman suspect confessed to the officer, he had searched her himself, behind closed doors.

Farmers took a hands-on approach to investigating their losses. Victims of theft living in towns sometimes spoke to suspects and then fetched a police officer. Farmers, however, because they were on farmland, away from other people's eyes and away from the nearest police station, adopted physical methods before going to the police. When farmer John Hotchkiss noticed that hens' eggs were regularly disappearing, he decided to root out the culprit himself.[84] He described how he trapped the man, who was one of his employees:

I myself went into the granary and concealed myself. I had not been there for a few minutes when prisoner entered the bin and shut the door after him. I then went back to the stable for a light and told the cowman Charles Bumford to follow me. I went into the bin. On my opening the door the prisoner was in the act of going into the cow house from the bin. When he got into the cow house he threw himself down into the straw and in a minute or so afterwards addressed the cowman, 'Didst thee see my jacket anywhere?' I called the prisoner to me. When he came I asked him, 'What have you got in your pocket?' He said, 'Nothing'. I put my hand in his coat pocket and felt, and I believe broke, an egg in it. He then drew away and was about running back into the cow house when I caught him by the leg and held him until another servant named Bumford came. I then had him out on the fold and commenced searching him again.

Farmer Richard Jones spotted a man on his land and grabbed him.[85] Jones was more forthcoming than Hotchkiss about his actions:

When I caught hold of the man he struggled to get loose but I told him I would not let him go but take him straight to the police man. I brought him along the road in the direction of Llanfair for about 150 yards. He did not speak a word but I felt something hit me across my arm twice and then it dropped to the ground. I picked it up the second time it dropped and found it was a hammer and I put it in my pocket and it is the one now produced. He then spoke and asked my pardon and to lose him. This was after a good struggle.

Whoever the victim was, he or she always brought in the police sooner or later. However, it was often the complainant, not the police, who prosecuted, usually when the victim was a man. People seemed to understand that the deposition of an officer at quarter sessions, even when it was only to describe a few main details of the apprehension and charging, gave their suits credibility and validity.

NOT GUILTY PLEAS

All the defendants in these theft cases were said to have confessed. In any case, the lost items were found on them, in their places of abode or were sworn by witnesses to have been in the hands of the accused at some point. However, all the suspects pleaded not guilty in court. Mary Morris did not have much hope of being found innocent, as the complainant positively identified her as the thief, and the item was found secreted in her lodgings.[86] But plead not guilty she did, and what is more, she was acquitted. It was common knowledge that prostitutes were often acquitted of thefts from their clients, or maybe she considered that if she was going to go down, she would take the man with her, in a sense, by humiliating him. She did this by providing intimate details that produced much laughter in court.[87] Elizabeth Hughes's words to Constable Crowden, 'What can they do to me as I have returned it?' show that she had an idea that returning the item would relieve her of the charge of theft. She may have wanted to pursue this in court. She also wanted it to be known that her employer had been underhand in giving her a wedding dress but taking the cost out of her wages. By pleading not guilty to the theft of twenty pairs of boots, and thereby having a trial, Owen Davies could tell the court about how his stock had earlier been stolen, and that he had suffered financially for it. It seems inexplicable that Mary Ann Nason would deny the charge of theft of her mistress's clothes. She had absconded to her home county of Warwickshire with them, and they were found on her person. Perhaps she was hoping against hope that she could avoid a return to the reformatory.

CONCLUSION

There was a generally downward rate of crime in Montgomeryshire across the 1870s, although crime was disproportionately high in Newtown and Welshpool. The most common single offence was theft, which occurred throughout the county and was not confined to urban districts. The gendered nature of offending was evident, reflected in the location and opportunities for crime, and the apparent motivations for some of the thefts. This was particularly notable in the purloining of clothing which, although stolen by both sexes, was generally sold on by men but retained by women. Females were more likely to steal in populated areas, and the goods they targeted were of a limited range. Males, however, through mobility and work, stole a wider range of items from much more disparate locations. For both gender groups, their patterns of offending highlighted their normal patterns of life, and reflected their different social boundaries. These meant that opportunities for evading the law also had a gendered nature. A determination was shown by victims of theft to seek out and bring to justice those people who had stolen from them. Complainants were prepared to meet the cost, both in time and money, of following through with a prosecution, even when their goods had been recovered.[88]

The following chapter explores the offences, treatment and experiences of a unique group of women who form a popular topic of historical study, namely prostitutes.

8

VICE

PUBLIC HOUSES, PROSTITUTION AND PLACE

Victorian prostitution and its place in society are well-studied historical topics, London and urban centres such as York and Portsmouth being particularly well covered.[1] This chapter investigates the degree to which prostitution contributed to crime, and in doing so, questions are asked about the life stories of these women, as well as their experience of the courts and the attitude of the wider community towards them. There will be investigations into whether the Bench and jury discretion seen before was apparent here also, and if the women's status disadvantaged them.

WHAT SORT OF WOMEN BECAME INVOLVED IN PROSTITUTION?

Dorcas Harding grew up in neighbouring Radnorshire, the daughter of a small farmer.[2] By 1861, she was living away from home, and by 1869, twenty-year-old Dorcas was known to the police in Newtown. She first appears in records when she faced charges of stealing a gold watch from a man. She was already known to the police, as Constable Richards knew who she was when notified of the theft by the victim, and found her within a short space of time.[3] The owner of the timepiece, Maurice Lloyd, told the magistrates he did not give her the watch as payment in kind, and said, 'I had money in my pocket at the time, both before and after I met with the prisoner.' In a similar case heard twelve months earlier, eighteen-year-old Mary Morris, often known as 'Red Mary', appeared before the county Bench charged with stealing a gold ring from a client.[4] Theft was a crime that was one of a narrow range of offences committed by women.[5] Morris's and Harding's offence was a crime that was 'traditionally the crime of the prostitute',[6] and in Merthyr it had become a major activity and source of income.[7] Many prostitutes had respectable occupations before going onto the streets,[8] and journalist Kallow Chesney wrote:

> More and more of them depended on selling their labour on a highly unstable labour market, and the wages most of them earned were miserable enough to make them want to seize any means of raising cash. The very fact that women were paid so little meant that employers often used them to replace the men who might have supported them.[9]

A young seamstress said: 'There isn't one young girl who can get her living by slop work [making cheap garments]', and makes the point that only those whose parents kept them in food and shelter could afford to remain virtuous. A girl in Carmarthenshire told Llanelli magistrates that it was impossible to be respectable on ten shillings a week when rent alone was eight shillings.[10] There are insufficient records to explain what Morris and Harding were doing before going onto the street, but Harding's elder brother, John, had worked as a carter on a farm near Newtown in the 1860s,[11] and it is possible that his sister had followed him to work in one of the flannel factories. The mechanization of spinning and its removal from cottages to manufactories deprived women of small but important incomes unless they followed the work to the towns,[12] and Newtown was becoming increasingly famous for dressmaking enterprises where girls could find employment. In larger factories, women represented a cheaper and more docile workforce than men, and were less costly to employ.[13] George Bernard Shaw commented, when discussing his 1893 play, *Mrs Warren's Profession*:[14]

> the truth that prostitution is caused, not by female depravity and male licentiousness, but simply by underpaying, undervaluing, and overworking women so shamefully that the poorest of them are forced to resort to prostitution to keep body and soul together.[15]

Mary Morris (Red Mary) may have been the daughter of a Radnorshire labourer shown living with her family in 1851 but described as a house servant in the Albion pub on Park Street ten years later. Another possibility for Red Mary was the daughter of a carpenter, living at home with her parents. Many craftsmen were highly vulnerable to poverty;[16] therefore this girl cannot be discounted as being Red Mary even though she had a father who could have been bringing in a reasonable income at times. Of the two, the former seems the more likely candidate, as prostitutes were often the unskilled daughters of the unskilled classes.[17] Circumstantially, the placing of the former candidate in a pub on Park Street is telling, as this area was well known for vice, particularly in public houses.

HOW DID PROSTITUTES CONTRIBUTE TO LEVELS OF CRIME?

Both Mary Morris's and Dorcas Harding's thefts took place on the street and, as expected from earlier discussion of police reaction to street crime, Constable Richards was quickly involved. The prostitutes' clients might have found him patrolling the streets,[18] or they may have gone to report their losses at the police station, which at that time was in Crescent Street, just a little to the north of the river.[19] Some thefts from clients took place indoors, however, and contributed to the chief constable's assertion that there were 'upwards of sixty prostitutes' in 'houses of ill fame' that were 'miserable haunts'.[20] Some of these haunts were public houses where, repeatedly, thefts took place. For example, in April 1869 – shortly after the chief constable's invective – farmer Richard Bache transacted agricultural business in Newtown and set off for home along Park Street.[21] He called in at the Picton Arms for a drink and was invited into the parlour by Sarah Lewis.[22] They spent fifteen minutes on the sofa together, after which time Bache noticed that most of his money was gone from his pocket. The landlady was present in the parlour initially and was well aware that Lewis and the farmer were together, giving the Picton Arms the appearance of a brothel.[23] Public houses were disreputable places, and commonly associated with crime and vice. In Shrewsbury, the notorious red light district of Roushill was enclosed by three public houses and a beer shop that were continually linked to prostitute crime. For example, in 1843 the Shrewsbury Chronicle reported:

On Tuesday, Thomas Downs, landlord of the King's Head, was charged by Constable Thomas with suffering notorious bad characters to assemble in his house ... he found about a dozen of the '*femmeélite* refreshing themselves after a trip on the light fantastic with about 30 gentlemen.[24]

A particularly unpleasant robbery took place in what was clearly a brothel in one of the rough parts of Newtown, near the road leading to Welshpool. This was the classic tale of an unsuspecting client being duped, and involved a known prostitute and her pimp, or 'bully'.[25] On Good Friday 1870, farm labourer Henry Reese had received his pay from his employer in the nearby village of Kerry. He spent some of the money, and then walked to Newtown where he spent time in the company of Ann Lloyd and Stephen Higgs at the house. He later left but returned and negotiated a price with Lloyd to spend the night with her. During the course of the evening, Higgs grabbed Reese and assaulted him, throwing him down the stairs and kicking him. The labourer eventually retrieved his trousers but the remainder of his pay, which he claimed to be about thirty shillings, was gone from his pocket.[26] Reese was the sort of client described as the prostitutes' 'easy pickings', with cash in their pockets and often 'simple fellows from Montgomeryshire or Pembrokeshire with harvest money in their pockets'. It was common for 'bewildered clients to fall downstairs with watches, wallets and trousers in their hands only to lose them to young men waiting at the bottom'.[27] Prostitutes often exploited men described as 'foolish young farm labourers' because the more innocent and inexperienced the client, the greater the opportunity for the prostitute to exploit him.[28] This observation does not include pimps in the exploitation. Crimes could be associated with the presence of prostitutes and their pimps, though not directly with the women. For example, a serious assault took place at the Queen's Head public house when Stephen Higgs was present. The victim described to the court how he entered the pub, intending to go through to the rear of the building but was set upon by another man. He went on: 'John Davies and some of the women of the house separated us ... At that time, Stephen Higgs came on and separated us.'[29] 'Women of the house' could have been barmaids or cleaners,

but Higgs' presence means that they were probably prostitutes. Higgs assisted in breaking up the assault in the Queen's
Head, which means he was the sort of bully commonly
employed by landlords, ostensibly to act as doormen to the
establishment thus keeping undesirables away from the
tenants. However, in reality, the bully's job was to ensure the
punters did not leave without paying their dues.[30] The
Queen's Head was not the only venue at which Higgs could
be found involved with trouble. At about the same time as
the Queen's Head case, he appeared at petty sessions charged
with fighting at the centre of town. The report said, 'They
fought two or three rounds near the shop of Mr Lewis, the
mercer. John Richards used very foul language, then Higgs
struck him down. Some woman eventually came and took
Higgs away.'[31] The court records show that other men, too,
were living off the proceeds of vice. After Sarah Lewis had
picked the pocket of her client, farmer Richard Bache, in the
parlour of the Picton Arms, she handed over the money to
two men. Lewis herself was described by one witness as
'intoxicated' and another as 'tipsy', and although she later
tried to retrieve the coins in order to return them to Bache
when he threatened to fetch a policeman, she did not have a
hope of getting the money back. Witness Mrs Mary Ann Lowe
testified:

> Sarah Lewis many times said to him, 'Dan, give me that money
> for the old man or else I shall be in the lock up'. He swore at
> her and lifted up his hand to strike her, saying to her, 'I'll not
> g'ie it'. Atkinson on that said, 'Hold fast Dan, her has got two
> shillings in her pocket, that is enough for her'. Atkinson and
> Walsh then walked into the slack hole, and while they were
> there for a few minutes, Sarah Lewis (drunk) fell asleep.
> [Witness observed the men with gold sovereigns] I then said,
> 'Now I see who had the money', to which Atkinson replied,
> 'Shut thy mouth Mary'. They then went out leaving Sarah
> Lewis sleeping in the shop.[32]

This description of the men's behaviour suits the word
'bully'. It also follows the pattern of the Victorian 'prostitute
melodrama', involving loss of virtue leading to a cycle of
alcohol and vice, and drinking to forget a sin committed

under the influence of drink. It probably contributed to the grand jury's dismissal of the case.[33]

As drinking places attracted working men, especially on pay day, it was not surprising that they attracted prostitutes too. Walmgate, the principal thoroughfare in the red light district of York, contained the most public houses and beer shops in the city, and in 1843, one-sixth of the city's prostitutes lived there.[34] In Montgomeryshire, there were regular and frequent calls for public house reform, addressing drunkenness and prostitution simultaneously, although the latter was not named specifically. The calls for reform included newspaper correspondence such as this letter:

> Public houses are the curse of our land. I hardly ever see a sign, 'Licensed to sell spirits and ale' without thinking that it is a licence to ruin souls. They are the yawning avenues to poverty and rags in this life, and as one has said, 'the short cut to hell'.[35]

The temperance movement in the county exerted a pressure on the law-enforcement agencies, although they did not always achieve their aims. This is shown by a letter published in *The Newtown and Welshpool Express* from the disappointed honorary secretaries of Newtown Temperance Society:

> That the magistrates should have paid so little attention to the strongly expressed opinion of the inhabitants of Newtown is to us a matter of regret; and the temperance committee cannot but express their surprise that the publican interest should have resorted to such subterfuge [saying that a temperance petition had been signed by many children] to deprive the principal ratepayers and overwhelming majority of the working classes of what they petitioned the magistrates to grant [a reduction in licences].[36]

Here the writers perceived that invoking the working classes in the call for change would carry some extra weight. It is relevant that the Second Reform Act of 1867 had recently enfranchised many lower-class men in the town, who could now vote in parliamentary elections. A branch of the Reform League had been established in Newtown, and although disbanded by the 1870s, former members were determined to continue campaigning for further democracy.[37] An editorial in the same issue of the newspaper said:

> By the report of the Newtown petty sessions which appears in another column, it will be seen that the magistrates, whilst giving notice of their intention next year to limit the number of licences granted to the supposed requirements of the population, have renewed all licences where objections were not made by the police.[38]

The magistrates were thus aware that they could not remove licences on an ad hoc basis, but only if there was a demonstrable reason for doing so in the form of police objections. There is an element of disapproval in the tone of the editorial. The temperance movement had grown in response to public concern at alcohol-fuelled disorder. The temperance society in Newtown included some prominent citizens, including town clerk and schoolteacher William Cooke, and Edwin Dixon who was a boot manufacturer and employer. Sergeant Hudson also admitted being a member of the 'Good Templars' when giving evidence about drunkenness in the Eagles public house.[39] The defence lawyer in that case had suggested that the sergeant's motivation for bringing the prosecution was temperance.[40] From the 1830s, the Nonconformists had moved towards teetotalism rather than mere moderation in alcoholic consumption, and by the 1870s, this new movement had become a 'social and political force of amazing dimensions' within Wales.[41] From the words in the editorial quoted, however, the same political and social sensibilities were not present in the majority of the Newtown Bench, where it was likely that the majority were Anglicans. Prostitution and its effect on public well-being were at the front of public consciousness during the 1870s. This was following the 1864, 1866 and 1869 Contagious Diseases Acts that had been passed in an effort to control the spread of venereal disease, particularly among enlisted men.[42] In 1857 William Acton had published his best-selling *Prostitution*, with a second edition published in November 1869, containing provocative comments such as 'a [prostitute] ... is free to spread among [her clients] deadly contagion.' There was also detail that some readers might have found titillating.[43] Earlier in the nineteenth century legal methods existed which allowed for the imprisonment of prostitutes, and some authorities took advantage of this gratefully.[44] When this law was changed in 1824, the University of Oxford's solicitor wrote of a fear of

> the streets of Oxford being thronged with prostitutes and bullies so that unless other means can be employed to remedy the evil, its consequences to the morals and credit of the university must daily become more deplorable.[45]

Some Montgomeryshire prostitutes were prosecuted under the new 1824 Act. According to *The Justices' Manual* of 1862, the following guidance was given, detailing the legislation:

> 5 George IV, chapter 83, section 3: Prostitutes behaving indecently – every common prostitute wandering in the public streets or public highways or in any place of public resort and behaving in a riotous or indecent manner, to be deemed an idle and disorderly person. Being found on premises for any unlawful purpose: Every person being found in or upon any dwelling house, warehouse, coach house, stable or outhouse or in any enclosed yard, garden, or area for any unlawful purpose to be deemed a rogue and a vagabond.[46]

Table 8.1 lists the offences attributable to prostitutes that were dealt with under the vagrancy laws at sessions during the course of a sample period 1869–70.

Night time in the centre of Newtown had no shortage of sights of women with their clients. Chief Constable Danily reported 'upwards of sixty prostitutes infesting [Newtown]' and 'their abominable haunts becoming a nuisance'.[47] But whereas the University of Oxford has plentiful extant records giving information about the response of the university and the city, there is little information about any public concern or reaction in Newtown. This may be due to local sensibilities finding any involvement with prostitution to be unacceptable. When a new law to address the issue of serious disease was being discussed at quarter sessions in 1869, the

Newspaper date	Crime	Names	Details	Sentence
30 Nov. 1869	Disorderly conduct	Eliza Oliver. Margaret Davies, Mary-Ann Richards	Unspecified location in Welshpool. Charged by Sup. Strefford	14 days in lock-up
4 Feb. 1870	Being in town for an unlawful purpose	Ann Jones	Seen by Sgt Ross with men. Later seen 'consulting' with man next to doctor's surgery	Fined 1s. and costs
5 Apr. 1870	Drunk and indecent	Ann Edwards (alias 'Sugar')	On the street somewhere in Welshpool	Fined 5s. or seven days in custody
17 Apr. 1870	Wandering streets late at night	Elizabeth Roberts, Elizabeth Edwards	Had followed militiamen to Welshpool	Discharged on condition that they left town

Table 8.1 Vagrancy offences attributable to known prostitutes, 1869–70

newspaper made clear that it was the Contagious Diseases (Animals) Act that was being debated, clearly distinguishing it from the law regarding disease spread by intimate contact.[48] Earlier in the same year, the local board held an *in camera* meeting with its agenda kept secret and the press forbidden to attend. However, *The Newtown and Welshpool Express* published a comment about the reporter's exclusion, which reveals that the content of the meeting was leaked. The comment was written in typical Victorian language that skirts around the issue and uses euphemisms, yet there are clues in the report's language that indicate the topic discussed was prostitution and how to address the matter:

> The exclusion of the reporters was no guarantee that the matter then discussed or resolved upon would remain a secret ... Those whose duty is essentially and vitally truth-telling would not for any meagre consideration prostitute the position they occupy in order to realise a condition of things which is far below their profession. [A member of the Board's] suggestion is really valuable and meets with the full approval of the medical officers and medical profession of the district. All that is really wanted is an immunity, so far as human means can ensure it, against those evils which again and again distress the community and turn many a happy family into a domestic Ramah.[49]

Ramah was the city in ancient Israel where captured Israelites were held before being taken to wicked Babylon. It was also the city where Rachel was said to be heard 'weeping for her lost sons'. Church or chapel attendees would have been familiar with these biblical references,[50] and analysis of clergymen's use of religion as a means of social control suggests that this letter was written by such a man.[51] The letter appealed directly to people's moral sensibilities. This was an example of the ethical campaign against prostitution that was prevalent during the Victorian period and which the *Express*, founded and edited by Welsh-speaking Wesleyan Methodist, Henry Parry,[52] was happy to publish. During the 1870s, the crusade was overtaken by more onus being put on the client,[53] and there will be examples of this new approach in due course. There is some evidence that steps were taken by the local board to improve conditions on the streets to control unacceptable behaviour. Charles Booth was to suggest in the 1880s that: 'The use of dark back streets ... by the lowest class of women can only be checked by better lighting and patrolling.'[54] Newtown local board was ahead of Booth, for in 1869 they had already plans in place to extend gas lighting to the canal area, a known location of prostitution and disorder. In November 1869, Ellen Griffiths, wife of a labourer living at the canal basin, was charged with being drunk and riotous. She claimed to suffer from fits and that she had been in one of these fits when the police found her lying prostrate on the ground.[55]

Although a large section of the public, particularly lower-class women, had little input into the administration of justice, the courts nevertheless provided them with a theatre in which they could give their opinions informally. This happened in a trial involving child prostitution at a time when the age of consent was twelve years. Coming before quarter sessions in March 1872, it concerned theft from the person by two twelve-year-old girls by the names of Eliza Oliver and Elizabeth Ellis.[56] The man concerned was a travelling salesman from Liverpool, going by the name of Drennan, who had been in Welshpool on business. After spending time with the girls, the man noticed that his money was gone. As in the case of 'Red Mary' in Newtown, the officer knew the alleged thieves and where to find them, and proceedings subsequently took place. The outcome was a conviction, with the girls sent to prison for twenty-one days followed a reformatory school for five years.[57] No charges of any sort were laid against the man, but the case was as much a popular trial of him as of the girls. The spectators in the court gave vent to their outrage by shouting out comments and objections during the proceedings, and later Drennan had to be escorted by police to the railway station in order to protect him from the crowd. *The Newtown and Welshpool Express* reported:

> It was evident from the excited condition of the audience that when the prosecutor left the court he would be roughly treated and steps were taken accordingly. A detachment of police officers was sent with him out; when he made his

appearance there was a tremendous burst of execration
outside and this was followed by a regular stampede ... [It
was] imperative that he should take shelter down one of the
passages but this was not effected without many blows and
kicks being inflicted and for some time the streets were in the
greatest commotion.

The chairman of the Bench made the point that had the girls
not reached the legal age, Drennan would have been alongside them in the dock facing charges himself. It was cases
such as this and the attendant public outcry, and the efforts
of reformers including Josephine Butler and William Stead,
that led to the age of consent being raised to thirteen years in
1875 and to sixteen years in 1885.[58] Thus the courtroom
could be a public forum for highlighting current matters,
with the resulting newspaper coverage of public response
and Bench comments helping to add to the debate.[59] The
justice system also allowed for a collective protest at the end
of the courtroom proceedings that was tolerated and was not
seen as a subversive action needing to be put down.[60]

WHAT WERE PROSTITUTES' EXPERIENCES OF THE COURTS?

Mary Morris pleaded not guilty to the charge of theft from
the person. Although she admitted taking the ring, she
claimed to have always intended to return it. When the
presiding magistrate addressed the jury, he pointed out that
her client was aware that she had taken the ring and did not
attempt to stop her. The jury found Morris not guilty.[61] Upon
the verdict being given, Morris's supporters, taking advantage of the forum provided by the court, made vocal
comment. This was one of the few opportunities they ever
had of giving vent to an expression of feeling in front of the
upper orders in society without being arrested for disorder.
Sarah Lewis pleaded not guilty to the larceny of gold coins
from the person of farmer Richard Bache. The two men who
took the sovereigns from her appeared alongside her in the
dock, charged with receiving money knowing it to be stolen.
They too pleaded not guilty. There was plenty of evidence
against Lewis: Bache positively identified her, and described

in detail the time they spent together in the parlour of the public house. He was certain that he was in possession of the money before the encounter, and that it was gone immediately after. Two witnesses confirmed seeing Lewis with the co-accused, and one confirmed seeing the men with the same amount of money that was missing. This witness also confirmed that Lewis had asked the men to return the money to her so that she could give it back to Bache. There was nothing to form a defence for Lewis except an absolute denial, but the case did not reach the trial stage, as the grand jury decided to throw it out. If the grand jury had received only the main prosecution case, the trial might well have gone forward. Earlier in the nineteenth century, this would have been the situation, and led to many complaints that appraising cases without access to witness depositions was unsatisfactory.[62] The fact that the grand jury here ignored the case means that they had access to the depositions, for within these lay the words of witness Mrs Lowe. It was she who described Welsh's rough words to herself and Sarah Lewis, and that the young woman wanted to return the money. By throwing out the case against Lewis, the grand jury had to find the men not guilty of receiving the money knowing it to be stolen.[63] There was strong prosecution evidence against Sarah Lewis. She may have been fortified in her stance against the charges by Mary Morris's acquittal a few months earlier, but there is a darker possibility. It could have been that the men used force against her, making her deny the charge because a guilty plea from her would mean a conviction for them.

Dorcas Harding was another who pleaded not guilty to a seemingly watertight prosecution case. She made a defence that must have seemed hardly credible to the grand jury – that the complainant gave her the gold watch – and, indeed, the grand jurymen did send the case forward to trial.[64] The petty jury, too, found for the prosecution but recommended her to mercy, and the magistrates agreed, deeming the man to be partly to blame. Harding received fourteen days with hard labour and was told that she would have received a heavier penalty 'had not the man been blameable'.[65] There is thus a picture emerging of juries being sympathetic to the women who appeared in the dock. They were willing to give the prostitutes the benefit of the doubt and to take into consideration the part played by the client in initiating the whole course of events. The magistrates, too, in their sentencing accepted the contributing role of the man.[66]

Sentences were heavier when the stolen item was clothing. A notable case involved the theft of a paisley shawl and a bonnet in March 1869.[67] The shawl belonged to prostitute Ann Lloyd, who was herself to be convicted for theft the following year with Stephen Higgs. The bonnet belonged to Esther Thomas, the woman Sergeant Ross had found drunk when clearing a disorderly public house. The perpetrator was Ann Williams, aged seventeen years, who was lodging in the same house as Lloyd.[68] Her sentence was one day in prison for the theft of the shawl and seven years penal servitude for the theft of the bonnet.[69] She had a previous conviction for theft from a year earlier but it appears that the aggravating feature resulting in the severe sentence was the element of deception, where Williams led Esther Thomas to believe that the bonnet was for the use of Lloyd.[70] Commonly penal servitude was given for repeat offenders but, on the whole, Williams's two thefts with a previous conviction are very similar to those of Sarah Rowlands who appeared in court the following year.[71] Why did Williams, who was very young albeit a repeat offender, receive such a severe sentence when Rowlands received only six months for a repeat offence?[72] It is known that the jury in the Rowlands case asked for mercy, and the Bench nearly always abided by such requests, but Williams was only seventeen years of age, which could have been considered worthy of some leniency.[73] An answer to the question is that different magistrates assigned different weightings to similar offences. Table 8.2 shows the magistrates dealing with Williams's and Rowlands's cases, and here is a feature noted before, that Major Drew's and Canon Herbert's presence on the Bench had a lowering effect on the level of sentence, and could reflect their personalities. Demonstrated here is the clear difference in levels of sentence when the theft was from a woman, not a male client. In 1871, when Sarah Rowlands – who had been convicted

Defendant/offence	Court	Magistrates	Sentence
Ann Williams: theft of shawl and bonnet from women	Midsummer 1869	Sir Watkin Williams-Wynn, J. R. Jones, Malcolm Crewe-Read, W. Fisher	1 day plus seven years' penal servitude
Sarah Rowlands: theft of stockings from headmistress	Hilary 1870	Lord Powis, Sir Watkin Williams-Wynn, J. R. Jones, Canon Herbert	Three months' hard labour
Sarah Rowlands, theft of petticoat from widow	Midsummer 1870	Sir Watkin Williams-Wynn, J. R. Jones, Major Drew, Canon Herbert	Six months

Table 8.2 Magistrates sitting at Williams's and Rowlands's trials at quarter sessions

twice in 1870 of theft from women – was charged with theft from a client, the case was ignored by the grand jury.[74]

WAS THE JUSTICE SYSTEM ACCESSIBLE TO THE PROSTITUTES THEMSELVES?

Prostitutes used the law, as for example in a case of prostitute-on-prostitute violence when Sarah Lewis assaulted Catherine Matthews in Ladywell Street.[75] Matthews reported this to the police and the case went to petty sessions. A witness was called to give evidence on behalf of Matthews and when the case was proved, Lewis received a fine of one shilling or seven days' imprisonment. It is not clear from the newspaper report which sentence of the two was carried out. One shilling appears to be a token amount, equivalent to eight copies of *The Newtown and Welshpool Express* and reflected a feeling of the magistrates that an assault on a prostitute by another was no crime at all, or that 'each was as bad as the other'. This was seen in a petty sessions case from May 1869, when a similar assault took place between two married women in Mount Street, Welshpool. Neither woman was a prostitute, but they had a very long history of ill feeling towards each other, described in the newspaper as 'bickering'. The sentence imposed was the same as in the Lewis–Matthews case.[76] In October of the same year, an altercation between two respectable married women in Ladywell Street, involving a physical assault and abusive language, also resulted in a conviction against one of them.[77] In this case, the fine was only sixpence, reflecting the defendant's financial means, or that costs were allowed. The costs were not mentioned in the newspaper account but were likely to amount to a high figure as there were four witnesses who would lose pay to attend court.[78] At the same set of hearings, a woman accused her neighbour of throwing scalding water over her, and the convicted woman was fined five shillings. This seemingly random set of sentences meant that the justices were considering several factors, including whether the defendant pleaded guilty or not guilty, whether there were previous convictions, and any aggravating or mitigating circumstances, as well as income and ability to pay.[79] A sentence,

Item	Value
Complete set of false teeth	£5.
First class return train ticket Newtown–Aberystwyth	4s.
Good seat at amateur concert in Welshpool town hall	5s.
1 day's pay for woman farm worker	1s. 3d
Small bottle of cough mixture	1s. 1½ d
Back row seat at Welshpool concert	1s.
1lb pot of honey	8d
8 eggs	6d
Copy of *The Newtown and Welshpool Express*	1½ d

Table 8.3 Prices of a range of items shown in advertisements in the *Newtown and Welshpool Express* 1869–1870

therefore, was not *per se* an indication of the crime, as two different defendants could receive very different sentences for the same offence. Fines that the prostitutes received ranged from one to five shillings. In comparison, in Shrewsbury the range that prostitutes received was between one and ten shillings.[80] In order to put the fines in context, Table 8.3 shows prices for a range of items during the second half of the nineteenth century.[81]

AN UNUSUAL OFFENCE

Victorian prostitution was considered by some to be the preserve of the female, but there is undoubted evidence of male prostitution.[82] An incident in Welshpool in 1870 indicates that the practice was going on there, for the hallmarks of female prostitution considered hitherto in this chapter were present. The man involved was known by the nickname 'Spango', met with a man in a public house in the evening, went with him down a side street, and subsequently picked the man's pocket while sitting close to him.[83] The depositions and cross-examination give details of the events of the night, but nothing to identify sexual intercourse between men unequivocally, which was at that time, illegal. Such acts were considered such a bad 'crime against nature' that they were usually referred to in Latin.[84] Similarly, *The Newtown and Welshpool Express* carried no details about a so-called 'unnatural offence', which was ignored by the grand jury at assizes in 1874.[85] The feature indicating that the Spango incident included something regarded as particularly offensive was the sentence. For the theft of £3 15s. he was given six months with hard labour. This was the same punishment awarded to a man who stole £25 from the pocket of his employer in a daytime offence, and a woman who embezzled £15.[86] There is evidence here that this man's pickpocketing offence was treated differently, and less favourably, from those by known, female, prostitutes.

CONCLUSION

Offences committed by prostitutes took place in the urban centres of Newtown and Welshpool. There was a connection between prostitution and public houses, and a corresponding effort from some sections of the community towards curbing both. Magistrates in petty sessions faced many offences that arose from alcohol consumption, but they frustrated the efforts of temperance proponents by not removing licences except when requested to do so by the police. The local boards were more proactive in undertaking measures to reduce vice.

The crimes committed by prostitutes were typically those of theft from their clients, which supports a view that financial constraints had initially sent them onto the streets. Other people benefited from their offending, including public house keepers, who sometimes were akin to brothel keepers, and pimps, who could be violent to both the women and their clients. The acquittals and small fines given to the women give an impression of generous tolerance, with juries and magistrates using their discretion to put responsibility for prostitute crime into the hands of their patrons. Here they were following the new shift towards highlighting the role of the client in prostitution.[87] A difference was seen when a similar offence was committed by a man. In that case, the defendant was convicted at quarter sessions and given a severe sentence. Lower-level prostitute offending included street disorder often involving other women. When they used the justice system to sort out their disputes, the fines imposed were either displays of tolerance or a reflection of the women's income. There were several severe sentences handed out at quarter sessions and, again, the differing personalities of justices were observed with Sir Watkin Williams-Wynn and John Robinson Jones often harsh in their judgements whereas Major Drew and Canon Herbert tended to be kinder.

CONCLUSION

CRIME, COURTS AND COMMUNITY

This study of the criminal justice system has helped to throw light upon social relations, as well as the place of the courts in people's lives. The aim was to consider individuals' contribution to legal proceedings and to analyse those people's actions and experiences. The work gives a view from all sides and assesses the input and participation of all court users. It explores mid-Wales – hitherto so little studied – from the viewpoint of nineteenth-century crime and legal history.[1] We have looked closely at women and gendered differences, and the effects they had on courtroom events. The project moved away from previous investigations of particular types of court – petty or quarter sessions, police court or assizes – and looked instead at all the criminal courts to make comparisons and to study similarities and variances. Newspaper reports and other records illuminated the character of people and places, and calls have been answered for furthering investigations on the effect of the environment, gendered and class experiences, and identity.[2] Comparisons have been made between the nature of offending in contrasting rural and urban areas, and certain themes and individuals were found to traverse chapters.

The initial assessment of Montgomeryshire at once established the several dualities of environment: the rural and the urban, the agricultural and the industrial, the decayed and the prosperous, the hills and the valleys. The polarities went on into the popular culture of the time, for there was a distinct English character in the east, and strong Welshness in the west. The Church of England, which was the established religion in Wales until the twentieth century, was strongly represented in decision-making bodies, and although Nonconformists were far greater in number, they were less well represented. Conservatives were more equated with Anglicans, while Liberals in Wales were historically aligned with Nonconformity. Employment opportunities encouraged movement of people, resulting in the demographic mixes that were present in most localities and in the constantly changing communities in towns. There were signs of control, such as when the local board in Newtown called for reform of open sewers that offended Sunday worshippers. There were indications of community segregation, with employers and gentry being associated with salubrious locations in notable houses, contrasting with many of the lower classes living in a mass of standardised housing, often near stagnant filth. Two environments that facilitated criminal activity were seen in the contrasts between townscapes and countryside. In the urban areas were pawnshops and close-packed dwellings, unemployment and itinerant labourers, and such situations were recognised as genitors of crime. Featuring too were canals, roads and railways, facilitators of a thief's opportunity for offending and getaway. The rural areas conversely contained isolated farms, livestock and crops in unattended fields, and hills across which to escape. Signs of control were apparent when landowners restricted access by enclosure, and there were indicators of conflict when new gentry and landed clergymen changed or usurped the rights of old families.

There was a duality on the Bench whereby the county justices held a superiority over their borough colleagues via noble connections, landed interests and wealth. Property owning and income allowed unrepresentative appointment to decision-making bodies. This raised issues about the appointment of Nonconformist ministers to such bodies, which led to debate and Chartist-like disagreement over reform.[3] Appointment to the magistracy increased a man's prestige, although social ranking differentiated the Bench and was enhanced by county roles made available by a man's position in society. The constabulary could be assessed in a similar manner, but here the discrimination was given named ranks, and further distinguished by housing and pay. This marks a difference between the motivating factors of the magistrates and the police: whereas the policemen could climb ranks and pay scales through hard work, the justices took on their roles because of who they were. Some men, however, became magistrates through their appointment to the local board in Welshpool, a status that immediately marked them out as those who had to earn a living. Social divisions were present in the form of housing, and the system of justice stamped its mark on society through architecture, and reinforced the social stratification with features such as balconies and higher-status entrances for magistrates.[4]

Police operations, although desired and appreciated by many, could cause conflict, especially where they were perceived to be acting in an underhand, overbearing or biased way. Residents with the ability to protest in writing could effect a change in police behaviour, whereas those who could respond only with fists, feet or verbal retorts were likely to feel the weight of the stave followed by a court appearance. People feeling aggrieved by the police could stand up for themselves by turning the law onto the officers or through letters to the local newspaper. There was less of a police presence in the countryside, and when combined with the many hillsides and long distances between settlements, this entailed opportunities for getting away with offences or meting out personal retribution. The distances travelled by a country policeman in the course of his duty, and the amount of time this travelling took, left scope for offending to go undetected, and the lack of officers in rural areas caused concern to some residents. Reaction to the police was differentiated and depended on whether police intervention was required or not. Some used the police as scapegoats for a wider dissatisfaction with lack of influence and decision-making ability, and some reacted negatively to police control when the deference they considered appropriate was not shown.[5]

The study of petty sessions saw the first appearance of women, although they were in no sense involved in the administration of justice. They were in the witness box, dock or public gallery, and could bring a dispute to court that had crossed a boundary into the criminal sphere. Often the offence was one that occurred in domestic space, exacerbated by the close-packed and constricting environment in which they lived. The women, and all the others involved in lawsuits, were judged by their social superiors; but there was little, if any, sign of ruling-class hegemony or collusion overshadowing the roles played by the lower classes. In fact, prosecutors often used the court to conspire against each other. The justices were aware of this and remarked upon it in open court. Some prosecutors also used the court to establish their rights, obtain retribution or restrain another party. Petty sessions therefore enabled a degree of control for those involved in legal proceedings and could offer protection against, for example, a violent employer or spouse, or heavy-handed landlord.[6] The police used the court to control disorder that very often resulted from the consumption of alcohol. Thirty per cent of the offences brought to the sessions by the constabulary were those of drunkenness or street disorder, rising to over 70 per cent in Welshpool and Newtown, showing how the influence of the new police had changed the justice system. In the remainder of the county, drunkenness and disorder accounted for around 30 per cent of court appearances, though this could have been due to under-reporting because of the lower availability of policemen in the countryside. The justices often gave the chief constable the result he wanted, inflicting stiff penalties particularly when an officer was injured during his work. However, the notable discretion shown by the various Benches in their judgements meant that in some cases, particularly when prostitutes were charged with street offences, the police did not achieve the outcomes they wanted, and there were early indications of the new approach to vice where the client was held responsible. The magistrates used their discretion to suit local needs, which sometimes included giving the defendant the benefit of any doubt, or overriding advice from the clerk. There were a few occasions when a Bench was biased towards members of a particular group. Analysis of fines indicated that these were based on ability to pay, showing that the Welshpool area was more affluent than the rest of the county, and the county as a whole was poor. Indeed, in some ways late nineteenth-century Montgomeryshire resembled eighteenth-century Essex, giving the Welsh county an appearance of economic underdevelopment.

Quarter sessions had a very different complexion from the summary courts, first because theft was the predominant offence brought before the magistrates, and secondly because men of the more ordinary sort had major influence in the decisions made. Discretion was in the hands of a more substantial part of the community, and choices were taken away from the upper classes and placed in the hands of middle-class juries. Hierarchies contributed to a man's sense of identity; status was symbolised in a very visible way by his seat in the jury box and through jury members' names being listed in the local newspaper. This identity was changeable, however, as a man could appear in different juries on two successive occasions.[7] Jury members were often people who actively pursued prosecutions against offenders, and there were jurors who were also members of felons' associations. This introduced the phenomenon of ability to pay for justice, with available funds enabling and facilitating the pursuance of prosecutions. Cooperation between better-off farmers and poorer ones was seen. The presence of two active felons associations suggests dissatisfaction with the police service, although Welshpool borough corporation gave a dinner in recognition of the force. Some members of the community were clearly more determined than others to see offenders brought to justice, and the felons associations were an extra support to the police.[8]

At quarter sessions, policemen often represented women, with the protection of a respectable woman's sensibilities being important. There were also occasions when police took actions to keep middle-class men – jury material – on their side, and deference to women could have been part of this, as the women had spouses and other family members who were potential jurors. Although much discretion was removed from the magistrates in quarter sessions, the high sheriff was able to manipulate the jury lists. This allowed more non-farmers into the box, and the system permitted the Bench to hand over the judging of a problematic situation from themselves to the jurors. There were still opportunities for magistrates to exercise their own judgement in dispensing sentences. There were indications of different judicial personalities appearing, also observed at petty sessions, with the leniency or kindness of Major Drew and Canon Herbert contrasting with the perhaps heavy-handedness of Sir Watkin Williams-Wynn and John Robinson Jones.[9]

The assize court had a direct effect on status as the magistrates were relegated to the grand jury box, and this may explain why aristocratic justices were not seen in the court, seeming to turn their backs on it. A domino effect occurred as those men who sat in the grand jury at quarter sessions were now in the petty jury at the assizes, and the class of man who formerly occupied the petty jury in quarter sessions no longer had any role. Women met the challenge of appearing at this highest-status theatre of justice. With the assistance of legal representation, they were generally not cowed and could win their cases.[10] Females were active throughout the public arenas of the court scene, even though they had no part in the administration of justice. They were often key players in jurisdictional situations despite being disadvantaged in day-to-day life. Women encouraged other females within the court building and immediately outside, showing that the court system could act as a support for gendered solidarity. There were many instances where reputations were established, bolstered or changed by the judicial system. The exact point at which barristers gained right of attendance at quarter sessions was identified, with the change being a direct consequence of solicitors losing their good standing. Control was exercised in various forms, most notably with his lordship directing procedures and making judgements, but also with many lower down the social scale – including tramps – being able to exert themselves at times. The assize court was not an 'upper-class conspiracy to evoke deference' from the lower orders, even if at times some pompous language or behaviour was used.

There was clear difference between the offending of men and women, particularly in regard to the locus of the offending event. Women rarely offended in isolated areas but often did so in their home locality, whereas men's offences took place in more disparate locations. Men stole clothing largely for financial gain but women usually retained the purloined items. The gendered nature of opportunity resulted in contrasting ranges of items stolen. The environment played a large part in these offences. Not only were women's opportunities constrained to narrowly defined locations, but their opportunities for making off after the event were limited and largely confined to known areas with physiology and clothing having a distinct bearing on this. The gendered nature of location and getaway necessarily had implications for policing because women were easier to track down and apprehend. A deep level of trust existed among some employers which often meant that goods could be stolen with ease by employees. Determination was subsequently shown by the victims, often setting traps or cooperating with policemen to track down the guilty party. Many suspects confessed readily when apprehended but pleaded not guilty in court, and it seems likely that the initial ready confession was sometimes brought about violently by the complainant or the police.

The chief constable showed a determination to root out prostitution and its associated crime and disorder. The women involved were often protected or controlled by rough men, but sometimes they worked alone. They had a distinct identity, and the language directed at them by others on the street or when referring to them in newspapers, along with the chief constable's crusade, engendered a separateness that defined such women as a distinct group. The location of prostitute offences, and the disorder related to them, was often at or near public houses that resembled brothels, and contributed to the chief constable's campaign against such drinking places. A new attitude towards prostitutes, noted by other historians, whereby the client was deemed responsible for theft offences, was apparent at this time, with many instances of low penalties or acquittals. Sometimes the Bench told the victim that it was his own fault. These thefts were regarded differently from other similar offences because prostitute thefts from other women, such as neighbours, were given considerably higher penalties. The women were thus accorded a degree of confidence when defending themselves against charges of theft from a man. Prostitutes themselves regularly brought charges against other women, and the justices gave them the same degree of discretion shown to others.

This book constitutes a microhistory, or rather a collection of narrative and interpretative microhistories, and whereas many historians prefer to take a wider view,[11] it has been found that individuals' actions become more visible and understandable when examined in such close focus.[12] Illuminated by the methods and detail of localised and individualised study, three main general themes have pervaded: class, status and gender. Power was exercised at various levels within the justice system of the 1870s, most notably via the court system, which made issues of class and gender visible in the Welsh society being studied. The close focus expounded here allows us to examine local issues of 'exploitation', and the evidence does not really suggest that a Marxist interpretation based upon conflict between classes was warranted in this region. The formal proceedings in court were certainly the preserve of men from relatively high on the social scale, for example those who controlled manufacturing. One can see this in appointments of borough justices and former factory owners to the Bench. Further, the overwhelming majority of cases involved the lower orders or working classes. Middle-class defendants and witnesses were often given the undoubted social privilege of avoiding petty sessions. There were occasions when attempts at class subjugation were visible, and these can be described in such terms, yet these remained nothing but attempts, and often thwarted ones. The circumspection and discretion that was demonstrated at every level by magistrates and juries helped avoid social and class discord. Where antipathy existed towards tithe payments for example, Canon Herbert used his careful judgement to temper the adversarial situations that would probably have arisen from his role in the established Church. When conflict did arise, it was very often in the form of intra-level strife and frequently in response to police action. One could argue that the police were the tools of the upper orders, and yet Chief Constable Danily often organised his men to suit his own sensibilities, and sentences handed out by justices sometimes went against police desires.

In contradiction of Marxist interpretations, the Welsh working classes in this region manifestly used the petty courts for their own ends. Common prostitutes could sometimes be confident that the system would judge in their favour. Such findings and readings of the evidence do not sit easily with class-exploitative or Marxist models of conflict, yet class and social position did play a large part, particularly in perceived or imposed identities.[13] Here a terminology of 'social stratification' derived from Max Weber may be more appropriate, in which 'status groups' and external perceptions of status and repute by others influenced actions and outcomes. In many cases, such status was derived initially by birth. It was then reinforced or modified by lifestyle, status roles and by the local attainments of social capital[14] – a concept that harmonises well with microhistory as an approach to rural Welsh interpersonal relations – even if social repute, 'honour' and standing could vary between those of differing social positions and genders, and may not have been widely agreed upon. Economic differentials between people using the justice system certainly played their part; yet the prestige, moral status or influence of an individual – often irrespective of wealth – were frequently visible in court outcomes, in how influence was exercised, and in how people of different social positions and genders were treated. Status and moral differentials were often made visible and clearly affected interpersonal judgements, for example between police and drinkers, workmen and prostitutes, landowners and tramps. One thinks of insults such as 'thou art nothing but a prostitute'. Status theory, and the attendant social capital and reputations pervading a morally Nonconformist and localised Welsh culture – one that could overshadow English or Anglican ideas of morality, social standing or class – help one to see that conflicts owed much to individuals (of whatever social position or moral dispensation) not receiving acknowledgement of their reputation or self-assumed status. Such theoretical directions, as an alternative to sometimes less nuanced Marxist interpretations, fit well with the nature of the local mid-Welsh society and its justice system with which we have been concerned.

'Women's history' now offers a new perspective on the past,[15] no longer overlooking female importance and influence through their everyday work and activities. The findings here shed new light on the offending event, for example by analysing the gendered getaway part of the offence, and giving a new context for further investigations of police work and methods. They also provide an answer to questions about women's influence,[16] as gendered bias in sentencing has been observed, and women's involvement in tracking down and apprehending suspects was explored. It was often only the women in court who observed discrepancies or tried to bring an issue to the attention of the presiding magistrate or judge. Edwin Ardener has argued that women were able to express their ideas only through the language of dominant males, and in this project too, time and again, the voice of the woman has come through in the records of the male-controlled courts. Yet although Ardener argued that women's silence in many areas could be related to the 'deafness' of men towards them,[17] the findings of the present investigation found many instances where, in court, women were listened to and note was taken of their points of view. This was true regardless of class, and the court therefore provided an enabling environment for them.

The justice system has proved to be an excellent and illuminating vehicle for the study of social relations. Further work could be done on the changing input of women into the system in Wales, including the arrival of women on the Bench,[18] and in the police force after the Second World War.[19] Magistrates lost their control of county administration when elected county councils appeared after 1888, and it would be rewarding to investigate whether their control in court also changed, and if jury decisions altered from this time. To date, most historical studies of crime have focused on assessments within England, and the field of Celtic comparison has yet to be opened up.[20] A comparative study of Montgomeryshire and an Irish county, such as Kilkenny, would contribute to existing important work, and provide cultural insight into differences in courts, crime and community. Montgomeryshire criminal history would also repay study in connection with land and tenant issues during the early twentieth century, when many great estates were sold, and the Great War impacted on communities via conscription and horse requisitioning.[21] Moreover, further studies are needed on the effects during later periods of Welsh

Nonconformity on the justice system. As always, the agendas and questions seem to grow with each new study, yet it is hoped that this book sheds fresh light on the history of criminal justice and community in a fascinating and often overlooked part of Britain.

NOTES

INTRODUCTION

[1]   B. Short, 'Conservation, class and custom: life space and conflict in a nineteenth-century forest environment', *Rural History*, 10 (1999), 127–54; B. Short, 'Environmental politics, custom and personal testimony: memory and life space on the late Victorian Ashdown Forest, Sussex', *Journal of Historical Geography*, 30 (2004), 145–61; B. Cowell, 'The Commons Preservation Society and the campaign for Berkhamsted Common, 1866–70', *Rural History*, 13 (2002), 145–61. For analyses of the special dimension of crime see N. Blomley, 'Making private property: enclosure, common right and the work of hedges', *Rural History*, 18 (2007), 1–21; and P. King, 'The impact of urbanization on murder rates and on the geography of homicide in England and Wales, 1780–1850', *Historical Journal*, 53 (2010), 671–98.

[2]   On the history of crowd actions, see E. J. Hobsbawm, *Primitive Rebels: Studies in Archaic Forms of Social Movement in the 19th and 20th Centuries* (Manchester, 1959); G. Rudé, *The Crowd in the French Revolution* (Oxford, 1959); G. Rudé, *The Crowd in History: A Study of Popular Disturbances in France and England, 1730–1848* (New York, 1964); M. Harrison, *Crowds and History: Mass Phenomena in English Towns, 1790–1835* (Cambridge, 2002).

[3]   Among many notable exponents of micro-history, see B. Reay, *Microhistories: Demography, Society and Culture in Rural England, 1800–1930* (Cambridge, 1996); C. Ginzburg, *The Cheese and the Worms: The Cosmos of a Sixteenth-Century Miller* (Baltimore, 1980). See also A.-M. Kilday and D. Nash (eds), *Law, Crime and Deviance since 1700: Micro-studies in the History of Crime* (London, 2017).

[4]   D. Hay, P. Linebaugh, J. G. Rule, E. P. Thompson and C. Winslow, *Albion's Fatal Tree: Crime and Society in Eighteenth-Century England* (London, 1975).

[5]   Hay, *Albion's Fatal Tree*, p. 13. Juvenile offenders, gender issues, customary rights and assaults were explored in P. King, *Crime and Law in England, 1750–1850* (Cambridge, 2006).

[6]   J. H. Langbein, 'Albion's fatal flaws', *Past and Present*, 98 (1983), 96–120.

[7]   For comments see Langbein, 'Albion's fatal flaws', 105–8.

[8]   See arguments against the 'elite' approach in P. J. R. King, 'Decision-makers and decision-making in the English criminal law, 1750–1800', *Historical Journal*, 27 (1984), 25–58. For the wide range of cases that were seen in earlier courts see P. J. R. King, 'The summary courts and social relations in eighteenth-century England', *Past and Present*, 183 (2004). King studied small time periods involving about

2,500 cases: Becontree, 1810–13; Chelmsford, 1801–3; Colchester, 1770–2 and 1799–1800; Lexden and Winstree, 1788–93; Tendring, 1794 and 1804. See also Jennifer Davis's work on police courts involving a study of about 5,000 cases in London, and J. Davis, 'A poor man's system of justice: the London police courts in the second half of the nineteenth century', *Historical Journal*, 27 (1984), 309–35

9   E. P. Thompson, *The Making of the English Working Class* (London, 1963).

10   See for example S. Rowbotham, *Hidden from History* (London, 1977); L. A. Tilley and J. W. Scott, *Women, Work and Family* (London, 1977); J. Scott, *Gender and the Politics of History* (New York, 1988); J. Thomas, 'Women and capitalism: oppression or emancipation?', *Comparative Studies in Society and History*, 30 (1988), pp. 534–49; B. Taylor, *Eve and the New Jerusalem: Socialism and Feminism in the Nineteenth Century* (New York, 1983); A. Clark, *The Struggle for Breeches: Gender and the Making of the British Working-Class* (Berkeley, 1995); S. O. Rose, *Limited Livelihoods: Gender and Class in Nineteenth-Century England* (Berkeley, 1992); G. Walker, *Crime, Gender and Social Order* (Cambridge, 2003). Peter King makes the comment: 'Historians working on major indictable crimes were, like most criminologists, slow to pick out gender as an important variable'; P. King, *Crime and Law*, p. 196. See also comments in 'Why gender and crime?', in M. L. Arnot and C. Usborne (eds), *Gender and Crime in Modern Europe* (1999; London, 2003), pp. 1–43.

11   A. Charlesworth, 'An agenda for historical studies of rural protest in Britain, 1750–1850', *Rural History*, 11 (1991), 235. See also P. Jones, 'Finding Captain Swing: protest, parish relations and the state of the parish mind in 1830', *Southern History*, 22 (2010), 429–58.

12   K. Hunt, 'Gender and labour history in the 1990s', *Mitteillungsblatt des Institut fur soziale Bewegungen*, 27 (2002), 185–200. Leonore Davidoff and Catherine Hall investigated the middle classes which have been largely ignored by historians mainly studying the working classes; L. Davidoff and C. Hall, *Family Fortunes: Men and Women of the English Middle Class, 1740–1850* (Oxford, 2002).

13   See S. D'Cruze, *Crimes of Outrage: Sex, Violence and Victorian Working Women* (London, 1998). Courtroom interactions have been used to analyse legal proceedings: see M. Wiener, 'Judges v. jurors: courtroom tensions in murder trials', *Law and History Review*, 17 (1999), 467–506; M. Wiener, *Men of Blood: Violence, Manliness and Criminal Justice in Victorian England* (Cambridge, 2004); P. Handler, 'The law of felonious assault in England, 1803–61', *Journal of Legal History*, 28 (2007), 183–206.

14   Laws made by men, and the administration of those laws, are said to have constituted the focus of women's intense anger during the late nineteenth and early twentieth centuries; S. Kingsley Kent, *Sex and Suffrage, 1860–1914* (1987; London, 1990), p. 140.

15   David Phillips discusses the roles of these two arms of the legal system in D. Phillips, *Crime and Authority in Victorian England: The Black Country, 1835–1860* (London, 1997), pp. 53–140. See also P. King, *Justice and Discretion in England 1740–1820* (Oxford, 2000), pp. 82–128; B. S.

Godfrey and P. Lawrence, *Crime and Justice, 1750–1950* (Cullompton, 2005), pp. 9–26; D. D. Gray, *Crime, Policing and Punishment in England, 1660–1914* (London, 2016); C. Emsley, *Crime and Society in England, 1750–1900* (1987; Harlow, 2005), pp. 138–200; C. Steedman, *Policing the Victorian Community: The Formation of the English Provincial Police Forces, 1856–80* (London, 1984); C. Emsley, *The Great British Bobby* (London, 2009); see also C. Emsley, *Policing and its Context* (London, 1983); D. Taylor, *The New Police in Nineteenth-Century England* (Manchester, 1997). See also D. Taylor, *Policing the Victorian Town: The Development of the Police in Middlesbrough c. 1840–1914* (Basingstoke, 2002) and D. Taylor, *Crime, Policing and Punishment in England, 1750–1914* (Basingstoke, 1998); D. J Cox and B. S. Godfrey (eds), *Cinderellas and Packhorses: A History of the Shropshire Magistracy* (Woonton Almeley, 2005).

16 D. J. V. Jones, *Crime in Nineteenth-Century Wales* (Cardiff, 1992); see also D. J. V. Jones, 'The Welsh and Crime: 1801–1891', in C. Emsley and J. Walvin (eds), *Artisans, Peasants and Proletarians, 1760–1860* (Beckenham, 1983), pp. 81–103.

17 For example, D. J. V. Jones, *Crime, Protest, Community and Police in Nineteenth-Century Britain* (Boston, 1982). Richard Ireland's highly readable work is focused on west Wales; R. W. Ireland, 'A second Ireland? Crime and popular culture in nineteenth-century Wales', in R. McMahon (ed.), *Crime, Law and Popular Culture in Europe, 1500–1900* (Cullompton, 2008), pp. 239–61; R. W. Ireland, '"Perhaps my mother murdered me": child death and the law in Victorian Carmarthenshire', in C. Brooks and M. Lobban (eds.), *Communities and Courts in Britain, 1150–1900* (Hambledon, 1997), pp. 229–43; R. W. Ireland, 'Putting oneself on whose country? Carmarthenshire juries in the mid-nineteenth century', in T. G. Watkin (ed.), *Legal Wales: Its Past, Present and Future* (Cardiff, 2001), pp. 63–87; R. W. Ireland, 'An increasing mass of heathens in the bosom of a Christian land: the railway and crime in the nineteenth century', *Continuity and Change*, 12 (1997), 55–78.

18 D. J. V. Jones, 'Crime, protest and community in nineteenth-century Wales', *Lafur*, 3 (1974), 110–20.

19 N. Woodward, 'Burglary in Wales, 1730–1830: evidence from great sessions', *Welsh History Review*, 24 (2008), 60–91; N. Woodward, 'Horse stealing in Wales, 1730–1830', *Agricultural History Review*, 57 (2009), 70–108; N. Woodward, 'Seasonality and sheep stealing in Wales, 1730–1830', *Agricultural History Review*, 56 (2008), 3–47; N. Woodward, 'Infanticide in Wales, 1730–1830', *Welsh History Review*, 23 (2007), 94–125; S. Howard, 'Crime, communities and authority in early-modern Wales: Denbighshire, 1660–1730' (unpublished Ph.D. thesis, University of Wales, 2003); S. Howard, *Law and Disorder in Early-Modern Wales: Crime and Authority in the Denbighshire Courts, c.1660–1730* (Cardiff, 2008).

20 M. Humphreys, 'Harmony, crime and order', in *The Crisis of Community* (Cardiff, 1996),

21 See comments in B. S. Godfrey and D. J. Cox, *Policing the Factory* (London, 2013), especially in the Foreword and Chapter 1.

[22]　P. O'Leary, 'Masculine histories: gender and the social history of modern Wales', *Welsh History Review*, 22 (2004), 259.

[23]　See also R. Davies, *Secret Sins* (Cardiff, 1996), pp. 161–2; Jones, 'Crime, protest'; F. Finnegan, *Poverty and Prostitution* (Cambridge, 1979); J. Walkowitz, *Prostitution and Victorian Society* (Cambridge, 1980).

[24]　See D. J. V. Jones, 'Greater and lesser men', in D. J. V. Jones, *Rebecca's Children* (Oxford, 1990).

[25]　R. Jones, 'Maria Humphreys-Owen: Montgomeryshire's champion of women's rights', *Mont. Colls*, 99 (2011), 109–21. See also *Montgomeryshire Express*, 13 February 1894 for a list of some of the members of the women's group including Mrs Humphreys-Owen.

[26]　'Pryce-Jones: pioneer of the mail-order industry', *http://www.bbc.co.uk/legacies/work/wales/w_mid/ article_1.shtml* (14 April 2012).

[27]　This follows a common methodology in justice history studies. For example, Barbara Weinberger mainly used the 1860s and 70s in her 'The police and the public in mid-nineteenth-century Warwickshire', in V. Bailey (ed.), *Policing and Punishment in Nineteenth-Century Britain* (London, 1981), pp. 65–93.

[28]　For an indication of the complexity of reading back shorthand, see, for example, I. C. Hill and M. Bowers, *Teeline* (London, 1983).

[29]　Observations about this are in S. Devereaux, 'From sessions to newspaper? Criminal trial reporting, the nature of crime and the London press, 1770–1800', *The London Journal*, 32 (2007), 2; A. B. Rodrick, 'Only a newspaper metaphor: crime reports, class conflict and social criticism in two Victorian newspapers', *Victorian Periodicals Review*, 29 (1996), particularly pp. 1–4. See also P. King, 'Newspaper reporting and attitudes to crime and justice in late eighteenth- and early nineteenth-century London', *Continuity and Change*, 22 (2007), 73–112; P. King, 'Making crime news: newspapers, violent crime and the selective reporting of Old Bailey trials in the late eighteenth century', *Crime, History and Societies*, 13 (2009), 91–116; J. Sharpe, 'Reporting crime in the north of England eighteenth-century newspaper: a preliminary investigation', *Crime, Histoire et Société*, 16 (2012), 25–45; C. Kent, 'The editor and the law', in J. H. Wiener (ed.), *Innovators and Preachers: The Role of the Editor in Victorian England* (Westport, 1985), pp. 99–119; L. Brown, *Victorian News and Newspapers* (Oxford, 1985). See also D. J. Robinson, 'Crime, police and the provincial press: a study of Victorian Cardiff', *Welsh History Review*, 25 (2011), 551–75.

[30]　T. Shakesheff, *Rural Conflict, Crime and Protest: Herefordshire, 1800–1860* (Woodbridge, 2003), p. 146.

[31]　Journal of PC Edward Jones, Constable of Llanfyllin, NLW, MS 6227D.

[32]　PCA, M/Q/SR; M/Q/AC7; M/Q/SO/11.

[33]　See the analysis of families in B. S. Godfrey, D. J. Cox and S. D. Farrall, *Criminal Lives: Family Life, Employment and Offending* (Oxford, 2007), pp. 109–41 and details of Michael Maynard's life in B. Short, 'Environmental Politics', 484–5. See also P. Tilley, 'Creating life histories and family trees from nineteenth-century census records, parish registers and other sources', *Local Population Studies*, 68 (2002), 63–81; B. S.

Godfrey, D. J. Cox and S. D. Farrall, *Serious Offenders: A Historical Study of Habitual Criminals* (Oxford, 2010); B. Godfrey and G. Dunstall, 'The growth of crime and crime control in developing towns: Timaru and Crewe, 1850–1920', in B. Godfrey and G. Dunstall (eds), *Crime and Empire, 1840–1940: Criminal Justice in Local and Global Context* (Cullompton, 2005), pp. 135–44.

34 A. Rees, *Life in a Welsh Countryside: A Social Study of Llanfihangel yng Ngwynfa* (1950; Cardiff, 1996). This community is in north Montgomeryshire.

35 G. A. Williams, *When Was Wales? A History of the Welsh* (Harmondsworth, 1985); S. Brooks, *Why Wales Never Was: The Failure of Welsh Nationalism* (Cardiff, 2017).

36 R. Williams, *The Country and the City* (London, 1973). Much of Raymond Williams's own experience and writing was based upon areas in Monmouthshire, Wales, notably around Abergavenny.

37 B. S. Godfrey, S. Farrall and S. Karstedt, 'Explaining gendered sentencing patterns', *British Journal of Criminology*, 45 (2005), 696–720. Note also the general editor's comment in *Criminal Lives*: 'Highly original ... applying modern concepts ... and visiting them upon the late nineteenth and early twentieth centuries'; Godfrey, *Criminal Lives*, p. vii.

CHAPTER 1

1 *Census of England and Wales, 1871*, PP, Vol. 3, Table 17, p. 596 'Occupations of males and females aged 20 years and upwards', p. 535. The total population of that age group is given as 41,904.

2 The Welsh Office, quoted in B. Poole, 'Agriculture' in D. Jenkins (ed.), *The Historical Atlas of Montgomeryshire* (Welshpool, 1999), p. 103.

3 J. M. Wilson, *The Imperial Gazetteer of England and Wales*, 5 (Edinburgh, Glasgow and London, 1874), p. 368.

4 P. Phillips, *A View of Old Montgomeryshire* (1977; Swansea, 1978), pp. 125–37; Poole, 'Agriculture', pp. 103–7.

5 Wilson, *Imperial Gazetteer*, p. 369.

6 K. D. M. Snell, *Annals of the Labouring Poor* (1985; Cambridge, 1995), pp. 15–103.

7 For a fascinating account of the history of the woollen industry see P. Hudson, 'The limits of wool', *Cardiff Historical Papers* (2007), 1–40.

8 D. Moore, *Wales in the Eighteenth Century* (Swansea, 1976), pp. 92–3.

9 A. H. Dodd, *The Industrial Revolution in North Wales* (Cardiff, 1951), p. 14.

10 'Welshpool' was commonly spelled 'Welch Pool' or 'Welchpool'. 'Welch' was originally added to distinguish the town from Poole in Dorset; J. Davies, N. Jenkins, M. Baines, P. I. Lynch, *The Welsh Academy Encyclopaedia of Wales* (Cardiff, 2008), p. 944.

11 D. Defoe, *A Tour Thro' the Whole Island of Great Britain, divided into Circuits or Journeys* (Letter 6, Part 3: Worcester, Hereford and Wales), *www.visionofbritain.org.uk* (5 June 2013).

[12]   T. Pennant, *A Tour in Wales* (1778; Caernarvon, 1883), pp. 184–6.
[13]   Dodd, *Industrial Revolution*, p. 12.
[14]   J. Evans, *Letters Written during a tour of North Wales in the Year 1798, and at Other Times* (London, 1804), pp. 31–3.
[15]   D. Moore, *Wales in the Eighteenth Century*, pp. 94–5.
[16]   J. Aitkin, *England Described: Being a Concise Delineation of Every County in England and Wales* (London, 1818), p. 469.
[17]   See note 1.
[18]   J. E. Roberts and R. Owen, *The Story of Montgomeryshire* (Cardiff, 1916), p. 5; E. R. Morris, 'Woollen Industry', in Jenkins, *Historical Atlas*, pp. 98–9; W. Scott Owen, 'A parochial history of Tregynon', *Mont. Colls*, 30 (1898), 14–15.
[19]   Phillips, *A View*, p. 131.
[20]   A. S. Davies, *The Ballads of Montgomeryshire: Life in the Eighteenth Century* (Welshpool, 1938), pp. 35–6. The ballad continues for a further sixteen lines.
[21]   The rise and fall of the flannel industry in mid-Wales is well documented; see for example J. G. Jenkins, 'The woollen industry in Montgomeryshire', *Mont. Colls*, 58 (1963–4), 50–69.; J. M. Pearson, 'The decayed and decaying industries of Montgomeryshire', *Mont. Colls*, 37 (1915), 15–30. See also an excellent discussion in an editorial 'The population in Newtown, 1871', *NWE*, 23 April 1871. For interesting comparative studies of the changing fortunes of the weaving industry see E. Jones, 'Missing out on an industrial revolution', *World Economics*, 9 (2008), 104–8 and J. H. Clapham, 'The transference of the worsted industry from Norfolk to the West Riding', *Economic Journal*, 20 (1910), 195–210.
[22]   National Census, 1871.
[23]   Fiona Rule in her book *The Worst Street in London* (Horsham, 2008) and Sarah Wise in *The Blackest Streets* (London, 2009) both discuss the decline of the Huguenot weaving industry, immigration and poverty, worsening living conditions and associated crime. See also comments about 'non-gentrified' areas being associated (perhaps mistakenly) with crime in B. S. Godfrey, D. J. Cox and S. D. Farrall, *Criminal Lives: Family Life, Employment and Offending* (Oxford, 2007), pp. 50–1.
[24]   I. Trant, *The Changing Face of Welshpool* (Welshpool, 1986), p. 5.
[25]   Pigot and Co., *Directory of North Wales* (1835); Slater, *Directory of North Wales* (1850 and 1868).
[26]   'A Brief History of Welshpool', *www.cpat.org.uk/ycom/wpool/wplhis.htm* (15 May 2010).
[27]   Robson, *Directory of North Wales* (1840).
[28]   See 'Earlier studies on economic crisis and crime', in Council of Europe, *Economic Crisis and Crime* (Strasbourg, 1985), pp. 9–11.
[29]   Worrall, *Directory of North Wales* (1874).
[30]   Jane Norton, the author of a guide to directories, wrote that it would be misleading to think of them as either precise or accurate; J. E. Norton, *Guide to the National and Provincial Directories of England and Wales, Published before 1856* (London, 1950), pp. 16–24.

31 *NWE*, 23 February 1869.
32 *NWE*, 9 March 1869.
33 M. Richards (ed.), *A Study of Newtown in 1881*, Part 1 (Newtown, 1987), p. 4.
34 *NWE*, 9 June 1874. For analysis and comment on sanitary inspections see C. Hamlin, 'Sanitary policing and the local state, 1873–4: a statistical study of English and Welsh towns', *Social History of Medicine*, 18 (2005), 39–61.
35 Wise, *Blackest Streets*, pp. 65–6 and 98.
36 J. B. Willans, *The Byways of Montgomeryshire* (London 1905), p. 31.
37 G. Rademan, 'The story of Milford Road', *Newtonian*, 30 (2007), 10–17.
38 See for example, G. R. Boyer and T. J. Hatton, 'Migration and labour market integration in late nineteenth-century England and Wales', *Economic History Review*, 50 (1997), 697–734; D. Friedland and R. J. Roshier, 'A study of internal migration in England and Wales, Part 1', *Population Studies*, 19 (1966), 239–79; N. Spencer and D. A. Gatley, 'Investigating population mobility in nineteenth-century England and Wales', *Local Population Studies*, 65 (2000), 47–57.
39 See K. J. Cooper, *Exodus from Cardiganshire: Rural–Urban Migration in Victorian Britain* (Cardiff, 2011); J. Saville, *Rural Depopulation in England and Wales, 1851 to 1951* (London, 1957); A. Redford, *Labour Migration in England, 1800–1850* (Manchester, 1976).
40 See National Census, 1851.
41 See comments in Jenkins, *Historical Atlas*, p. 59.
42 These features of the county's education are covered in R. Jones, 'Private schools in nineteenth-century Montgomeryshire', *Mont. Colls*, 102 (2014), 121–30. On nineteenth-century educational provision in Montgomeryshire, see Phillips, *A View*, pp. 150–9 and Jenkins, *Historical Atlas*, p. 85. On the place of quality education in the lives of the middle classes see 'Education', in D. Hay (ed.), *The Oxford Companion to Local and Family History* (Oxford, 1996), pp. 141–9.
43 R. Haslam, *The Building of Wales: Powys* (1979; London, 2003), pp. 76–80.
44 D. W. Smith, *Aberriw to Berriew: The Story of a Community* (Newtown, 1992), p. 11.
45 Smith asserts that such intercommoning has not been found elsewhere; Smith, *Aberriw to Berriew*, p. 13.
46 D. J. V. Jones, 'The poacher: a study in Victorian crime and protest', *Historical Journal*, 22 (1979), 838. See also his comments in D. J. V. Jones, *Crime, Protest, Community and Police in Nineteenth-Century Britain* (Boston, 1982), p. 116.
47 The owners of the Vaynor Estate in Berriew carried out a major programme of restoration in the 1880s and some restoration work may have been going on in the 1860s; also R. Haslam, *Building of Wales*, p. 78.
48 On this topic see W. T. R. Pryce, 'Changing language geographies of Montgomeryshire', in Jenkins, *Historical Atlas*, pp. 118–24; E. M. White, 'The established church, dissent and the Welsh language', in G. H. Jenkins (ed.), *The Welsh Language before the Industrial Revolution* (Cardiff,

1997), pp. 253–4 on the flow of bilingualism across northern Montgomeryshire; J. Edwards, *Language and Identity: An Introduction* (Cambridge, 2009).

49 D. Jones, *Statistical Material Relating to the Welsh Language, 1801–1911* (Cardiff, 1998).

50 Pryce, 'Changing language', 119.

51 Pryce, 'Changing language', 120. The critical government reports, entitled *Report of Commission of Enquiry into the State of Education in Wales, 1847*, are held at the National Library of Wales. The data on Montgomeryshire is in volume 3.

52 J. I. Davies, 'The history of printing in Montgomeryshire, 1789–1960', *Mont. Colls*, 70 (1982), 72.

53 Pryce, 'Changing language', 121.

54 E. G. Ravenstein, 'On the Celtic Languages in the British Isles: a statistical survey' quoted in Jones, *Statistical Material*, p. 224. Linda Colley describes how industrialization sucked in migrants and changed Welsh identity by weakening the grip of the Welsh language and by bringing people from north and south Wales into greater contact: L. Colley, 'Acts of union and disunion: Wales', BBC Radio 4, 15 January 2014.

55 E. R. Morris, 'Hugh Jerman', *Mont. Colls*, 72 (1984), 47–52.

56 Jones, 'Victorian schools'. For a description of the contribution of eisteddfodau to Welsh culture see H. Richard, *Letters and Essays on Wales* (London, 1884), pp. 44–52.

57 For comprehensive detail and discussion on all of the following, see K. D. M. Snell and P. S. Ell, *Rival Jerusalems: The Geography of Victorian Religion* (Cambridge, 2000). See also C. Davis, *Religion and Society: Essays in Social Theology* (Cambridge, 1994).

58 Tithe riots took place during the 1880s when Montgomeryshire farmers revolted against paying taxes to Church of England landlords. See D. W. Smith, 'The tithes to their end in Montgomeryshire: an introduction', *Mont. Colls*, 84 (1996), 134–5; *Minutes of Evidence of the Commission of Inquiry as to Disturbances Connected with Levying of Tithe Rent Charge in Wales* (House of Commons, 1887), pp. 157–67. For an excellent discussion on the reasons for the decline in popularity of the Church of England in Wales see 'The established church', in D. G. Evans, *A History of Wales, 1815–1906* (Cardiff, 1989), pp. 80–5. See also H. Richard, *Letters on the Social and Political Condition of the Principality of Wales, Reprinted from the Morning and Evening Star* (London, 1866).

59 T. W. Pritchard, 'The Church in Wales', in Jenkins, *Historical Atlas*, pp. 67–73. See also J. Johnes, *Causes of Dissent in Wales* (1832; London, 1870), which argues that the main reasons for the decline of the established Church was not so much the popularity of the Dissenting chapels but the unpopularity of the Church. (Discussed in Phillips, *A View*, p. 145. Phillips also states that by 1880, Nonconformists made up 80 per cent of the population, p. 149).

60 P. Jenkins, *A History of Modern Wales, 1536–1990* (London, 1992), p. 190; Evans, *A History of Wales*, pp. 76–80. See also Richard, *Letters and Essays*, pp. 1–35.

61 A. Jones, *Welsh Chapels* (Stroud, 1984), p. 49. Jones states that by the mid-1850s the vast majority of the population of Wales was in some way directly associated with a chapel.

62 Jones, *Welsh Chapels*, p. 46.

63 See maps in Jenkins, *Historical Atlas*, pp. 73–82.

64 Phillips, *A View*, p. 150.

65 Davies, 'The history of printing', 72.

66 White, 'The Established Church, dissent and the Welsh language', 239.

67 M. Jarman. 'The Welsh language and the courts', in T. G. Watkin and N. S. B. Cox (eds), *Canmlwyddiant, Cyfraith a Chymreictod: A Celebration of the Life and Work of Dafydd Jenkins, 1911–2012* (Bangor, 2013), p. 171.

68 R. L. Brown, 'The Reverend David Davies, Rector of Llansilin, 1876–1901', *Mont. Colls*, 101 (2013), 109–16.

69 Shrewsbury School Register, 1874–1908.

70 White, 'The Established Church', 241.

71 M. Humphreys, *The Crisis of Community* (Cardiff, 1996), p. 42.

72 Pritchard, 'The Church', 72.

73 Reported in *NWE*, 23 March 1869.

74 Voting became secret in 1872, giving the enfranchised more ability to vote as they pleased; R. Woodall, 'The Ballot Act of 1872', *History Today*, 24 (1974), 464–71. See also a description of voting tenants being persecuted by unscrupulous landlords in 'Territorial Tyranny in Wales', *The Bradford Observer*, 9 July 1869, p. 2; 'Political oppression by Welsh landlords', *The Wrexham Advertiser*, 10 July 1869, 6.

75 R. Wallace, 'Wales and the parliamentary reform movement', *Welsh History Review*, 11 (1983), 483.

76 R. Jones, 'The Gregynog state, 1880–1920' (unpublished MA dissertation, University of Leicester, 2007). Copy at Newtown (Powys) library and the Powysland Club library, Welshpool.

77 See also lists of denominations present in the county; Jones, *Statistical Material*, pp. 451–2. For comment see 'Roman Catholicism and Irish immigration', in Snell and Ell, *Rival Jerusalems*, pp. 173–84.

78 Jones, *Statistical Material*, p. 452.

79 P. O'Leary, 'The Irish and crime', in P. O' Leary, *Immigration and Integration: The Irish in Wales, 1789–1922* (Cardiff, 2000), pp. 165–7. Protestant clergymen also blamed 'immoral teachings of Dissent'; see comments in Richards, *Letters and Essays*, pp. 36 and 52.

80 'Riot on the Mid-Wales Railway', reprinted in G. Roberts (ed.), *Pencambria*, 23 (2013), 34–5.

81 P. O'Leary (ed.), *Irish Migrants in Modern Wales* (Liverpool, 2004), pp. 121–4. Note also that anti-popery riots had taken place in Birmingham (about eighty miles away) in the late 1860s; V. Bailey (ed.) *Policing and Punishment in Nineteenth-Century Britain* (London, 1981), p. 70. See also R. Swift and S. Gilley (eds), *The Irish in Victorian Britain: The Local Dimension* (Dublin, 1999); J. Maclaughlin, 'Pestilence on their backs, famine in their stomachs: the racial construction of Irishness and the Irish in Victorian Britain', in C. Graham and R. Kirkland (eds), *Ireland and Cultural Theory: The Mechanics of Authenticity* (Basingstoke, 1999), pp. 50–76.

CHAPTER 2

1   D. Taylor, *Crime, Policing and Punishment in England, 1750–1914* (Basing-
    stoke, 1998), p. 106.
2   Great Britain, of course, included Wales. Note Richard Ireland's argu-
    ment that the legal and constitutional status of Wales being identical to
    that of England may have led to Welsh legal history receiving little
    attention, despite its cultural differences which may have had a distinct
    bearing on crime and its prosecution; R. Ireland, 'A second Ireland?
    Crime and popular culture in nineteenth-century Wales', in R.
    McMahon (ed.), *Crime, Law and Popular Culture in Europe, 1500–1900*
    (Cullompton, 2008), pp. 239–61.
3   For a comprehensive history of the magistracy, see T. Skyrme, *History of
    the Justices of the Peace*, 1–3 (Chichester, 1991); D. J. Cox and B. S. Godfrey
    (eds), *Cinderellas and Packhorses: A History of the Shropshire Magistracy*
    (Woonton Almeley, 2005).
4   See H. Johnston, 'The Shropshire magistracy and local imprisonment:
    networks of power in the nineteenth century', *Midland History*, 30
    (2005), 68.
5   'Justices of the peace', in D. Hey (ed.), *The Oxford Companion to Local
    and Family History* (Oxford, 1996; 1998), p. 253; P. J. Stead, *The Police of
    Britain* (London, 1985), pp. 11–13; Skyrme, *History of the Justices of the
    Peace*, 1, pp.1–40. See also H. Johnston, 'The Shropshire magistracy' for
    possible motivations for men taking on these roles. For a comprehen-
    sive description and discussion of the history and role of the magistracy
    see S. and B. Webb, *English Local Government: Parish and County* (London,
    1924), pp. 35–60 and pp. 484–8.
6   PCA, Justices Qualifications Rolls, 1843–1900, M/QS/JQ/3 and 4.
7   Most of these were members of the Bench for the whole period. Only a
    handful joined or left during the period under study.
8   See F. M. L. Thompson, *English Landed Society in the Nineteenth Century*,
    (London, 1963), pp. 109–11 for a discussion on admission to the county
    Bench.
9   For comments on this topic, see Thompson, *English Landed Society*, p.
    185.
10 Jones found that in the mid-1880s in the rural counties of Anglesey,
    Cardiganshire and Radnorshire, out of a total of 286 justices, 228 were
    gentry, 24 clergy, 27 ex-military, 3 medical and 4 lawyers. There were no
    justices with trade occupations; D. J. V. Jones, *Crime in Nineteenth-Century
    Wales* (Cardiff, 1992), p. 17.
11 By an Act of 1723, county justices had to own or occupy land in the
    county worth £100 or more (with a few exceptions, such as eldest sons
    of peers and Privy Councillors); D. Bentley, *English Criminal Justice in the
    Nineteenth Century* (London, 1998), p. 20.
12 There are short biographies of Robert Jasper More and Sir Thomas
    Gibbons Frost at *http://en.wikipedia.org/wiki/Robert_Jasper_More* and
    www.british-history.ac.uk (11 March 2011). George Hammond Whalley
    has an entry in *DNB*. For information about the Revd William Bishton

Garnett Botfield see 'Decker Hall' at *www.anatpro.com/index_files/Annie_Augusta_Garnett_Botfield.htm* (15 March 2014).

13 Landed ownership became fashionable at the time of the Industrial Revolution amongst wealthy families looking to acquire social status. The trend was to buy so-called 'villa estates' with land that gave them the status of gentry; 'Landowners', in *The Oxford Companion to Local and Family History*, p. 264.

14 Some of the magistrates' houses are in R. Haslam, *The Buildings of Wales: Powys (Montgomeryshire, Radnorshire, Breconshire)* (New Haven and London, 2003). Listed buildings can be found easily on the British Listed Buildings website: *www.britishlistedbuildings.co.uk* and Frost's and Hilton's houses in the north of England were found by using an internet search engine.

15 Figure from Census of England and Wales (1871), PP, 1, population summary table V.

16 See Thompson, *English Landed Society*, p. 185. Cox and Godfrey found a similar composition on the Shropshire Bench on which the Earl of Powis also had a seat; Cox and Godfrey, *Cinderellas*, pp. 43–7.

17 See quote by Bagehot in Thompson, *English Landed Society*, p. 186.

18 For comment on modern-day debates about representation on magisterial Benches see 'Equality laws should aid the working classes', *Daily Telegraph*, 13 December 2013.

19 Times correspondent, Thomas Campbell Foster, after spending three months interviewing people in south-west Wales after the Rebecca Riots, wrote, 'It cannot be denied that people look upon the landlords, and the gentry and the magistrates as a class, with hatred and suspicion'; quoted in D. J. V. Jones, *Rebecca's Children* (Oxford, 1990), p. 96.

20 See G. B. A. Finlayson, 'The politics of municipal reform, 1835', *English Historical Review*, 81 (1966), 673–92.

21 Reflected in the adjective 'county' defined as 'having social status or characteristics of county families: those having an ancestral seat in a particular county'; 'County', in *Concise Oxford Dictionary* (Oxford, 1982).

22 Griffiths describes how social status was an issue when selecting potential magistrates; W. P. Griffiths, *Power, Politics and County Government in Wales* (Llangefni, 2006), pp. 68–9. John Hammond wrote that manufacturers were 'a class that many of them [country gentlemen] despised'; J. L. Hammond and B. Hammond, *The Town Labourer, 1760–1832* (London, 1917), p. 64. See C. H. E. Zangerl, 'The social composition of the county magistracy in England and Wales, 1831–1887', *Journal of British Studies*, 11 (1971), 115 for a useful table showing how the composition of the county and borough Benches changed between 1841 and 1887. The etymology of the word 'gentleman' is interesting. The Latin term for 'born', *genitus*, passed into Old French as 'gent', gaining the additional sense of 'being of noble birth'. When the word was taken up in English as 'gentle', it described someone of good breeding, as 'gentleman' was originally a man entitled to bear arms. Such 'gentle' people were expected to have equally graceful manners, and the adjective soon came to mean 'delicate'; *OED*.

23 *NWE*, 2 March 1869. Details about the encroachment affair began on 5 January 1869.

24 *NWE*, 30 March 1869.

25 Haslam, *The Buildings of Wales*, p. 79

26 W. S. Owen, 'A parochial History of Tregynon', *Mont. Colls*, 30 (1898), 14–15.

27 See Highways Act 1835, *www.legislation.gov.uk* (5 May 2011).

28 M. Humphreys, *The Crisis of Community* (Cardiff, 1996), p. 204.

29 This matches Jones's finding from south-west Wales in the 1840s: 'proceedings were dominated by up to a score of well-known figures'; Jones, *Rebecca's Children*, p. 89.

30 See Zangerl, 'Social Composition', 118–19 for a comprehensive review of the appointment of clerical justices.

31 Jones, *Rebecca's Children*, p. 85.

32 Zangerl quoting Webb in 'Social Composition', 120. Griffith explains how in mid-nineteenth-century Anglesey, 'the burgeoning Nonconformist culture ... set itself apart from an anglicized landed elite', and the majority of the magistracy were increasingly unresponsive to Nonconformist agitation; W. P. Griffith, *Power, Politics and County Government*, pp. 75–6. Humphreys discusses political machinations that took place around the appointment of magistrates in the eighteenth century but does not consider religious differences; Humphreys, *Crisis*, pp. 201–3.

33 See R. Williams, 'Montgomeryshire Nonconformity: extracts from gaol files, with notes', *Mont. Colls*, 27 (1893), 55–6.

34 'George Hammond Whalley', in *DNB*.

35 Montgomeryshire residences (or residences in other counties in locations close to the Montgomeryshire border) are known for 80 per cent of the magistrates.

36 Alternatively known as Epiphany quarter sessions.

37 *NWE*, 12 January 1869.

38 *NWE*, 6 July 69.

39 Initial impressions of Vane's character are reinforced upon viewing a very large portrait of himself hanging in Plas Machynlleth. It shows him standing in his robes, holding an enormous ceremonial sword erect in front of himself.

40 King describes how sessions being held at Chelmsford discouraged attendance by magistrates from outlying areas, and how in 1872 only 40 per cent attended even one sitting; P. King, *Crime, Justice and Discretion in England, 1740–1820* (Oxford, 2000), p. 111.

41 In 1784 the author of *The Magistrate's Assistant* wrote of the difficulties of persuading gentlemen to dedicate some portion of their leisure hours to the preservation of the peace; quoted in King, *Crime, Justice*, p. 112.

42 King, *Crime, Justice*, p. 111.

43 Shropshire Archives, Shropshire Quarter Session Order Book, 1840–89 shows the Earl's attendances. As an example of the sense of elevation gained after meeting aristocracy see M. N. Cohen, *Lewis Carroll: A*

Biography (London, 1995), p. 509. For comment on Victorian social
climbing, see Cohen, *Lewis Carroll*, pp. 512–3.

44 Griffiths, *Power, Politics*, pp. 63–4. See also pp. 57–71 for a description
and discussion on the activity, or otherwise, of Anglesey justices which
shows the same pattern found in the present study.

45 For an overview of the role of the Lord Chancellor see J. Cannon (ed.),
The Oxford Companion to British History (1997; Oxford, 2002), p. 593. See
also Griffiths, *Power, Politics*, p. 67 for an example of the Lord Chancellor's influence on the county Bench.

46 J. D. K. Lloyd, 'The lieutenants of Montgomeryshire', *Mont. Colls*, 63
(1973), 114–18. Note Francis Dodsworth's comments about the hierarchy present in local government in F. Dodsworth, 'Liberty and order:
civil government and the common good in eighteenth-century
England', *CRESC Working Paper Series*, 21 (2006), 5.

47 *Oxford Companion to British History*, pp. 59–60; D. Phillips, 'The Black
Country magistracy, 1835–60', *Midland History*, 3 (1976), 165.

48 Lloyd, 'The lieutenants', p. 117. Zangerl notes that 90 per cent of lords
lieutenant in 1875 were aristocrats; Zangerl, 'Social composition', 116.

49 'Charles Hanbury-Tracy, 1st Baron Sudely' viewed at *http://en.wikipedia.
org/wiki/Charles_Hanbury-Tracy,_1st_Baron_Sudeley* (5 May 2011); see
also Lord Sudeley, 'Gregynog before 1900', *Mont. Colls*, 62 (1972),
116–82.

50 The Webbs noted that the office was one of 'pure social dignity'; S.
Webb and B. Webb, *English Local Government from the Revolution to the
Municipal Corporations Act: The Parish and the County* (London, 1963),
pp. 286–7.

51 Humphreys quoting J. V. Beckett in *Crisis*, p. 205. See E. Jones, 'Missing
out on an industrial revolution', *World Economics*, 9 (2008), 107 for a
succinct description of the newly rich man's move to the country and
subsequent gentrification.

52 See Bentley, *English Criminal Justice*, pp. 51–2 for a description of events,
and pp. 81–2 for a description of the role.

53 See A. Briggs, 'The language of class in early nineteenth-century
England', in A. Briggs and J. Saville (eds), *Essays in Labour History in
Memory of G. D. H. Cole* (London, 1967), pp. 44–5 for discussion on
movement between social groups. Briggs asserts that 'the most
successful of them [middling sorts] were easily absorbed into the
gentry'. For interesting comment on Montgomeryshire gentry see M.
Humphreys, 'Gentry', in Jenkins, D. (ed.), *Historical Atlas of Montgomeryshire* (Welshpool, 1999), pp. 58–60.

54 See any quarter sessions coverage, *NWE* and *ME*, 1869–78.

55 There was a similarity with the names and areas of the administrative
Hundreds; see E. R. Morris, 'The Hundreds', in Jenkins, *Historical Atlas*,
pp. 65–6.

56 See for example *ME*, 4 September 1877 (Newtown special sessions).

57 C. Emsley, *Crime and Society in England, 1750–1900* (1987; Harlow, 2005),
p. 195; B. S. Godfrey and P. Lawrence, *Crime and Justice, 1750–1950*
(Cullompton, 2005), p. 53. The provincial police courts were slightly

different in operation and organisation; see J. Davis, 'A poor man's system of justice: the London police courts in the second half of the nineteenth century', *Historical Journal*, 27 (1984).

58 E. Moir, *The Justice of the Peace* (Harmondsworth, 1969), p. 44; *Oxford Companion to British History*, p. 746. According to Godfrey and Lawrence in *Crime and Justice*, p. 53, most defendants 'faced one magistrate or however many troubled to turn up'.

59 Moir, *Justice of the Peace*, p. 65.

60 Preamble to 'Flintshire Petty Sessions Records' viewed at *www. archiveswales.org.uk* (13 January 2011).

61 P. King, 'The summary courts and social relations in eighteenth-century England', *Past and Present*, 183 (2004), 125–72. King also explains how a range of other administrative tasks were performed at petty sessions including bastardy, settlement examinations, contracts and the swearing of oaths.

62 Douglas Hay argues that the justices' work at sessions helped to show their superiority in moral and religious terms by their apparent concern for humanity, and an image that 'ensured the continuation of traditional attitudes and ideas and reinforced the dominance of the establishment'; D. Hay quoted in Johnston, 'Shropshire magistracy', p.78.

63 Hammond, *The Town Labourer*, p. 65.

64 See P. Bourdieu, 'The forms of capital', in I. Szeman and T. Kaposy (eds), *Cultural Theory: An Anthology* (Oxford, 2011), p. 86.

65 See Neale's analysis in R. S. Neale, 'Class and class consciousness in early nineteenth-century England: three classes or five?', *Victorian Studies*, 12 (1968), 5.

66 R. Moore-Colyer, 'Gentlemen, horses and the turf in nineteenth-century Wales', *Welsh History Review*, 16 (1992), 60.

67 See C. Griffiths, *The Police Forces of Mid and West Wales, 1829–1974* (Llandybie, 2004) and H. K. Birch, *The History of Policing in North Wales* (Pwllheli, 2008), pp. 85–90. Jones mentions a borough police force in Montgomery in the 1830s; D. J. V. Jones, *Crime in Nineteenth-Century Wales* (Cardiff, 1992), p. 204. The five borough towns must have had police forces following the Municipal Corporations Act of 1835. Newtown had lost its borough status in the seventeenth century and therefore did not need to form a force. The Welshpool force remained separate from the county force until 1857 or 1858 and was able, therefore, to concentrate on local concerns until that time. Griffiths in *The Police Forces* gives 1857 as the date of amalgamation of Welshpool borough force with the county force. However, in the clerk of the peace's notes at Powys County Archives, the date is 1858 (PCA, MQ/CX/2).

68 E. Parry, 'The bloodless wars of Montgomeryshire: law and disorder, 1837–41', *Mont. Colls*, 97 (2009), 123–64; O. R. Ashton, 'Chartism in mid Wales', *Mont. Colls*, 62 (1971), 10–57; E. R. Morris, 'Who were the Montgomeryshire Chartists?', *Mont. Colls*, 58 (1963–4), 27–49.

69 D. Foster, *The Rural Constabulary Act, 1839* (London, 1982), p. 14; K. D. M. Snell, *Annals of the Labouring Poor: Social Change and Agrarian England, 1660–1900* (1985; Cambridge, 1987), pp. 135–6.

70 P. Phillips, *A View of Old Montgomeryshire* (1977; Swansea, 1978), p. 140;
    B. Owen, 'The Newtown and Llanidloes poor law union workhouse,
    Caersws 1837–1847', *Mont. Colls*, 78 (1990), 120.
71 See C. Emsley, *The Great British Bobby* (London, 2009), for life stories of
    policemen, especially Chapter 6.
72 See C. Steedman, *Policing the Victorian Community: The Formation of the
    English Provincial Police Forces, 1856–80* (London, 1984), pp. 69–91.
    Steedman writes of the rapid expansion of forces after 1856 drawing on
    working-class recruits, often those who could not find work in factories,
    and a 'great army' who would otherwise have worked the land. Gorer
    argues that the Metropolitan commissioners originally recruited agri-
    cultural labourers to ensure a constable's status as an agent of imper-
    sonal authority, free from local or class ties; G. Gorer quoted in D.
    Hobbs, *Doing the Business* (Oxford, 1988), p. 35.
73 D. Taylor, *The New Police in Nineteenth-Century England* (Manchester,
    1997), p. 47.
74 Steedman, *Policing the Victorian Community*, p. 112. Taylor quotes the
    chairman of the Bristol watch committee who stated: 'Our recruits all
    come from districts where work is bad and wages light. A large number
    of them come from lower parts of Somersetshire and Devonshire where
    wages are notoriously considerably below average'; Taylor, *The New
    Police*, p. 49.
75 Report of Her Majesty's Inspector of Constabularies, PP 1871, (23),
    p.59; Gregynog Estate Labour Books, 1866–73, NLW, 1957112/55.
76 The term 'white collar' is thought to originate in the early twentieth
    century but it is possible it was used earlier; *http://en.wikipedia.org/wiki/
    White-collar_worker* (29 November 2010).
77 Other workers featuring in the Gregynog labour books would have
    received payments in kind too. For example, the land agent's house
    went with the job, as did the schoolmaster's, although it is not clear
    whether the occupants paid rent.
78 F. Clements, 'Sergeant W. R. Breese: a policeman in rural nineteenth
    century Denbighshire', *Transactions of Denbighshire Historical Society*, 56
    (2008), 126.
79 The clerk of the peace's record book records that between 1869 and
    1873 twelve of the constables studied here received promotion. (PCA,
    MQ/CX/2).
80 Some rural workers entered the workhouse during winter months,
    putting them even further down the league table and making the
    policeman's pay seem even better. However, Stead makes the point that
    the pay was small for the hours worked; Stead, *Police of Britain*, p. 60;
    and Weinberger states that in the interests of ratepayers, pay was kept at
    the lowest rate possible that could attract literate men; B. Weinberger,
    'The police and the public in mid-nineteenth century Warwickshire', in
    V. Bailey (ed.), *Policing and Punishment in Nineteenth-Century Britain*
    (London, 1981), p. 83. In Warwickshire, the chief constable had great
    difficulty filling posts throughout the 1870s, but this could reflect the
    pay available for other occupations in this county, which was a relatively

diversified economic area (*http://en.wikipedia.org/wiki/History_of_Warwickshire* (12 December 2010). See 'Development of the long-term policeman', in D. Taylor, *The New Police in Nineteenth-Century England* (Manchester, 1997), pp. 61–77.

[81] Taylor recognises that there was a hierarchy within the police; Taylor, *New Police*, p. 53.

[82] Steedman's analysis of Buckinghamshire shows a man joining as a constable in 1857 who became deputy chief constable thirty years later. Steedman found that promotion within the classes of constables was considerably faster than in Montgomeryshire, typically four months to rise from third class to second, and a year to rise to first class; Steedman, *Policing the Victorian Community*, pp. 106–7. Montgomeryshire rates of promotion are detailed in the clerk of the peace's records, PCA, M/Q/CX/2.

[83] *ME*, 26 January 1915.

[84] Weinberger, 'The police and the public', p. 70.

[85] *NWE*, 5 January 1869. In terms of social hierarchy, dialect can reveal shared values among both rich and poor; P. Joyce, *Visions of the People: Industrial England and the Questions of Class, 1848–1914* (Cambridge, 1991), p. 299; K. D. M. Snell (ed.), *The Regional Novel in Britain and Ireland, 1800–1990* (Cambridge, 1998), pp. 32–5, 47–52.

[86] Police houses were not rent-free. An amount was deducted from the men's pay. See Police Committee discussion, *NWE*, 24 October 1876.

[87] A descendant of Sergeant Owen has produced a detailed website about his life and work: *www.owen.cholerton.org* (4 November 2010).

[88] The HMIC report of 1870 gives a first-class constable's pay in Liverpool as 26s. per week (equivalent to 3s. 8d. per day, a penny a day more than a sergeant in Montgomeryshire). Pay was laid down by government circular; Steedman, *Policing the Victorian Community*, p. 108; but it was quarter sessions that fixed the rate; W. C. Maddox, *A History of the Montgomeryshire Constabulary, 1840–1948* (Carmarthen, 1982), p. 2. Borough police wages were dependent on local revenues; hence boroughs that were more prosperous could pay more. Birch explains how Liverpool's first chief constable was offered £650 and Manchester's £550; Birch, *The History of Policing in North Wales*, p. 90. By 1870, Liverpool's chief constable's pay was £1,000 per annum.

[89] *NWE*, 16 November 1869.

[90] *NWE*, 12 January 1869.

[91] *NWE*, 26 October 1869.

[92] PCA, Clerk of the Peace's records, M/Q/CX2.

[93] Memorandum on the construction of police stations 1875, PCA, MQ/AC/7. This was written by Edmund du Cane, surveyor-general of prisons and designer of forts on the south coast of England, and a former Royal Engineer (*DNB*).

[94] For background information on police pay scales, superannuation and standards of lock-ups, see R. Cowley, R. Todd and L. Ledger, *The History of Her Majesty's Inspectorate of Constabulary: The First 150 Years* (no place, no date).

95 Examination of the 1871 census suggests that Constable Richards's residence was across the road and some fifty yards from the building known as the Public Rooms which housed the cells at that time. A flannel measurer and a warehouseman were living in the Public Rooms, which also served as a flannel exchange.
96 PCA, M/Q/AC/6. Charles Augustus Cobbe had been chief constable of the West Riding of Yorkshire before being appointed HM inspector (from 1861 census).
97 The architect's drawings are in PCA, M/Q/AC/6, dated 17 November 1877.
98 PCA, M/Q/CX/2; M/Q/AC/2. The building still stands, now used as a hostel for homeless people.
99 A former magistrate has said, 'There was a feeling of distance from the other people in the court. That was probably the whole idea'; personal correspondence with A. Pugh (16 April 2013).
100 *NWE*, especially 5 January 1869, 23 February 1869 and 5 October 1869.
101 *NWE*, 12 January 1869.
102 *NWE*, 13 January 1874.
103 Note that quarter sessions had earlier been held at various towns around the county, including Welshpool, Llanfyllin (until possibly 1830); Montgomery, Newtown, Machynlleth and Llanidloes; E. A. Lewis, 'A schedule of the quarter sessions records of the county of Montgomery at the National Library of Wales', *Mont. Colls*, 46 (1940), 157.
104 In fact, this came about twenty years later when the Local Government Act of 1888 led to Montgomeryshire County Council being established in 1889. According to Hey, elected county councils (and county borough councils in borough towns with populations of over 50,000) lasted for nearly a hundred years, being abolished in 1974; D. Hey, *Local and Family History*, p. 115.
105 The following were the locations of 1869 quarter sessions: Hilary: Welshpool; Easter: Welshpool; midsummer: Newtown; Michaelmas: Welshpool.
106 *NWE*, 26 January 1869. The whole letter is reproduced here because of the wealth of evidence contained in it.
107 'Up the valley' and 'down the valley' were terms used locally when referring to the differentials in prosperity often found along the Severn valley, and are still in use in the twenty-first century.
108 E. Bredsdorff, *Welshpool in Old Photographs* (Stroud, 1993), p. 46.
109 The architect was Benjamin Lay of Welshpool. Haslam describes the amended town hall as 'vaguely French Renaissance'; Haslam, *Buildings of Wales*, p. 210.

CHAPTER 3

1 Philip Jenkins puts it bluntly: 'It was in the early Victorian era that Welsh communities first developed professional police forces, in response to the public order problems faced by industrialisation'; P.

Jenkins, *A History of Modern Wales, 1536–1990* (London, 1992), pp. 254–5. See also D. J. V. Jones, *Crime in Nineteenth-Century Wales* (Cardiff, 1992), p. 201; R. D. Storch, 'The plague of the Blue Locusts: police reform and popular resistance in northern England, 1840–57', *International Review of Social History*, 20 (1975); 62; D. Taylor, *The New Police in Nineteenth-Century England* (Manchester, 1997), p. 36. See also C. Emsley, 'A typology of nineteenth-century police', *Crime, History and Society*, 3 (1991), 29–44 for a comprehensive coverage of the development of European police forces; also R. Cowley, *A History of the British Police: From its Earliest Beginnings to the Present Day* (Stroud, 2011).

2   B. Owen, 'The Newtown and Llanidloes poor-law union workhouse, Caersws 1837–1847', *Mont. Colls*, 78 (1990), 120; P. Phillips, *A View of Old Montgomeryshire* (1977; Swansea, 1978), p. 140. Carmarthenshire and Cardiganshire established their county forces as a direct result of tollgate riots. The Montgomeryshire forces had been established earlier and this may be why the rioting did not spread further into the county than the southernmost area. A report of the tollgate events in the Rhayader area was written by the chief constable of Montgomeryshire and submitted to quarter sessions. The report is reproduced in part in Maddox, *History of Montgomeryshire Constabulary, 1840–1948* (Carmarthen, 1982), pp. 10–11. See also the Journal of PC Thomas Jones, PCA, M/SOC/7/42. Jenkins argues that the slump seen in mid-Wales textile towns contributed to the unrest of the 1840s; Jenkins, *A History*, pp. 266–7.

3   For descriptions of the working lives of nineteenth-century policemen in disparate locations around Britain, see C. Emsley, *The Great British Bobby* (London, 2009), especially chapter 5. See also I. Channing, *The Police and the Expansion of Public Order Law in Britain, 1829–2013* (London, 2015), and B. S. Godfrey and D. J. Cox, 'Policing the industrial north of England, 1777–1877: the control of labour at work, and in the streets', *Crime, History and Society*, 20 (2016), 129–47.

4   Information from the Report of Her Majesty's Inspector of Constabularies, 1871.

5   See the map in D. Jenkins (ed.), *The Historical Atlas of Montgomeryshire* (Welshpool, 1999), p. 92. Llanrhaiadr ym Mochnant, the most northerly location of a policeman on the map, is partly in Denbighshire. Although Constable Thomas Vaughan stationed here is mentioned in newspaper reports of Montgomeryshire crime (e.g. the case of theft by Robert Hughes, *NWE*, 26 October 1870) he later became deputy chief constable of Denbighshire. Therefore, it is possible that in 1871 he was a constable with Denbighshire Constabulary rather than Montgomeryshire.

6   'Repeal of turnpike laws' at *www.lawcom.gov.uk/docs/turnpikes.pdf*, p.11 (18 November 2010).

7   Advertisement for auctions at which leases were to be sold for the 1869–70 period, *NWE*, 9 February 1869.

8   *NWE*, 9 February 1869, 1 June 1869, 3 May 1870, 14 July 1870, 6 September 1870, 10 January 1871, 16 May 1871 (two incidents), 20 May 1873; *ME*, 19 September 1876.

⁹   For discussion on attitudes taken to tramps in the north of England see
     D. Taylor, *Beerhouses, Brothels and Bobbies: Policing by Consent in Hudders-
     field and the Huddersfield District in the Nineteenth Century* (Huddersfield,
     2016).
¹⁰   Home Secretary George Grey used public fear of the vagrant criminal
     to promote his 1856 County and Borough Police Bill which became law
     and made the establishment of county police forces compulsory; C.
     Steedman, *Policing the Victorian Community: The Formation of the English
     Provincial Police Forces, 1856–80* (London, 1984), p. 25.
¹¹   Maddox, *History of Montgomeryshire Constabulary*, p. 13.
¹²   In neighbouring Radnorshire, the number of vagrants relieved in 1868
     was 3,687. The number had been growing steadily in recent years, and
     the 1869 figure was an increase of nearly 500 per cent on that of 1864.
     The chief constable of Radnorshire said that the vagrants preferred
     'the comforts of gaol to the [Radnorshire] poorhouse [and] committed
     crime in order to go to gaol and were often clever enough to avoid hard
     labour'; Maddox, *A History of Radnorshire Constabulary* (Llandrindod
     Wells, 1959), p. 16. There were three workhouses in Radnorshire.
     Clements proposes that Denbighshire's chief constable deployed
     constables at strategic points that provided optimal surveillance oppor-
     tunities; F. Clements, 'Sergeant W. R. Breese: a policeman in rural
     nineteenth-century Denbighshire', *Transactions of Denbighshire Historical
     Society*, 56 (2008), 127.
¹³   HMIC Report, *PP* (26), 1870, p. 4
¹⁴   F. Clements, 'Vagrancy in Victorian Denbighshire', *Transactions of
     Denbighshire Historical Society*, 58 (2010), 64.
¹⁵   *NWE*, 30 May 1871. From inspection of a map of Montgomeryshire
     parishes, the writer's parish could be Llanwyddyn. This parish later
     became the location of a new reservoir, begun in 1881 when an extra
     policeman was paid for by Liverpool Corporation; letter from Liverpool
     Town Clerk, PCA, M/Q/AC/7; see also R. Kretchmer, *Llanfyllin: A
     Pictorial History* (Welshpool, 1992), p.173. See D. Phillips and R. D.
     Storch, *Policing Provincial England, 1829–1856* (London, 1999), p. 38 for
     a comment on the country gentry attitude to rural policing. It has been
     said that during this period, vagrants showed a marked antagonism
     towards Montgomeryshire farmers; D. J. V. Jones, 'A dead loss to the
     community: the nineteenth-century vagrant in mid-nineteenth century
     Wales', *Welsh History Review*, 8 (1977), 312–44.
¹⁶   'John Verniew' appears to be a *nom de plume* giving a clue to his home
     location as the River Verniew (Vyrnwy) flows through northern Mont-
     gomeryshire, and there are several properties in the area with names
     such as Glan Verniew and Verniew Cottage.
¹⁷   Jenkins argues that political and religious dissent was 'able to grow on
     the fringes of shires, far from the agents of justice'; Jenkins, *A History*, p.
     6. This is exactly the same argument Verniew was making regarding
     trouble relating to tramps.
¹⁸   Report of the attack *NWE*, 2 May 1871. Details of the promotion are in
     the chief constable's report to quarter sessions; *NWE*, 11 January 1870
     and PCA, MQ/SO11.

19 HMIC Report, PP 1871 (28), p. 59; HMIC Report, PP 1872 (30), p. 70.
20 Jones highlights the steep decline in vagrancy at the beginning of the 1870s and notes Montgomeryshire's method of moving tramps on. He identifies the new police as making a significant difference to the statistics of vagrancy crimes; Jones, *Crime*, pp. 162–4.
21 C. Emsley, *The English and Violence since 1750* (London, 2005), pp. 131–2.
22 *ME*, 27 August 1878. The pseudonym 'cat o' nine tails' indicates vividly the degree of punishment this writer thought of as suitable for the stone throwers.
23 *NWE*, 30 December 1873.
24 *NWE*, 13 January 1874, 27 January 1874.
25 *NWE*, 27 April 1875. According to the *University of Wales Dictionary* (2002), the word *heddlu* (the Welsh word for police, literally meaning peace force) was first used in 1858. Before this, the word for constable was *heddswyddog* (peace officer) or *heddgeidwadd* (peacekeeper); personal correspondence, Thomas Glyn Watkin (29 October 2012).
26 The same issues as those raised here are present in the twenty-first century, as similar newspaper correspondence shows. For example, the *Daily Telegraph* published a report entitled 'Be polite to the public, police told' (9 July 2013). A response to this reads: 'Public sector workers [including police] should take pride in providing the best service they can to their fellow citizens, rather than by treating them with indifference or contempt.' Another letter suggesting a different point of view reads: 'What about the public being told to be polite to the police?', *Daily Telegraph*, letters page, 10 July 2013.
27 As a comparison of modern thinking to that of the nineteenth century, see guidance sent by the Senior Presiding Judge and Lord Chancellor to magistrates 18 February 2014 stating that it is deemed inappropriate for magistrates to take any part in the selection of police officers in order to maintain public confidence in the impartiality of the magistracy.
28 R. D. Storch, 'The plague of the Blue Locusts: police reform and popular resistance in northern England, 1840–57', *International Review of Social History*, 20 (1975), 71. The picture of working-class policemen enforcing the law and the ruling elite handing out sentences is well illustrated in C. Emsley, 'Mother, what did policemen do when there weren't any motors? The law, the police and the regulation of motor traffic in England, 1900–1939', *Historical Journal*, 36 (1992), 357–81.
29 See for example Storch, 'Blue locusts', p. 65 and P. Rawlings, *Policing: A Short History* (Cullompton, 2002), p. 143.
30 *NWE*, 15 April 1873.
31 Bryan was a horse dealer and substantial farmer, employing live-in domestic servants and farm workers; National Census, 1871 and 1881.
32 The new police routinely subjected pubs and beerhouses to closer surveillance; Phillips, *Policing Provincial England*, p. 225.
33 Comparison of newspaper reports to court records held at Powys County Archives shows that both types of written report used identical

terminology for the policeman's reference to the named individual. Therefore, it seems that the language reported in the press was the same as used in court, and not the reporter's choice.

[34] Apart from financial contributions from ratepayers, there was also a grant from the Treasury to forces deemed efficient by HMIC. For more information on this see D. Philips, *Crime and Authority in Victorian England* (London, 1978), p. 83.

[35] B. J. Davey, *Lawless and Immoral: Policing a Country Town, 1838–1857* (Leicester, 1983), p. 46.

[36] *NWE*, 3 February 1874.

[37] *NWE*, 18 May 1869.

[38] *NWE*, 16 August 1870.

[39] For a discussion on nineteenth-century police methods of dealing with difficult working-class areas of London see C. Bowlby, 'Do difficult areas need special police attention?', *BBC History* (September 2012), 49.

[40] Emsley writes: 'There were still some areas where the police did not go except in pairs. Cavanagh [a London policeman] recalled being advised by an old Irishman to keep out of the slum and cul-de-sac of Ewer Street; if there was a fight it was best to let them get on with it'; Emsley, *The Great British Bobby*, p. 126.

[41] *NWE*, 16 November 1869, 14 June 1870, 16 August 1870. Constable Arthur Howell Williams, Denbighshire Constabulary, was given this advice when starting his police career: 'Think to get your back to the wall if you're threatened. If you can't get your truncheon out remember that your helmet is just as good for belting them with!'; I. Niall, *The Village Policeman* (London, 1971), p. 4.

[42] For example, when Constable Richards went in pursuit of a thief (*NWE*, 18 October 1869) or when Constable Hudson followed the trail of four suspects over the county boundary into Shropshire (*NWE*, 11 January 1870).

[43] An example is when Constable Hudson received information of an indecent assault (*NWE*, 5 July 1870).

[44] For example, on 19 July 1870 (*NWE*, 19 July 1870).

[45] Announcement of the annual police dinner given by Welshpool Corporation, *NWE*, 29 August 1871.

[46] A notable petty offender was a young lad who cut the buttons off worshippers' coats in chapel. Constable Sibbold reported frequent complaints to him about the boy from the chapelgoers (*NWE*, 16 March 1869)

[47] Private prosecutions continued after the establishment of the paid police force. Philips describes and discusses this in chapter 4 of *Crime and Authority in Victorian Britain*.

[48] *NWE*, 4 May 1869.

[49] *NWE*, 19 October 1869.

[50] *NWE*, 23 February 1869.

[51] *NWE*, 7 June 1870.

[52] Textile Museum, Commercial Road, Newtown.

[53] *NWE*, 14 June 1870.

54 *NWE*, 26 April 1870.
55 For an example of reporter/police collaboration see F. Rule, *The Worst Street in London* (2008; Horsham, 2010), pp. 128–9.
56 Discussed in more detail in the chapter on prostitution and related crime.
57 *NWE*, 8 December 1874.
58 *NWE*, 19 October 1875.
59 *NWE*, 14 May 1872.
60 See Storch's discussion in 'The policeman as domestic missionary: urban discipline and popular culture in Northern England, 1850–1880', *Journal of Social History*, 9 (1976), 481–509.
61 B. Weinberger, 'The police and public in mid nineteenth-century Warwickshire', in V. Bailey, *Policing and Punishment in Nineteenth-Century Britain* (London, 1981), p. 65.
62 B. Reich and C. Adcock, *Values, Attitudes and Behaviour Change* (London, 1976), pp. 50–7.
63 *NWE*, 3 February 1874.
64 Storch, 'Domestic missionary', 482.
65 Reich, *Values*, p. 52.
66 *NWE*, 10 February 1874.
67 The defendant was lodging at the doctor's house on The Bank, a genteel part of central Newtown. Questions arise as to whether the police were proactive in this case because there might be trouble at a middle-class person's property.
68 For accounts of similar events see 'Policing the working class', in Emsley, *Great British Bobby*, pp.148–53.
69 *NWE*, 14 March 1871 and 21 March 1871.
70 National Census, 1881.
71 *NWE*, 27 October 1874.
72 For a discussion of the contribution of newspaper reporting to public knowledge and attitudes to police effectiveness see P. King, 'Newspaper reporting and attitudes to crime and justice in late eighteenth- and early nineteenth-century London', *Continuity and Change*, 22 (2007), 73–112. For information about detectives, see C. Emsley and H. Shpayer-Makov (eds), *Police Detectives in History, 1750–1950* (Aldershot, 2006).
73 *NWE*, 8 December 1872.
74 *NWE*, 17 August 1871.
75 J. Briggs, C. Harrison. A. McInnes and D. Vincent, *Crime and Punishment in England: An Introductory History* (London, 1996), p. 151.
76 D. Hobbs, *Doing the Business* (Oxford, 1988), p. 36.
77 Hobbs, *Doing the Business*, p. 37.
78 *ME*, 5 June 1906.
79 See H. Shpayer-Makov, *The Ascent of the Detective* (Oxford, 2011), p. 43.
80 *NWE*, 6 June 1871.
81 Hobbs asserts: 'When this presence becomes invisible, covert and indistinguishable in appearance from the policed, it has been traditionally perceived as un-British, and therefore threatening'; Hobbs, *Doing the*

Business, p. 36. For a description and comment on a particular case, see Emsley, *Great British Bobby*, pp. 56–8.

82 Storch, 'Blue locusts', 71.

83 Emsley, *Great British Bobby*, p. 58; Storch, 'Domestic missionary', 489. In urban areas, it was plain-clothes men who apprehended most criminals; Briggs, *Crime and Punishment*, p. 152.

84 *County Times*, 17 March 1906.

85 P. J. Stead, *The Police of Britain* (London, 1985), p. 52. According to Stead, this was the character of Inspector Bucket in *Bleak House*; C. Dickens, *Bleak House* (London, 1853).

86 Journal of PC Thomas Jones, PCA, M/SOC/7/42, entry for 6 December 1843.

87 Constable Edward Jones's journals are at the National Library of Wales, NLW MS 6227D, 6228D and 6229D. Whereas the Metropolitan Police had a dedicated detective section, criminal investigations in Montgomeryshire remained in the hands of constables, as had been the situation in London during the first ten years of the Metropolitan force. For a comment, see Emsley, *The Great British Bobby*, p. 62, and p. 118 for a short discussion on the regulation of a policeman's life and the records he had to keep.

88 Journal of PC Thomas Jones, entry for 21 August 1843.

89 Forensics Timeline viewed at *www.umbc.edu/tele/canton/studentproj/May.A/timeline.htm* (15 December 2010).

90 This is reminiscent of the case, nine years earlier, of Constance Kent, who was accused of, and later confessed to, the murder of her baby brother. Blood stains found on a nightdress were deemed to be menstrual blood; R. Castleden, *Infamous Murders* (London, 2005), pp. 378–89.

91 M. Bauer and D. Patzelt, 'Evaluation of mRNA markers for the identification of menstrual blood', *Journal of Forensic Science*, 47 (2002), 1278–82; M. Bauer, D. Patzelt, 'Identification of menstrual blood by real time RT-PCR: technical improvements and the practical value of negative test results', *Forensic Science International*, 174 (2008), 54–8. Note especially the comments in Section 6 of K. Virkler and I. K. Lednev, 'Analysis of body fluids for forensic purposes: from laboratory testing to non-destructive rapid confirmatory identification at a crime scene', *Forensic Science International*, 188 (2009), 11.

92 Trial documents no longer exist, so any correspondence from the professor is lost. The importance of forensic techniques was recognised in Scotland throughout the nineteenth century, with a chair in medical jurisprudence being established in 1807; B. White 'Training medical policemen: forensics, medicine and public health in nineteenth-century Scotland', in M. Clark and C. Crawford (eds), *Legal Medicine in History* (Cambridge, 1994), pp. 145–66.

93 In Buckinghamshire in 1859, six hours per day was spent on walking, and this could be extended by an order from the chief constable; Steedman, *Policing the Victorian Community*, p. 122.

[94] David Jones identifies this contradiction in D. J. V. Jones, 'The new police, crime and people in England and Wales 1829–1888', *Transactions of the Royal Historical Society*, 33 (1983), 151–68.

CHAPTER 4

[1] See P. King, 'The summary court and social relations in eighteenth-century England', *Past and Present*, 183 (2004), 125–72 for a comprehensive summary of the workings of the court during the early modern period. Jennifer Davis describes a platform wherein magistrates used personal inclination, knowledge of context and of offenders to deal with these matters and to maintain social order; J. Davis, 'A poor man's system of justice: the London police courts in the second half of the nineteenth century', *Historical Journal*, 27 (1984), 309–35. Caution must be considered here, as the metropolitan situation could be very different from Montgomeryshire.

[2] See D. Hay, 'Property, authority and the criminal law', in D. Hay, P. Linebaugh, J. G. Rule, E. P. Thompson and C. Winslow, *Albion's Fatal Tree: Crime and Society in Eighteenth-Century England* (London, 1975), pp. 17–65.

[3] C. Emsley, *Crime and Society in England, 1750–1900* (1987; Harlow, 1996), p. 208. See also 'Summary Trial', in D. Bentley, *English Criminal Justice in the Nineteenth Century* (London, 1998), pp. 19–25.

[4] See also Godfrey's suggestion that it was police activity that brought about an increase in prosecutions of drunkenness during the period; B. S. Godfrey, D. J. Cox and S. D. Farrall, *Serious Offenders: A Historical Study of Habitual Criminals* (Oxford, 2010), p. 59.

[5] King, 'The summary courts', 139.

[6] Note Diane Drummond's comparison of Victorian Crewe to the wild west of America quoted in B. S. Godfrey, D. J. Cox and S. D. Farrall *Criminal Lives: Family Life, Employment and Offending* (Oxford, 2007), p. 11. The phrase was used in the context of the United States by 1826; *Online Etymology Dictionary*, www.etymonline.com (20 July 2014).

[7] Most theft cases were sent to quarter sessions, meaning that the proportions were different at the higher court. This will be examined in a later chapter.

[8] 26.4 per cent of male convictions and 36.5 per cent of female convictions involved drunkenness; see L. Zedner, *Women, Crime and Custody* (Oxford, 1991), pp. 309 and 221. Godfrey found that in Crewe, during the late Victorian age, the proportion appearing in court on drunkenness charges was also one-third; Godfrey, *Criminal Lives*, p. 41. See also discussions on drunkenness, violence and young, single men, in B. Godfrey and G. Dunstall, 'The growth of crime and crime control in developing towns: Timaru and Crewe, 1850–1920', in B. Godfrey and G. Dunstall (eds), *Crime and Empire 1840–1940: Criminal Justice in Local and Global Context* (Cullompton, 2005), pp. 135–44.

[9] D. Rabin, 'Drunkenness and responsibility for crime in the eighteenth century', *Journal of British Studies*, 44 (2005), 457.

[10] C. Emsley, *Crime and Society in England*, p. 15.

[11] See for example the cases of Mary Morris and Dorcas Harding which were prosecuted at quarter sessions. Records of the prosecutors' recognisances are in the records at Powys County Archives, M/Q/SR (Hilary 1869 and Hilary 1870 respectively).

[12] D. J. V. Jones, *Crime in Nineteenth-Century Wales* (Cardiff, 1992), p. 207.

[13] In his paper on drunkenness in Newcastle upon Tyne in the early 1900s, Bennison marks the 1870s as the high point in UK spirit consumption; B. Bennison, 'Drunkenness in turn-of-the-century Newcastle upon Tyne', *Local Population Studies*, 52 (1994), 14.

[14] Temperance has been said to have reached 'amazing dimensions' by the 1870s; P. Jenkins, *A History of Modern Wales, 1536–1990* (London, 1992), p. 202. See also Evans, *A History of Wales, 1815–1906* (Cardiff, 1989), pp. 85–9.

[15] See Bennison, 'Drunkenness', 20.

[16] The Order of Good Templars was founded in the USA in the early 1850s and was brought to England in 1868; thus Sergeant Hudson was one of its early members; 'IOGT: a brief history', *http://iogt-ew.org/history.html* (4 January 2013). See also reports of Good Templar meetings, *NWE*, 21 January 1873, 13 May 1873, 2 September 1873, 30 September 1873; 'Temperance lecture', *NWE*, 7 December 1869; letter to the editor, *NWE*, 30 September 1873.

[17] See the introduction in H. P. Jeffers, *Freemasons: Inside the World's Oldest Secret Society* (New York, 2005), pp. ix–xiiii.

[18] Report of Danily's funeral, *ME*, 26 January 1915; G. Rademan, 'The Cedewain Lodge of Freemasons', *Newtonian*, 32 (2008), 8–14. Robert Storch found that Leeds chief constables saw themselves as 'natural allies' of the temperance movement, and contemporaneously to Danily, Leeds Chief Constable Wetherell was similarly driven. R. D. Storch, 'The policeman as domestic missionary: urban discipline and popular culture in Northern England, 1850–1880', *Journal of Social History*, 9 (1976), 485.

[19] *NWE*, 6 April 1869.

[20] Danily's obituary, *NWE*, 26 January 1915.

[21] There was a recognised 'dark figure' of unrecorded crime (see C. Emsley, *Crime and Society in England*, p. 24); however, see graph in Godfrey, *Serious Offenders*, p. 59. See also B. Harrison, *Drink and the Victorians* (London 1971), pp. 179–347 for background information on the drink question during the 1870s. The Good Templars are described as 'a pseudo Masonic organisation of the most extreme temperance zealots', p. 241. David Taylor describes how numbers of arrests for drunkenness could reflect a particular chief constable's attitudes; D. Taylor, *The New Police in Nineteenth Century England* (Manchester, 1997), pp. 92–3. See also comments throughout J. S. Blocker, M. Fahey and I. R. Tyrrell (eds), *Alcohol and Temperance in Modern History: A Global Encyclopedia* (Santa Barbara, 2003).

[22] *NWE*, 18 May 1869.

[23] *NWE*, 5 July 1870. The Astley's Court area was crammed with small, terraced houses accommodating working-class people, most of them employed at the nearby flannel factories and an iron foundry, and many living in lodging houses. The area, lying along a quarter-mile stretch of Pool Road, took up thirty-five pages of the 1871 census, exactly the sort of area described by Rule as fostering prostitution and the fencing of stolen goods; F. Rule, *The Worst Street in London* (2008; Horsham, 2010), p. 78. See also Jones's comments in Jones, *Crime*, p. 195 and D. J. V. Jones, 'Where did it all go wrong? Crime in Swansea, 1938–68', *Welsh History Review*, 15 (1990), 240–74.

[24] Esther Thomas was a pump maker's wife, living a few doors away from The Wheat Sheaf; National Census, 1871.

[25] Ann Nock, wife of factory fitter, Richard Nock, National Census, 1871.

[26] Jones, *Crime*, p. 195.

[27] *NWE*, 16 January 1872.

[28] *NWE*, 1 January 1875.

[29] *ME*, 26 January 1915.

[30] See 'Summary Trial', in Bentley, *English Criminal Justice*, pp. 19–25.

[31] *NWE*, 7 May 1872 and 9 May 1871.

[32] *NWE*, 11 January 1870.

[33] *NWE*, 2 May 1871.

[34] *NWE*, 30 November 1869, 8 March 1870, 15 November 1870.

[35] King, writing about eighteenth-century England, says that many rural magistrates continued to conduct what were effectively semi-private hearings, and that legal technicalities did not take pride of place. Magistrates had a tendency to base their judgements on their own unauthorised ideas of equity. However, increasing pressure from defendants, their representatives and judges encouraged magistrates to become more precise about such matters; P. King, *Crime, Justice and Discretion in England, 1740–1820* (Oxford, 2000), p. 85.

[36] *NWE*, 1 February 1870. Jones was later convicted following a trial at which she was represented by a solicitor. (Also reported in *NWE*, 1 February 1870). Yet another show of leniency towards prostitutes was seen in May 1870 when two women who had followed the militia to Welshpool were discharged with a caution (*NWE*, 17 May 1870).

[37] *NWE*, 12 December 1871. Using modern parlance, some defendants might have viewed him as a 'soft touch'.

[38] King, 'Summary courts and social relations', p. 128.

[39] *NWE*, 6 April 1869.

[40] *NWE*, 15 November 1870

[41] D. J. V. Jones, 'The poacher: a study in Victorian crime and protest', *Historical Journal*, 22, (1979), 829.

[42] Shrewsbury School Register, 1874–1908.

[43] D. Jenkins, (ed.), *Historical Atlas of Montgomeryshire* (Welshpool, 1999), p. 69.

[44] See D. W. Smith, 'Tithe protests', *Mont. Colls*, 84 (1996), 134–5.

[45] M. Strathern, *Kinship at the Core: An Anthropology of Elmdon, a Village in North-West Essex in the Nineteen-Sixties* (Cambridge, 1981), p. 58; H.

Newby, 'The deferential dialectic', *Comparative Studies in Society and History*, 17 (1975), 158.

46 *NWE*, 12 April 1870. The chairman quoted from *The Law Journal*, 32 (1863), 186: 'A conviction cannot be sustained where a farmer under a claim of right kills a pigeon doing mischief, that is, picking up seed on his land.' Otherwise they could have imposed a fine of up to £2 above the value of the pigeon. However, see H. Stephens, *The Book of the Farm*, 3 (Edinburgh, 1844), p. 261 for the comment regarding an 1832 case in which a tenant farmer failed to prove his defence that his landlord's pigeons had been destroying his crops: 'This decision proves the fallacy of a common opinion that a farmer may shoot pigeons in the act of destroying his crops provided he does not carry them away after they have been shot. If this opinion were supported by law, any tenant that had a grudge against his landlord might lure his pigeons by various means and there shoot them and let them lie.' See also 'The eclipse of *mens rea*', *Law Quarterly Review*, 60 (1936), 60.

47 Davis, 'A poor man's system of justice', 331.

48 *NWE*, 19 January 1875.

49 B. Short, 'Environmental politics, custom and personal testimony: memory and life space on the late Victorian Ashdown Forest, Sussex', *Journal of Historical Geography*, 30 (2004), 480–4.

50 S. Stone, *The Justices' Manual* (n.p., 1880), NLW item number 94MA16717.

51 *NWE*, 16 November 1869, 14 October 1869, 17 May 1870.

52 According to Bentley, 'The clerk himself might know little of the law. Some had no legal qualifications at all'; Bentley, *English Criminal Justice*, p. 23.

53 See J. G. Jones, 'The Welsh language in local government: justices of the peace and the courts of quarter sessions *c*.1536–1800', in G. H. Jenkins (ed.), *The Welsh Language before the Industrial Revolution* (Cardiff, 1997), pp. 181–206; R. Suggett, 'The Welsh language and the court of great sessions', in Jenkins (ed.), *The Welsh Language*, pp.153–80. Note, however, in 1576, Sir William Gerard, the Justice of South Wales, recommended to the government that, with the appointment of a second justice to each of the four great sessions circuits, one of the justices on each circuit should be fluent in Welsh. Thus, the importance of the Welsh language to local justice was recognised and accepted at that time; personal correspondence, Thomas Glyn Watkin (20 June 2013).

54 See comment on the rule in M. Jarman, 'The Welsh language and the courts', in T. G. Watkin and N. S. B. Cox (eds), *Canmlwyddiant, Cyfraith a Chymreictod: A Celebration of the Life and Work of Dafydd Jenkins, 1911–2012* (Bangor, 2013), p. 171. Note that it was not until 1993 that a law was enacted which led to Welsh being equal to English in courts; Jarman, 'The Welsh language', p. 172.

55 *NWE*, 30 January 1872. Bards kept alive the poetic forms of Welsh which could have died out after the Acts of Union. They were highly trained professionals who had undergone intense instruction in the complex poetic forms; Jenkins, *A History*, pp. 61–6.

56 Dr Richard Woosnam, the Revd John Evans and Edmund Cleaton, flannel manufacturer.

57 T. Skyrme, *History of the Justices of the Peace* (Chichester, 1991), 3, p. 40.

58 See also a case when clerk Mr Jenkins translated a Welsh-speaker's evidence into English for the benefit of the defendant who was monoglot English, *NWE*, 2 May 1872, and an occasion when the defendant made a lengthy closing statement in Welsh, *NWE*, 3 September 1872.

59 *NWE*, 1 June 1869.

60 R. J. Harrison, 'Royal Montgomery Regiment of Militia', *Mont. Colls*, 17 (1884), 211.

61 The Webbs noted that the office of deputy lieutenant was one of 'pure social dignity', furthering the idea that many men pursued county roles related to status; S. Webb and B. Webb, *English Local Government* (London, 1963), pp. 286–7.

62 'Lists of deputy lieutenants, and correspondence', *Mont. Colls*, 16 (1883), 120–1.

63 Godfrey and Cox identified that JPs 'frequently betrayed their own self-interested bias'; B. S. Godfrey and D. J. Cox, *Policing the Factory* (London, 2013), p. 153.

64 See for example Mary Ann Pugh, *NWE*, 7 July 1874; Sarah Payne, *NWE*, 10 January 1871; William Davies, *NWE*, 7 June 1870.

65 *NWE*, 1 January 1870.

66 See comments 'Perceptions of judicial partiality' and 'The impact of judicial bias' in Godfrey, *Policing the Factory*, pp. 151–7.

67 Level of fine based on ability to pay is the case in the modern magistrates' court; see Judicial Studies Board, *Adult Court Bench Book* (n.p., 2005), pp. 3–50.

68 *ME*, 2 January 1877.

69 *NWE*, 13 May 1873.

70 *NWE*, 31 May 1870.

71 Amount recoverable was allowed up to a maximum of £10; Stone, *Justices' Manual* (1862), p. 769. See also D. Hay, 'England 1562–1875: the law and its uses', in D. Hay and P. Craven (eds), *Masters, Servants and Magistrates in Britain and the Empire* (London, 2004), pp. 59–116.

72 *ME*, 14 May 1878.

73 There are good summaries of nineteenth-century educational provision in Montgomeryshire in P. Phillips, *A View of Old Montgomeryshire* (1977; Swansea, 1978), pp. 150–9, and L. H. Williams, 'Education', in Jenkins, *Historical Atlas*, p. 85.

74 This could be analysed using the modern concept of 'strain theory'. The families' opportunities for earning money were reduced, leading to criminal avenues being followed to gain the desired goal. See R. White and F. Haines, *Crime and Criminology* (1998; Oxford, 2002), pp. 52–71.

75 See for example, 'Newtown petty sessions', *NWE*, 16 May 1876, and 'school board prosecutions,' *NWE*, 20 January 1874. See S. Auerbach, 'The law has no feeling for poor folks like us!' Everyday responses to legal compulsion in England's working-class communities, 1871–1904',

Journal of Social History, 45 (2012), 686–708 for a discussion on how working-class parents dealt with the authorities regarding school attendance.
76 C. Emsley, 'Mother, what did policemen do when there weren't any motors? The law, the police and the regulation of motor traffic in England, 1900–1939', *Historical Journal*, 36 (1992), 360.
77 *Adult Court Bench Book*, pp. 3–110. There is also the restraining order which does not involve a bond.
78 J. Rowbotham referencing the work of A. C. Plowden in 'Turning away from criminal intent: a reflection on Victorian and Edwardian strategies for promoting distance amongst petty offenders', *Theoretical Criminology*, 13 (2009), 115–16.
79 See P. King, 'Punishing assault: the transformation of attitudes in the English courts', *Journal of Interdisciplinary History*, 27 (1996), 43–74 for a discussion of early modern treatment of this sort of offence.
80 Godfrey, *Crime and Justice*, p. 63.
81 Quoted in Godfrey, *Crime and Justice*, p. 64. For a good discussion of this topic see A. Clark, 'Domesticity and the problem of wifebeating in nineteenth-century Britain: working-class culture, law and politics', in S. D'Cruze (ed.), *Everyday Violence in Britain, 1850–1950: Gender and Class* (Abingdon, 2014), pp. 27–40.
82 *NWE*, 6 December 1870.
83 Davis, 'A poor man's system of justice', p. 322.
84 C. Emsley, *The English and Violence since 1750* (London, 2005), p. 64.
85 Davis, 'A poor man's system of justice', p. 322. See also N. Tomes, '"A torrent of abuse": crimes of violence between working-class men and women in London, 1840–1875', *Journal of Social History*, 11 (1978), 333–4.
86 *NWE*, 4 October 1870.
87 Modern guidelines indicate that magistrates may give a suspended sentence if the defendant shows a genuine willingness to reform his or her behaviour; *Adult Court Bench Book*, p.177.
88 Twenty-first century domestic assaults often are treated as common assault, but there are supplementary guidelines including consideration of the history of the relationship and patterns of behaviour; *Adult Court Bench Book*, p. 177.
89 King states that as summary court decisions were rarely scrutinised, it is easy to be misled by the guidelines given in legal handbooks; King, *Crime, Justice and Discretion*, p. 82.
90 *NWE*, 19 August 1869. For discussions on this topic see L. Ryan, 'Publicising the private: suffragists' critique of sexual abuse and domestic violence', in L. Ryan and M. Ward (eds), *Irish Women and the Vote: Becoming Citizens* (Dublin, 2007); M. May, 'Violence in the family: an historical perspective', in J. P. Martin (ed.), *Violence in the Family* (Chichester, 1978). See also Tomes, '"A Torrent of Abuse"', 338–40 for discussion on how individual magistrates' views influenced sentencing in domestic abuse cases.
91 *NWE*, 3 May 1870.

92 B. S. Godfrey, S. Farrall and S. Karstedt, 'Explaining gendered sentencing patterns', *British Journal of Criminology*, 45 (2005), 702.
93 Godfrey, 'Explaining gendered sentencing patterns', p. 714.
94 *NWE*, 28 May 1872.
95 *NWE*, 21 December 1869 and *ME*, 15 January 1878.
96 *ME*, 1 January 1878 and *NWE*, 28 May 1872.
97 *NWE*, 20 July 1869.
98 *NWE*, 17 January 1871, 10 September 1872.
99 See M. A. Riva, L. Tremolizzo, M. Spicci, C. Ferrarese, G. De Vito, G. C. Cesana and V. A. Sironi, 'The disease of the moon: the linguistic and pathological evolution of the English term "lunatic"', *Journal of the History of the Neurosciences*, 20 (2011), 65–73.
100 Stone, *Justices' Manual*, pp. 766–7.
101 *NWE*, 19 January 1875.
102 *NWE*, 19 September 1871.
103 *NWE*, 5 September 1871.
104 Sarah Beedles, *NWE*, 31 May 1870; Ann Jenkins, *NWE*, 19 January 1869.
105 *NWE*, 18 January 1875.
106 *NWE*, 13 May 1873.
107 D. Phillips, *Crime and Authority in Victorian England: The Black Country, 1835–1860* (London, 1997), pp. 177–219.
108 For this sample, complete data from all the petty sessions in January, May and September 1869–78 were used.
109 *NWE*, 3 September 1872.
110 *NWE*, 17 September 1878.
111 See D. Hay, 'Property, authority and the criminal law', in *Albion's Fatal Tree*, pp. 17–65.
112 *NWE*, 9 November 1869.
113 *ME*, 8 May 1877.
114 *NWE*, 9 September 1870.
115 *NWE*, 16 May 1871. See also for examples of neighbour disputes that were bound over or dismissed: Ann Williams and Eliza Evans, *NWE*, 7 September 1869; Jane Thomas and Margaret Davies, *NWE*, 16 May 1876; Sarah Evans and Eliza Owens, *NWE*, 7 September 1869.
116 *NWE*, 3 September 1872.
117 *NWE*, 31 May 1870.
118 Davies, 'A poor man's system of justice', p. 331.
119 *ME*, 22 May 1877.
120 *ME*, 9 January 1877.
121 *NWE*, 20 May 1873.
122 *ME*, 17 September 1878.

CHAPTER 5

1 B. S. Godfrey and P. Lawrence, *Crime and Justice, 1750–1950* (Cullompton, 2005), p. 29; also comments in D. Phillips, *Crime and Authority in Victorian England: The Black Country, 1835–1860* (London, 1997), p. 96.

2 King's mainly eighteenth-century investigations identify the victim as the one who provided the driving force that moved a dispute to a trial, and describes the multifarious opportunities for discretion on the way to the court, and the various options that could allow the victim to obtain satisfaction; P. King, *Crime, Justice and Discretion in England, 1740–1820* (Oxford, 2000). pp. 17–35. Barry Godfrey commented that if it were not for the substantial activity of victims, there would be little recorded crime at all before the late Victorian period; B. S. Godfrey, 'Changing prosecution practices and their impact on crime figures, 1857–1940', *British Journal of Criminology*, 48 (2008), 171.

3 M. Humphreys, *The Crisis of Community* (Cardiff, 1996), pp. 224–5.

4 Quarter Sessions Minute Books at Powys County Archives name the prosecutor in each case; Quarter Sessions Minute Books, PCA, M/QS/SM/3. Phillips's calculations from Staffordshire in 1860 show that police were handling less than half of all prosecutions, and Jones argues that it was only very late in the century that the police became the main initiators of criminal cases at the higher courts; Phillips, *Crime and Authority*, p. 130; D. J. V. Jones, *Crime in Nineteenth-Century Wales* (Cardiff, 1992), pp. 20–1. See also comments in Godfrey, 'Changing prosecution practices', pp. 171–86.

5 C. Emsley, *Crime and Society in England, 1750–1900* (1987; Harlow, 1996), p. 196.

6 *NWE*, 11 January 1870.

7 *NWE*, 16 March 1869. In this case, a labourer sold a horse on behalf of the owner but disappeared with the money. He was located in Maentwrog two weeks later. Finding him might well have involved the use of the *Police Gazette*. This publication at that time was published weekly and contained details of absconded persons suspected of crimes, and was circulated to police stations. For information about the *Police Gazette* see D. T. Hawkings, *Criminal Ancestors* (1998; London, 2008), p. 155.

8 Jury List, midsummer 1869, PCA, M/Q/SR. More recently, in the 1970s, an experienced officer told a new recruit, 'When dealing with the public, bear in mind that at some time in the future that person could be a member of the jury when you are trying to convict a murderer or bank robber'; 'Letters', *Daily Telegraph*, 7 September 2016.

9 Eddowes: *NWE*, 25 October 1870; Hickman: *NWE*, 10 January 1871; Morris: *NWE*, 27 October 74; Sayce: *NWE*, 5 July 1869.

10 A. Shubert, 'Private initiative in law enforcement: associations for the prosecution of felons', in V. Bailey (ed.), *Policing and Punishment in Nineteenth-Century Britain* (London, 1981), pp. 25–41. See also Emsley, *Crime and Society in England*, p. 191.

11 Reports of the association's annual dinners in *NWE*, 9 March 1869 and 8 March 1870.

12 Godfrey, 'Changing prosecution practices', p. 175. See also A. Shubert, 'Private initiative in law enforcement: associations for the prosecution of felons', in Bailey, *Policing and Punishment*, p. 26.

13 B. S. Godfrey, S. Farrall and S. Karstedt, 'Explaining gendered sentencing patterns', *British Journal of Criminology*, 45 (2005), 701.

[14] *NWE*, 31 January 1972.
[15] C. E. Howells, 'The association for the prosecution of felons, Welsh-pool', *Mont. Colls*, 33 (1904), 95–105. Howells was a regular and frequent prosecuting lawyer at the sessions studied here.
[16] However the victim decided to proceed, pursuing the offender and collecting evidence was a challenge for the private prosecutor. Howard describes how victims of theft in early modern Denbighshire responded in a variety of ways. Some might go to great lengths to apprehend a suspect or else choose to ignore the loss, and some might be prepared to accept an informal deal with the offender rather than face the lengthy and possibly expensive legal process; S. Howard, 'Investigating responses to theft in early-modern Wales: communities, thieves and the courts'; *Continuity and Change*, 19 (2004), 410; King, *Crime, Justice and Discretion*, p. 30. Jones cites this as the alternative face of the supposedly merit-worthy British legal system; Jones, *Crime in Nineteenth-Century Wales*, p. 20.
[17] Shubert, 'Private initiative', p. 36.
[18] Landau argues that the enforcement of criminal law depended on the willingness of the private prosecutor to bring charges and that those prosecutors found the courts' mechanical and routine treatment of the people they accused very useful; N. Landau, 'Indictment for fun and profit: a prosecutor's reward at eighteenth-century quarter sessions', *Law and History Review*, 17 (1999), 32.
[19] *ME*, 6 February 1875.
[20] Landau, 'Indictment for fun and profit', 519.
[21] Godfrey and Cox discuss similar praise to magistrates given by people in Yorkshire in B. S. Godfrey and D. J. Cox, *Policing the Factory* (London, 2013), p. 152.
[22] Thorn passed his final examinations as an articled clerk in summer 1872 (*The Worcester Journal*, 14 June 1872); thus he had been fully qualified less than two years when appointed by the association.
[23] See also Godfrey's findings; B. S. Godfrey, D. J. Cox and S. D. Farrall, *Serious Offenders: A Historical Study of Habitual Criminals* (Oxford, 2010), p. 58. In King's study of eighteenth-century English summary courts, he found that about 33 per cent of the adult population of one rural Wiltshire parish was involved in judicial hearings as either victims or offenders, and that urban dwellers also made extensive use of summary courts. He found a huge contrast with quarter sessions, where, in an Essex parish, less than 5 per cent of households would have contained anyone who had performed any substantial role in a major court. In any given year, the average resident there was between ten and fifteen times more likely to be involved in a summary hearing than in a major court case; P. J. R. King, 'The summary courts and social relations in eighteenth-century England', *Past and Present*, 183 (2004), 133–4.
[24] Jones found that property offences constituted 75 per cent of quarter sessions cases compared to 25 per cent of petty sessions cases; Jones, *Crime in Nineteenth-Century Wales*, p. 105.
[25] Among the early modern Essex courts studied by King (note 23), property crimes constituted about 70 per cent of cases. His warning about

the manipulation of definitions brings caution into the picture, but it is possible to say that highway robbery, burglary, house breaking (i.e. daytime burglary), and sheep and horse stealing featured significantly in his studies, although the greatest single property offence was larceny (i.e. theft without aggravating features). But as these studies were of the eighteenth century, they might be very different from those found in the present study. In Phillips's nineteenth-century Black Country work, larceny constituted 85 per cent. There, industrial theft (tools, metal, coal etc. from places of work) was the greatest single offence, with theft of clothing, food and animals also being significant; Phillips, *Crime and Authority*, pp. 177–8. Humphreys's eighteenth-century calculations show that 66.5 per cent of all quarter sessions defendants faced assault charges, whereas 15.5 per cent of them faced property charges. He found that often the assault charges were brought by people in authority, such as bailiffs, who perhaps needed the support of the court. Humphreys warns that the quarter sessions records that he consulted were fragmented, and this could explain why his finding that only a small proportion of cases were property crimes is very different from King's, Phillips's, Jones's and the results found in the present study; Humphreys, *Crisis*, pp. 224–5.

26 Some offences such as assault or riot could be tried either summarily or on indictment. The Juvenile Offenders Acts of 1847 and 1850 allowed summary trial for larcenies if committed by juveniles under the age of sixteen. The Criminal Justice Act of 1855 allowed summary trial, for accused of all ages, for larcenies under the value of five shillings if the accused agreed to a summary trial, and for larcenies of 5 shillings and over if the accused pleaded guilty; Phillips, *Crime and Authority*, p. 97.

27 For discussions of thefts of different types in varying communities see Jones, *Crime in Nineteenth-Century Wales*, pp. 106–14.

28 See comments in Jones, *Crime in Nineteenth-Century Wales*, pp. 127–8.

29 N. Woodward, 'Horse stealing in Wales, 1730–1830', *Agricultural History Review*, 57 (2009), 103–4. See also N. Woodward, 'Seasonality and sheep stealing in Wales, 1730–1830', *Agricultural History Review*, 56 (2008), 30.

30 *ME*, 9 July 1878 and 19 March 1878; PCA, M/Q/SR, midsummer and Easter 1878.

31 See C. Emsley, *Crime and Society in England*, especially Introduction and chapters 6 and 7. In a case heard at the Montgomeryshire quarter sessions in 1871, a pawnbroker joined the lawful owner of twenty pairs of boots in setting up a trap for the suspect. This may have been in an attempt to disassociate himself from the theft; *NWE*, 4 July 1871, discussed more fully in a later chapter.

32 *ME*, 19 March 1878. The 1886 1:25,000 OS map shows the two farms, Brynmawr and Frongoch, about a quarter of a mile apart.

33 PCA, M/Q/SR, Michaelmas 1871.

34 Comparable with Woodward's findings about disposal over the border, the suspect and animal were found in neighbouring Denbighshire, en route to Wrexham. In agreement with Woodward's comment that horse theft was less prevalent, being difficult to execute and trace, out of a

total of twenty-seven livestock thefts during the period, only this single horse theft was recorded, and the animal was found within a matter of hours.

[35] Mrs Parry told the court that she knew the suspect, Thomas Jones, because he had worked for her until recently. He can be seen on the 1871 census as her unmarried farm servant, residing at the farm.

[36] Howells, 'Association for the prosecution of felons', 102. See comment about a woman's interests being those of her husband after the Reform Act of 1832, in S. D'Cruze and L. A. Jackson, *Women, Crime and Justice in England since 1660* (Basingstoke, 2009), p. 106.

[37] *NWE*, 5 July 1870, 15 March 1870.

[38] C. Emsley, *Crime and Society*, p.188.

[39] P. King, *Crime, Justice and Discretion*, p. 136.

[40] D. Bentley, *English Criminal Justice in the Nineteenth Century* (London, 1998), pp. 131–2.

[41] Owning land worth at least £10 a year; occupying a dwelling of at least £20 per year rateable value; or occupying a house with at least fifteen windows. This was laid down by the Juries Act of 1825; see Phillips, *Crime and Authority*, p. 106.

[42] For example, farmer Charles Langford of Berriew, present on the petty jury, Hilary 1874 and the grand jury, Michaelmas 1871; Montgomery butcher Charles Davies, petty jury, Hilary 1876 and grand jury, Michaelmas 1871; Kerry farmer William Alderson, petty jury, Michaelmas 1877 and grand jury, midsummer 1872.; PCA, quarter sessions rolls.

[43] R. J. Morris, 'Middle classes', in *The Oxford Guide to British History* (1997; Oxford, 2002), pp. 639–40. See also A. Briggs, 'The language of class', in R. S. Neale (ed.), *History and Class* (Oxford, 1983), pp. 2–29 and R. S. Neale, 'Class and class consciousness in early nineteenth-century England: three classes or five?', *Victorian Studies*, 12 (1968), 14.

[44] See also Ralf Dahrendorf's comment: 'Classes are based on the differences in legitimate power associated with certain positions, i.e. on the structure of social roles with respect to their authority expectations ... An individual becomes a member of a class by playing a social role relevant from the point of view of authority ... He belongs to a class because he occupies a position in a social organisation'; R. Dahrendorf, quoted in E. P. Thompson, *The Making of the English Working Class* (London, 1963), p. 11.

[45] Phillips, *Crime and Authority*, p. 106.

[46] King, *Crime, Justice and Discretion*, p. 242.

[47] Phillips, *Crime and Authority*, p. 102. However, Bentley states that the grand jury were not furnished with the depositions but had only the bill of indictment from which to work, along with the questioning of witnesses; Bentley, *English Criminal Justice*, p. 132.

[48] King, *Crime, Justice and Discretion*, p. 238. King found an 'ignoramus' result in about 17 per cent of cases in the early 1800s and in the present study it was found to be about 13 per cent. David Taylor found the percentage to be about 22 per cent in early modern Surrey, and about 10 per cent in the mid-nineteenth-century Black Country; D. Taylor,

Crime, Policing and Punishment in England, 1750–1914 (Basingstoke, 1998), p. 118.

49 See Chapter 3 of the present work on the Montgomeryshire Constabulary and *NWE*, 14 March 1871. In 1887, a Constable Endacott was charged with perjury following an acquittal; C. Emsley, 'Lessons from history: how worried should we be when the police close ranks?', *BBC History* (Christmas 2013), 12.

50 See J. J. Tobias, *Crime and Industrial Society in the Nineteenth Century* (Oxford, 1967), pp. 226–7 for a description of problems resulting from the secrecy of the grand jury proceedings.

51 See comment in Bentley, *English Criminal Justice*, footnote 7, p. 132, and Phillips, *Crime and Authority*, p. 103. See Bentley, *English Criminal Justice*, pp. 131–4 for an interesting discussion of contemporary opinions about the grand jury system.

52 See jury lists, quarter sessions rolls, 1869–78, PCA.

53 Phillips found that gentlemen, bankers and members of professions were not found among petty jurors in his studies of the Black Country; Phillips, *Crime and Authority*, p. 106. See also Ireland's analysis of different juries; R. Ireland, 'Putting oneself on whose country?', in T. G. Watkin (ed.), *Legal Wales: Its Past, Its Future* (Cardiff, 2001), pp. 68–70.

54 King, *Crime, Justice and Discretion*, p. 244; Bentley, *English Criminal Justice*, p. 93.

55 Ireland, 'Putting oneself', p. 70.

56 See comments in King, *Crime, Justice and Discretion*, p. 244.

57 Bentley asserts that the compilation of the lists was done by poorly paid sheriffs' clerks, but it is clear from a comparison of handwriting and signature on the Montgomeryshire lists, that these were drawn up by the sheriff himself. The names of potential jurors were supplied by the overseers of each parish and delivered to magistrates at petty sessions regularly. For example, it was reported that in Machynlleth petty sessions in September 1869: 'The jury lists for the different parishes were presented for verification and sworn to by the respective overseers of those parishes, as the law requires'; *NWE*, 5 October 1869.

58 *The Shrewsbury Chronicle*, 3 January 1873. See also Shropshire quarter sessions orders, 1840–89, Shropshire Archives.

59 Juvenile Offenders Acts of 1847 and 1850 (discussed in Phillips, *Crime and Authority*, p. 97). See also Bentley, *English Criminal Justice*, p. 19.

60 *NWE*, 5 July 1870.

61 The case of Henry Poole, *NWE*, 8 August 1870. The victim was farmer Thomas Hilditch who was a grand juror at Easter sessions 1873 and a petty juror at Hilary sessions 1875.

62 Charles Morris served at Hilary quarter sessions in 1870. For discussion of juvenile delinquency see H. Shore, *Artful Dodgers: Youth and Crime in Early 19th-Century London* (Woodbridge, 2002); M. May, 'Innocence and experience: the evolution of the concept of juvenile delinquency in the mid-nineteenth century', *Victorian Studies*, 17 (1973), 7–29; S. Margerey, 'The invention of juvenile delinquency in early nineteenth-century London', *Labour History*, 34 (1978), 11–25.

63 *NWE*, 5 January 1869 and 12 January 1869 respectively.

[64] *NWE*, 5 October 1869.
[65] M/Q/SR, Michaelmas 1869.
[66] *NWE*, 29 October 1869.
[67] For discussions on contemporary attitudes to the acceptability of corporal punishment see J. Middleton, 'Thomas Hopley and mid-Victorian attitudes to corporal punishment', *History of Education*, 24 (2005), 599–615. Randall McGowan recognizes that attitudes towards violence were selective, depended on who defined it and whether social control was an element; R. McGowan, 'Cruel inflictions and the claims of humanity in early nineteenth-century England', in K. D. Watson (ed.), *Assaulting the Past: Violence and Civilisation in Historical Context* (Newcastle, 2007), pp. 38–57.
[68] Greg Smith points out: 'Assault charges could arise from an extremely wide range of events, and for that reason it is difficult to draw specific conclusions about the nature of violence in society simply from patterns of assault prosecutions. Counting assault indictments across time as an index of levels of interpersonal violence in society might, then, seem highly problematic given the dark figure of unrecorded crime'; G. T. Smith, 'Violent crime and the public weal in England, 1700–1900', in R. McMahon (ed.), *Crime, Law and Popular Culture in Europe, 1500–1900* (Cullompton, 2008), p. 195.
[69] The indecent assaults were: *NWE*, Thomas Redge, 7 July 1874; John Stephens, 23 February 1869 and 16 March 1869; Edwin James, 5 July 1870; William Lewis, 6 July 1869; George Powell, 10 January 1871 and John Horton, 4 July 1871. In Emsley's *The English and Violence since 1750* (London, 2005), the crimes under consideration are those committed by males. Females feature only in discussions of victims. This suggests that the finding here – that males were the perpetrators of crimes that reached the higher courts – is the same as Emsley's. Note Rafter and Heidensohn's comment: 'Criminology remains one of the most thoroughly masculinised of all social science fields; certainly one of the last academic bastions in which scholars regularly restrict their studies to the activities and habits of men without feeling compelled to account for this'; quoted in D. M. Britton, 'Feminism in Criminology', in M. Chesney-Lind and L. Pasko (eds), *Girls, Women and Crime* (Los Angeles, 2004), p. 61. See Chapters 1 and 2 in *Girls, Women and Crime* for theories of why females offend less than males.
[70] Sharon Howard identifies the length of depositions relating to homicides as reflecting how seriously violent deaths were taken; S. Howard, 'Crime, communities and authority in early modern Wales: Denbighshire, 1660–1713' (unpublished Ph.D. thesis, University of Wales, Aberystwyth, 2003), 61. Peter King argues that the length of an assault deposition probably reflects the fact of interpersonal difficulty when establishing guilt as at least two persons were involved giving varying accounts which were difficult for courts to judge; personal correspondence, 9 May 2012. Shani D'Cruze explains that assault cases relied on the effectiveness of narratives; D'Cruze, *Crimes of Outrage: Sex, Violence and Victorian Working Women* (London, 1998), p. 48.

NOTES 235

71 Easter quarter sessions 1869. Smith argues that the individual thresholds regarding perceptions of violence mean that it is difficult to assign figures to the actual levels of violent crime; Smith, 'Violent crime', p. 194.
72 Margaret Mostyn's evidence was reported in *NWE*, 16 March 1869.
73 Perverse jury decisions are considered further in the assizes chapter.
74 *ME*, 9 July 1878, 8 January 1878.
75 *ME*, 9 July 1878; 12 March 1878.
76 This agrees with Bentley's statement that 'in 1854 courts were empowered to sentence offenders aged under sixteen to a term of at least fourteen days imprisonment, followed by two to five years in a reformatory school'; Bentley, *English Criminal Justice*, p. 16. See also comment in Chesney, *Victorian Underworld*, p. 144 and C. Kelly, 'Reforming juvenile justice in nineteenth-century Scotland: the subversion of the Scottish day industrial school movement', *Crime, History and Society*, 20 (2016), 129–47.
77 See *Royal Commission on Penal Servitude* (21), 1, 1863.
78 Data from Bailey, *Policing and Punishment*, p. 131. The Penal Servitude Acts of 1853–64 had been on the statute books for several years, and the Habitual Criminals Act became law during the period under study. The former provided a replacement for transportation and incarceration on hulks, and for the mandatory death penalty, which had come to an end for all offences except murder and treason; D. Hoffman and J. Rowe, *Human Rights in the U.K.* (2003; Harlow, 2010), p. 148; Bailey, *Policing and Punishment*, pp. 126–44. See also Bentley, *English Criminal Justice*, p. 13; M. H. Tomlinson, 'Penal servitude 1846–65: a system in evolution', in Bailey, *Policing and Punishment*, pp. 126–49. See also N. Woodward, 'Transportation convictions during the great Irish famine', *Journal of Interdisciplinary History*, 37 (2006), 59–87.
79 Moody describes in detail the treatment of Fenian Michael Davitt who was convicted at the Old Bailey in 1870; T. W. Moody, 'Michael Davitt in penal servitude', *Irish Quarterly Review*, 30 (1941), 517–30. His period of hard labour was spent at Dartmoor where he was a co-inmate with Newtown offender Stephen Higgs, the pimp of prostitute Ann Lloyd, convicted at the midsummer sessions 1870; Pentonville Register, TNA, HO24/192.
80 Hawkings, *Criminal Ancestors*, p. 23.
81 Bailey quoting evidence given to the 1856 Commission on Penal Servitude, in Bailey, *Policing and Punishment*, p. 134. See Taylor, *Crime, Policing*, pp. 120–1 and 160 for discussions about penal servitude. Jones states that penal servitude was given in exceptional circumstances, and gives examples of a poisoning case and the theft of five pounds of pork; Jones, *Crime in Nineteenth-Century Wales*, p. 231.
82 *NWE*, 15 March 1870.
83 *NWE*, 5 July 1870.
84 *NWE*, 15 March 1870.
85 Data from B. Owen, *Transportation by Montgomeryshire Courts, 1788–1868* (Llanidloes, 2003), pp. 86–213. Owen gives data from 1788, but the earliest data has not been used here as thoughts about transportation

being a substitute for execution may have affected the committing magistrates' thinking (no person was hanged in England except for murder after 1838; Bentley, *English Criminal Justice*, p. 13). The analysis here also does not use data originally given as penal servitude but which subsequently became transportation. See Jones, *Crime in Nineteenth-Century Wales*, pp. 227–9 for his discussion on the implications of transportation for Wales, and D. Beddoe, *Welsh Convict Women* (Cowbridge, 1979).

86 G. Pavlich, 'The emergence of habitual criminals in nineteenth-century Britain', *Journal of Theoretical and Philosophical Criminology*, 2 (2010), 8–11; V. Bailey, 'The fabrication of deviance: "dangerous classes" and "criminal classes" in Victorian England', in J. Rule and R. Malcolmson (eds), *Protest and Survival: The Historical Experience; Essays for E. P. Thompson* (London, 1993), pp. 221–56.

87 *NWE*, 25 October 1870.

88 Pavlich, 'The emergence', p. 10. The editorial appeared in *The Times*, 10 March 1869, p. 9.

89 For discussion see Godfrey, *Serious Offenders*, pp. 190–6.

90 Peter King makes a comment about this in P. J. R. King, 'Decision-makers and decision-making in the English criminal law, 1750–1800', *Historical Journal*, 27 (1984), 42.

91 *NWE*, 15 November 1870.

92 *NWE*, 5 July 1869.

93 *NWE*, 23 February 1869.

94 *NWE*, 16 March 1869.

95 An appeal hearing at Mold Crown Court, 16 August 2013, was allowed to take place partly because the convicting Bench had not given their reasons for the conviction. The appeal was upheld.

CHAPTER 6

1 See M. J. Wiener, 'Judges v. jurors: courtroom tensions in murder trials and the law of criminal responsibility in nineteenth-century England', *Law and History Review*, 17 (1999), 468.

2 The etymology of the word 'stereotyping' is given in J. Rendall, *Women in an Industrializing Society* (Oxford, 1990), p. 65: 'In the printing industry ... taking a mould of sections of type for mass production'.

3 The Church of England was the established church in Wales until the end of March 1920. Personal correspondence with Thomas Glyn Watkin (6 February 2017). Calculations made from the 1851 Religious Census show that at least 30 per cent of the county population were practising Nonconformists, whereas around 11 to 18 per cent were practising Anglicans (Census of Great Britain, 1851, Religious worship. England and Wales, 89, pp. 126 and 127). In her analysis of the bloody events in Paris at the time of the Revolution, Kate Berridge describes royal pageantry as spectacle of power, reinforcing the *ancien régime* of rule by a tiny, unrepresentative minority; K. Berridge, *Waxing Mythical* (London, 2006), p. 120.

⁴   *NWE*, 23 March 1869. One analysis of the religious service is that of Max
    Weber who commented: '… every physical contact with a member of
    any caste that is considered lower by the members of a higher caste is
    considered as making for a ritualistic impurity and to be a stigma which
    must be expiated by a religious act'; M. Weber, 'Class, status, party', in
    R. S. Neale (ed.), *History and Class* (Oxford, 1983), p. 65. There is no
    evidence here, however, that this is the reason for the pre-assizes service.
⁵   Originally a phrase used in the novel *Sybil, or The Two Nations* by Disraeli
    to describe the rich and the poor; B. Disraeli, *Sybil or the Two Nations*
    (1845; London, 1927). Used by David Ward to describe the residential
    patterns in nineteenth-century Leeds created by class difference; D.
    Ward, 'Environs and neighbours in the two nations: residential differ-
    entiation in mid nineteenth-century Leeds', *Journal of Historical Geog-
    raphy*, 6 (1980), 133.
⁶   *NWE*, 22 March 1870.
⁷   *NWE*, 17 March 1874.
⁸   *NWE*, 4 July 1876. The legislation referred to is the 1870 Education Act,
    which required local authorities to provide education for children aged
    5–13 years. See W. H. G. Armytage, 'The 1870 education act', *British
    Journal of Educational Studies*, 18 (1970), 121–33.
⁹   Lucia Zedner writes of nineteenth-century prison reformers looking
    back nostalgically to a time when religious faith, deference and commu-
    nity kept each in his place; L. Zedner, *Women, Crime and Custody in Victo-
    rian England* (Oxford, 1991), p. 96. The idea of the classes being kept
    separate was clear in an 1830 advertisement for a touring exhibition of
    Madame Tussaud's: 'arrangements [have been made] to admit THE
    WORKING CLASSES for Half Price during the time the exhibition
    remains … In this arrangement, sufficient time will be given for both
    classes to view the collection without interfering with each other';
    Berridge, *Waxing Mythical*, p. 22 (upper-case letters as in the original
    text). Note that here there was no recognition of a middle class.
¹⁰ The records of the spring 1875 assizes are missing. Spring 1874 was a
    maiden assize.
¹¹ Humphreys found that in Montgomeryshire during the previous
    century, assault accounted for 53 per cent of persons being prosecuted
    at great sessions, whereas property offences accounted for only 28.5 per
    cent. It has been said that industrialisation led to an increase in theft as
    people acquired goods; M. Humphreys, 'Harmony, crime and order',
    in *The Crisis of Community* (Cardiff, 1996), p. 225.
¹² *NWE*, 26 July 1870.
¹³ *NWE*, 25 July 1871.
¹⁴ Newtown solicitor William Beecham, and London barrister, magistrate
    and later MP, Morgan Lloyd.
¹⁵ D. Bentley, *English Criminal Justice in the Nineteenth Century* (London
    1998), p. 38. The prosecutor would have to present his case to the
    grand jury, with witnesses if any, and they would consider the bill in the
    usual way, finding a true bill or no true bill. If a true bill was found, the
    first the accused would know about it was when he was arrested on a

warrant, and he would have to stand trial without knowing anything about the evidence against him.

[16] This supports Woodward's comment that a belief in urban areas as nurseries of crime, offering plentiful targets and anonymity to opportunist thieves, should be treated with caution; N. Woodward, 'Burglary in Wales', *Welsh History Review*, 24 (2008), 65. The one burglary in a borough town was a case in which the burglar had a specific reason to steal from one particular house; *NWE*, 23 March 1869.

[17] The case of Edward Edwards, *NWE*, 18 October 1870, and George Wood and William Johnson, *NWE*, 22 March 1870.

[18] See for example Bill to Provide for the Appointment of Public Prosecutors, 1854 (15), *V*, 571; Bill for the Appointment of a Private Prosecutor, 1872 (28), *IV*, 583. When victims had to be prosecutors they might be intimidated or bought off; civil claims might be pursued through the criminal courts; cases might collapse for lack of funds; P. Rock, 'Victims, prosecutors and the state in nineteenth-century England and Wales', *Criminal Justice*, 4 (2004), 338. See also comments in B. S. Godfrey, 'Changing prosecution practices and their impact on crime figures, 1857–1940', *British Journal of Criminology*, 48 (2008), 175.

[19] D. Lemmings, 'Criminal trial procedure in eighteenth-century England: the impact of lawyers', *Journal of Legal History*, 26 (2005), pp. 73–4.

[20] Lemmings, 'Criminal trial procedure', p. 80. Bentley reports that there were countless cases in which judges could be found directing juries that guilt had to be found beyond reasonable doubt, e.g. *R. v. White*, 1865; Bentley, *English Criminal Justice*, p. 205 (footnote 3).

[21] Lemmings, 'Criminal trial procedure', p. 81; R. W. Ireland, 'Putting oneself in whose country? Carmarthenshire juries in the mid nineteenth century', in T. G. Watkin (ed), *Legal Wales, Its Past, Its Future* (Cardiff, 2001), pp. 70–3.

[22] D. Phillips, *Crime and Authority in Victorian England: The Black Country, 1835–1860* (London, 1997), p. 119.

[23] *NWE*, 25 July 1871.

[24] *NWE*, 4 July 1876.

[25] Bentley, *English Criminal Justice*, p. 148.

[26] *NWE*, 27 July 1869. William Wynn Ffoulkes had been called to the bar in 1847. In 1875 he was to become a county court judge on the Chester circuit. National censuses, 1861–1901; memorial inscription viewed at *http://members.tripod.com/caryl_williams/index-4.html* (3 November 2011).

[27] Of the thirty-seven females in the dock pleading not guilty, twenty-five (68 per cent) were undefended. This was a much higher proportion than males (47 out of 145 not-guilty pleaders, 32 per cent).

[28] *NWE*, 26 July 1870, 19 March 1872.

[29] B. Weinberger, 'The police and the public in mid-nineteenth-century Warwickshire', in V. Bailey (ed.), *Policing and Punishment in Nineteenth-Century Britain* (London, 1981), p. 85. For a comparison to modern public reaction to undercover policing see R. Evans and P. Lewis, *Undercover: The True Story of Britain's Secret Police* (London, 2013).

30 Biography of Channell, *DNB*
31 Peter King discusses how a judge's individual character and attitudes were important; P. King, *Crime, Justice and Discretion in England, 1740– 1820* (Oxford, 2000), p. 224.
32 Bentley explains that an officer's 'natural ambition to convict' meant that there was a fear of invented confessions, and twisting or distorting of a suspect's words; Bentley, *English Criminal Justice*, p. 231. The police also regularly used physical violence to control situations or to informally punish people they felt deserved a beating rather than arrest; B. S. Godfrey and P. Lawrence, *Crime and Justice, 1750–1950* (Cullompton, 2005), p. 102. See the Christmas street music letter, Chapter 3 of the present work.
33 *NWE*, 23 March 1869.
34 S. D'Cruze, *Crimes of Outrage: Sex, Violence and Victorian Working Women* (London, 1998), p. 149.
35 Zedner, *Women, Crime and Custody*, pp. 11–26.
36 Bentley, *English Criminal Justice*, p. 146.
37 The view of women being innately non-criminal was strongly propounded throughout the Victorian period and evidence included observations that women were less competitive than men and more likely to be religiously inclined. Zedner, *Women, Crime and Custody*, p. 23.
38 A. B. Rodrick, 'Only a newspaper metaphor: crime reports, class conflict and social criticism in two Victorian newspapers', *Victorian Periodicals Review*, 29 (1996), 5. See also J. Coleman, 'Incorrigible offenders: media representations of female habitual criminals in the late-Victorian and Edwardian press', *Media History*, 22 (2016), 143–58.
39 William Henry Davies, traced through the censuses. His brother Edward was living in Aberystwyth in 1901. They both attended Chester Street Grammar School, Wrexham, in the 1850s.
40 D'Cruze, *Crimes of Outrage*, p. 149.
41 *NWE*, 4 April 1876.
42 Mytton knew his place: in an address to the crowd on his return from honeymoon he said, 'The welcome you have this day given us is an assurance that there is a latent bond of sympathy existing amongst all classes in the neighbourhood, which only requires an occasion like the present to cause it to burst forth'; *NWE*, 18 March 1873.
43 The scandal first appeared in February 1875 when Mytton was taken to the County Court by two Shropshire nurserymen. They claimed £30 payment for garden trees ordered by Miss Jones, described as the housekeeper of one of Mytton's properties. She had given birth a year after being installed in this house on Mytton's estate but he denied being the father of the child although he admitted being a regular visitor to the hall; 'A Montgomeryshire magistrate and his dairymaid', *Western Mail*, 25 February 1875.
44 The Prisoner's Counsel Act of 1836 recognised the right of a defendant in a felony case to legal representation. See C. C. Griffiths, 'The Prisoner's Counsel Act, 1836: doctrine, advocacy and the criminal trial', *Law, Crime and History*, 2 (2014), 28–47.

[45] See a succinct comparison of civil and criminal law in S. Hester and P. Eglin, *A Sociology of Crime* (London, 1992), p. 170.

[46] P. Rock, 'Victims, prosecutors and the state in nineteenth-century England and Wales', *Criminal Justice*, 4 (2004), 331–54. At the end of the trial the judge made the point that this was a case of civil and not criminal liability. There is a question therefore, why it ever came to appear in a criminal court.

[47] Mytton had been present in the grand juries on the occasions when Barons Channell and Piggott addressed them regarding their roles with respect to the lower classes.

[48] J. Minkes, 'Wales and the Bloody Code', *Welsh History Review*, 22 (2006), 696.

[49] Bentley describes how the selection of trial jurors could be challenged; Bentley, *English Criminal Justice*, pp. 95–6; but it appears that grand jurors could not be challenged.

[50] Miss Jones was the stepdaughter of a farmer who owned his own land. He paid the rent that was owing to Mytton, so may well have funded her defence. The solicitor recruited Shrewsbury barrister Charles Chandler.

[51] For the full story see R. Jones, 'A Montgomeryshire magistrate and his dairymaid', *Mont. Colls*, 101 (2013), 101–8. Some people might have said that Mytton's actions in bringing the charge were verging on the criminal or, at least, bullying. Criminal theory states that crimes of the powerful are committed to enhance competitive advantage, with the individuals having access to superior social resources. This can be seen in the *Mytton v. Jones* case. See R. White and F. Haines, *Crime and Criminology* (1998; Oxford, 2002), p. 107. Note that the sending in of bailiffs unannounced has been prohibited by a statutory procedure that came into force in England and Wales in April 2014. Landlords must now serve at least seven days' notice before entering a commercial property. It has been said that this new procedure is 'not welcomed by commercial landlords'; 'New rent rules to impact on commercial landlords', *Agricultural Group News*, 1 (2014), 4. Mytton claimed that Miss Jones had taken on Trefnanney Hall to run as a business – a hostel for fishermen.

[52] 'Singular case of assault upon a tradesman', *Liverpool Mercury*, 24 December 1868. In 'Landed estates court', *Freeman's Journal and Daily Commercial Advertiser*, 29 April 1876, Nolan is listed as the lessee of land worth £500 in County Sligo.

[53] 'Welsh assize cases', *Liverpool Mercury*, 18 March 1869; *NWE*, 23 March 1869.

[54] Crimes involving Irish people were inevitably interpreted in British newspapers as a reflection of national character; C. Conley, *Certain Other Countries: Homicide, Gender, and National Identity in Late Nineteenth-Century England, Ireland, Scotland, and Wales* (Columbus, 2007), p. 43. Conley describes a violent offence resulting from a nose insult on p. 74.

[55] Golan discusses this in T. Golan, 'The history of scientific expert testimony in the English courtroom', *Science in Context*, 12 (1999), 1–12, and

names the case of *Folkes v. Chadd* in 1782 as the first instances of expert opinion being taken from a person who was not present at the time of the event. King describes how hearsay evidence was rejected earlier in the eighteenth century; P. King, *Crime, Justice and Discretion in England, 1740–1820* (Oxford, 2000), p. 225.

56 Golan, 'History of scientific expert testimony', p. 15. The midwife's evidence was likely to be brief. The transcribed examination of Mary Ranger, midwife, who appeared at the infanticide trial of Sarah Russell can be found in 'The Victorian medico-legal autopsy', *www.casebook.org. html* (6 January 2011), which shows that her testimony was to establish that the woman charged was the mother, and to describe the child and mother immediately after the birth. It was the surgeon who followed who was asked about medical details and his opinion about the cause of death. Landsman gives a league table of the medical professions, with physicians at the top and midwives at the bottom; S. Landsman, 'One hundred years of rectitude: medical witnesses at the Old Bailey, 1717–1817', *Law and History Review*, 16 (1998), 449. See comments about strategies of professionalisation ensuring that expertise was consolidated in the hands of males: D'Cruze and L. A. Jackson, *Women, Crime and Justice in England since 1660* (Basingstoke, 2009), p. 106.

57 Landsman, 'One hundred years', pp. 449–54.

58 R. W. Ireland, 'Perhaps my mother murdered me: child death and the law in late Victorian Carmarthenshire', in *Communities and Courts in Britain, 1150–1900* (London, 1997), pp. 234–6.

59 Bentley, *English Criminal Justice*, p. 38. See also E. T. Hurren, 'Remaking the medico-legal scene: a social history of the late-Victorian coroner in Oxford', *Journal of the History of Medicine and Allied Sciences*, 65 (2010), pp. 207–52; B. Heathcote, *Viewing the Lifeless Body: A Coroner and his Inquests held in Nottinghamshire Public Houses during the Nineteenth Century, 1828 to 1866* (Nottingham 2006); P. Fisher, 'An object of ambition? The office and role of the coroner in two Midland counties, 1751–1888' (unpublished Ph.D. thesis, University of Leicester, 2003). See N. Woodward, 'Infanticide in Wales, 1730–1830', *Welsh History Review*, 23 (2007), 119–23 for a discussion of the defendant's experiences in court.

60 *NWE*, 14 March 1871. The inquest on this case was reported in *NWE*, 8 November 1870.

61 A murder charge in the case of death of an infant often failed, but the jury could subsequently return a verdict of concealment of birth if the prosecution could prove that the child was existing independently of the mother at the time of death; H. Marland, 'Getting away with murder? Puerperal insanity, infanticide and the defence plea', in M. Jackson (ed.), *Infanticide: Historical Perspectives on Child Murders and Concealment, 1550–2000* (Aldershot, 2002), p. 168. See also H. Marland, *Dangerous Motherhood: Insanity and Childbirth in Victorian Britain* (Basingstoke, 2004) and G. K. Behlmer, 'Deadly motherhood: infanticide and medical opinion in mid-Victorian England', *Journal of Historical Medicine and Allied Sciences*, 34 (1979), 403–27.

[62] Margaret Arnot describes how potential witnesses in neonatal murder cases sometimes 'chose' not to see, and illustrates this with a case very similar to the Yearsley one in M. L. Arnot, 'Understanding women committing new-born child murder in Victorian England', in S. D'Cruze, *Everyday Violence in Britain, 1850–1950: Gender and Class* (2000; Harlow, 2004), pp. 55–69.

[63] Ann Williams is shown on the 1871 census living in one of the crowded passages in town called Mermaid Passage. Her neighbours were a mix of skilled workers such as tailor and carpenter, and unskilled charwomen and labourers.

[64] Barrett was also a Welshpool magistrate.

[65] Landsman, 'One hundred years', p. 476.

[66] Landsman, 'One hundred years', p. 467.

[67] Mayor, magistrate and surgeon; one of the extended family that included coroner R. D. Harrison; clerk of the peace J. P. Harrison; solicitor G. D. Harrison and Capt. Mytton.

[68] Montgomeryshire Jury Book, 1871–4, NLW, MSS 21843–4 E.

[69] For a comparison to eighteenth-century petty juries in Montgomeryshire and Essex see Humphreys, *Crisis*, p. 242 and King, *Crime, Justice and Discretion*, p. 243 respectively. For a comparison to nineteenth-century Staffordshire see Phillips, *Crime and Authority*, p. 106

[70] Bentley, *English Criminal Justice*, p. 92. Lewis Carroll put a lengthy satirical scene in *Alice in Wonderland*, taking up a whole chapter, in which he portrayed an incompetent jury. 'Who stole the tarts?', in L. Carroll, *Alice in Wonderland* (London, 1865).

[71] C. Emsley, *Crime and Society in England, 1750–1900* (1987; Harlow, 2005), p. 202.

[72] R. W. Ireland, 'Putting oneself on whose country?', pp. 70–1.

[73] In 1755, the Earl of Powis brought a prosecution against eight men for stealing and receiving lead from the roof of Powis Castle. The petty jury acquitted them when a flaw in the indictment was brought to their attention; Humphreys, *Crisis*, p. 244. In his contradiction of David Hay's argument that the legal system was a ruling-class conspiracy, Langbein writes: 'If I were going to organize a ruling-class conspiracy to use the criminal law to terrorize the lower orders, I would not interpose autonomous bodies of non-conspirators like the petty juries'; J. H. Langbein, 'Albion's fatal flaws', *Past and Present*, 98 (1983), 107.

[74] Zedner, *Women, Crime and Custody*, p. 29.

[75] Ireland, 'Perhaps my mother murdered me', pp. 236–8.

[76] R. Davies, *Secret Sins* (Cardiff, 1996), p. 174.

[77] Humphreys makes the comment: 'Of greater significance [than the grand jury] to the processes of trial and verdict was the petty or trial jury who decided on the guilt or innocence of the indicted'; Humphreys, *Crisis*, p. 242.

[78] Known as Baron Bramwell because he was a baron of the court of the exchequer; Bentley, *English Criminal Justice*, p. 65.

[79] King describes how, if the crime was one the judge considered must be suppressed, his neutrality might soon evaporate; King, *Crime, Justice and*

Discretion, p. 224. Note also that although Langbein states that having a jury removed a judge from the adjudication, he also describes 'progressive dethronement' of the jury via judges' directions; J. H. Langbein, 'The bifurcation and the bench: the influence of the jury on English conceptions of the judiciary', in P. Brand and J. Getzler (eds), *Judges and Judging in the History of the Common Law and Civil Law: From Antiquity to Modern Times* (Cambridge, 2012), pp. 77–80. When it was concealment of birth, Baron Bramwell was particularly strong-minded. He wrote in a letter that he 'had no doubt the legislature meant the judges to give a very severe sentence when there had been foul play with the child, and a nominal sentence when there was no suspicion of anything wrong. But the judges won't be parties to this kind of fraud – one can call it nothing less'; letter from Bramwell to Frederick Pollock, quoted in T. Ward, 'Legislating for human nature: legal responses to infanticide', in Jackson, *Infanticide*, p. 256.

[80] *The Exeter Flying Post*, 15 March 1871. King mentions a particularly sarcastic comment made by Judge Carter at Essex Lent assizes in 1739; King, *Crime, Justice and Discretion*, p. 224.

[81] Reprinted in *The Liverpool Mercury*, 16 March 1871. The Tarpey case was a diamond robbery that took place in London in 1870. The trial took place at the end of February 1871. One of the two accused was a young woman with a baby. She pleaded guilty but was deemed by the jury to be not guilty, and released. This trial took place at the Central Criminal Court before the recorder. The judge on the rota for attendance during the week was Bramwell; *The Times*, 21 February 1871.

[82] *NWE*, 21 March 1871. The comments of the judge were similar to those made by the Anglican commissioners who wrote the notorious reports on education, which became known as 'The Treachery of the Blue Books'. For a discussion on how the commissioners used language to establish superiority and to communicate their view of themselves as authoritative men see G. T. Roberts, 'Under the hatches: English parliamentary commissioners' views of the people and language of mid nineteenth-century Wales', in B. Schwartz (ed.), *The Expansion of the English Race: Race, Ethnicity and Cultural History* (London, 1996), pp. 171–97. The education reports were published in 1847, within the lifetime of many of the people attending the assizes during the period studied. 'Impression ... made by counsel' could be a reference to the performances made by counsel in court. Barristers knew they could acquire fame through their performances in court, and, in fact, barristers attended stage school to acquire presentation skills, and various bars from around the country had traditions of putting on plays. The public treated the court as a theatre, too, and it was not until 1860 that entrance fees to court were abolished; J. R. Lewis, *The Victorian Bar* (London 1982), pp. 13–15. There are descriptions of barristers' performances in D. Pugsley, 'The Western Circuit', *Bracton Law Journal*, 26 (1994), 43–54.

[83] Biography of Bramwell at *http://en.wikipedia.org* (1 November 2014).

[84] Landsman, 'One hundred years', 486.

85 *NWE*, 18 March 1873.

86 Although the judge referred to Edwards and Huddart as doctors, in the censuses both men gave their occupation as surgeon, normally addressed as 'Mr' (doctor of medicine, master of surgery). Doctors were university-trained scholars and expected to employ an analytical approach to deciphering the internal ills of their patients, while surgeons concentrated on external injuries, wounds and conditions amenable to manual or operative intervention; Landsman, 'One hundred years', p. 452; W. Byrnum, 'When did medical practitioners start to be called "doctor"?', *BBC History* (July 2013), 93.

87 J. H. Warner, 'Therapeutic explanation and the Edinburgh bloodletting controversy: two perspectives on the medical meaning of science in the mid-nineteenth century', *Medical History*, 24 (1980), 244–5.

88 *ME*, 19 March 1878.

89 K. D. M. Snell, *Annals of the Labouring Poor: Social Change and Agrarian England, 1660–1900* (1985; Cambridge, 1987), pp. 126 and 193. Osborne, however, has linked the pattern of poaching in the winter months to the availability, maturity and marketability of the animals, and although he accepts the economic and social motivations for the offence, he notes that poachers usually were skilled workers, rather than poor agricultural labourers, who mostly viewed poaching as a sport. H. Osborne, 'The seasonality of nineteenth-century poaching', *Agricultural History Review*, 45 (2000), pp. 28 and 34. Out of 267 offenders discussed by him, 31 per cent were general labourers, 20 per cent craftsmen, 17 per cent miners, 4 per cent railway workers, 4 per cent farmers/farm workers, and the remainder had a range of occupations including domestic servants and retailers.

90 T. Shakesheff, *Rural Conflict, Crime and Protest: Herefordshire, 1800–1860* (Woodbridge, 2003), p. 163.

91 John Archer has moved Shakesheff's and Snell's debates on by identifying armed night poachers as a particular breed, tending to be canal men, colliers and weavers, who were very likely to commit other offences; J. E. Archer, 'Poaching gangs and violence', *British Journal of Criminology*, 39 (1999), 29.

92 D. J. V. Jones, *Crime in Nineteenth-Century Wales* (Cardiff, 1992), p. 79.

93 Jones found that other crimes of a sexual nature such as bestiality or sodomy rarely appeared. In this study, there was one case of an 'unnatural offence', but this was dismissed, with no details except the defendant's name reported in the newspaper; *NWE*, 21 July 1874. Phillips found that the reticence of newspapers in nineteenth-century Staffordshire in reporting details of sexual offences was especially marked in cases 'of an unnatural nature'; Phillips, *Crime and Authority*, p. 269. See Phillips, *Crime and Authority*, p. 271 for a list of sentences given for rape convictions.

94 *NWE*, 27 July 1869, 14 March 1871, 18 March 1873 and 4 April 1876. Conley found that in nineteenth-century Kent 40 per cent of rape cases ended with a conviction, whereas in all other criminal cases it was 85 per cent; C. Conley, 'Rape and justice in Victorian England', *Victorian Studies*, 29 (1986), 521.

[95] The National Archives have assize records for the Chester and North Wales circuit from the 1870s but they are mostly from Chester assizes with a few from Caernarfonshire and Flintshire but none from Montgomeryshire; thus Professor Johnson's report no longer exists; TNA, ASSI (65/8, 65/9 and 65/10).

[96] *NWE*, 4 April 1876.

[97] The woman at the centre of the case in which John Pilot accused Sergeant Ross of perjury (see Chapter 3), left the area after a preliminary hearing before magistrates, in which intimate details were discussed and widely reported.

[98] *NWE*, 18 March 1873.

[99] Emsley, *Crime and Society in England*, p. 185.

[100] Conley, 'Rape and justice', pp. 526–30.

[101] S. D'Cruze, 'Sex, violence and local courts', *British Journal of Criminology*, 39 (1999), 39.

[102] J. H. Langbein, *The Origins of the Adversary Criminal Trial* (Oxford, 2003), pp. 106–7.

[103] Langbein, *Origins*, p. 110.

[104] D. Lemmings, 'Criminal trial procedure in eighteenth-century England', *Journal of Legal History*, 26 (2005), 73.

[105] Bentley, *English Criminal Justice*, p. 97.

[106] See Bentley, *English Criminal Justice*, pp. 98–101 for information about the sorts of men who became barristers, their backgrounds and training etc.

[107] *NWE*, 4 July 1871.

[108] Possibly a reference to Jones's 'strong denouncing of the injustice'. Note that this courtroom scene was one of the platforms where she could get away with shouting at (and possibly being abusive to) upper-class people.

[109] *NWE*, 4 July 1871.

[110] In King's study of pardons granted after Assize convictions in the two years 1787 and 1790, he found a variety of factors affecting pardoning decisions taken. These included previous good character, youth, old age, respectability and insanity. Sometimes it could be because the conviction was against evidence where it was clear that the prosecution was malicious, but never because the evidence presented had been appropriate for a different charge; King, *Crime, Justice and Discretion*, pp. 298–301.

[111] In contradiction to the barristers' claim, according to Bentley, solicitors retained their rights at four (unnamed) county sessions until the beginning of the twentieth century; Bentley, *English Criminal Justice*, p. 98.

[112] Lemmings discusses how barristers could not simply wait for work but had to actively look for it. They sometimes found business by creating and exploiting connections; D. Lemmings, *Gentlemen and Barristers* (Oxford, 1990), p. 113. Changing social and economic conditions encouraged individualists, and some barristers quickly took work wherever it was offered. Lemmings argued that these were often men from unconventional backgrounds and cites William Murray, the future Lord

Mansfield, who was Scottish and had benefited from a broad liberal education; Lemmings, *Gentlemen and Barristers*, p. 176. One is reminded of some famous Welsh barristers including Sir Ellis Jones, Ellis Griffiths and Sir Thomas Artemus Jones, *http://wbo.llgc.org.uk/en/s-elli-jon-1860. html*; *http://yba.llgc.org.uk/en/s2-jone-art-1871.html* (both 13 January 2012). See also T. A. Jones, *Without my Wig* (Blaenau Ffestiniog, 1944).

113 *NWE*, 24 October 1871.

114 J. Gerrard and V. Parrott, 'Craft, profession and middle-class identity: solicitors and gas engineers, c. 1850–1914', in A. Kidd and D. Nicholls, *The Making of the British Middle Class* (Stroud, 1998), pp. 15–51.

115 S. D'Cruze, *Crimes of Outrage*. See also the study of prostitute Charlotte Walker's repeated appearances and successful self-defences at the Old Bailey during the later eighteenth century, in M. Clayton, 'The life and times of Charlotte Walker, prostitute and pickpocket', *The London Journal*, 33 (2008), 3–19.

CHAPTER 7

1 Lynn Mackay investigated this using data from the late eighteenth century, and argued that differing patterns made a distinct difference; L. MacKay, 'Why they stole: women in the Old Bailey, 1779–1789', *Journal of Social History*, 32 (1999), 623–39. Note that the theory of criminological modernisation, which interprets the effects of socio-economic change on crime, includes consideration of changing opportunity; Council of Europe, *Crime and Economy: Reports Presented to the 11th Criminological Colloquium, 1994* (Strasbourg, 1995), pp.17–20.

2 For discussions on attitudes see S. Howard, *Studies in Welsh History: Law and Disorder in Early-Modern Wales, c. 1660–1730* (Cardiff, 2008) and S. Howard, 'Crime, communities and authority in early-modern Wales: Denbighshire, 1660–1713' (unpublished Ph.D. thesis, University of Wales, Aberystwyth, 2003).

3 D. V. J. Jones, *Crime in Nineteenth-Century Wales* (Cardiff, 1992), p. 32. See also V. A. C. Gattrell, 'The decline of theft and violence in Victorian and Edwardian England', in V. A. C. Gattrell, B. Lenman and G. Parker (eds), *Crime and the Law: The Social History of Crime in Western Europe since 1500* (London, 1980), pp. 238–370. Crime was declining over much of Europe at this time. See European Committee on Crime Problems, *Crime and Economy: Reports Presented to the 11th Criminological Colloquium, 1994* (Strasbourg, 1995), p. 25

4 See Jones, *Crime in Nineteenth Century*, pp. 37–45 for a detailed discussion.

5 C. Emsley, *Crime and Society in England, 1750–1900* (1987; Harlow, 2005), p. 114.

6 Thomas Plint (1851) quoted in Emsley, *Crime and Society*, p. 114. 'Flying' to urban areas may have been a reference to the new fashion for railway transport, described as 'railway mania', see 'Timeline of UK Railways', *www.stationbuffet.co.uk/history4.html* (5 August 2012). 'Flying' was later to be incorporated into the locomotive name *Flying Scotsman* when that

engine started travelling the London to Edinburgh route; *Flying Scotsman*, viewed at *www. bbc.co.uk/ahistoryoftheworld* (5 August 2012). The railways provided access to criminal opportunities and a quick getaway. See R. Ireland, 'An increasing mass of heathens in the bosom of a Christian land: the railway and crime in the nineteenth century', *Continuity and Change*, 12 (1997), 55–78 for a discussion on railway crime and increased mobility.

7 Brereton quoted in Emsley, *Crime and Society in England*, p. 115.

8 Reach quoted in Emsley, *Crime and Society in England*, footnote 3, p. 136. Biography of Reach, *DNB*.

9 Emsley, *Crime and Society in England*, p. 120 and footnote 28, p. 139.

10 Jones, *Crime in Nineteenth Century Wales*, pp. 171–6.

11 In cases where the defendant pleaded guilty, no trial followed and therefore the exact location of the offence is unclear. The data for this analysis are from the forty-nine cases where the woman pleaded not guilty, so that a trial ensued and more details were given.

12 MacKay, 'Why they stole', p. 629.

13 *NWE*, 5 July 1870. The present study found allegations of sexual assault in the workplace, private homes, on the street and in isolated areas. The lone woman was clearly vulnerable in any place. Louise Jackson briefly discusses the relation of social space and sexual assault in L. A. Jackson, 'Women professionals and the regulation of violence in interwar Britain', in D'Cruze, *Everyday Violence in Britain*, pp. 119–35. D'Cruze herself devotes a section to space in S. D'Cruze, *Crimes of Outrage: Sex, Violence and Victorian Working Women* (London, 1998), pp. 30–6. See also R. J. Barrow, 'Rape on the Railway: Women, Safety, and Moral Panic in Victorian Newspapers', *Journal of Victorian Culture*, 20 (2015), 341–56.

14 *ME*, 12 March 1878.

15 *NWE*, 6 July 1869.

16 *NWE*, 8 July 1873.

17 *NWE*, 22 August 1873.

18 J. Kermode, and G. Walker, *Women, Crime and the Courts in Early-Modern England* (London, 1994), p. 87.

19 R. Wynter, 'Good in all respects: appearance and dress at Staffordshire County Lunatic Asylum, 1818–54', *History of Psychiatry*, 22 (2011), 40–1.

20 *NWE*, 10 March 1874.

21 Information given in Ann Lloyd's witness statement, PCA, M/Q/SR, midsummer 1869, and the deposition of Constable John Gregory, PCA, M/Q/SR, Easter 1869.

22 For comments see M. Bellanta, 'Looking flash: disreputable women's dress and "modernity", 1870–1910', *History Workshop Journal*, 78 (2014), 58–81.

23 E. Wilson and L. Taylor, *Through the Looking Glass: A History of Dress from 1860 to the Present Day* (London, 1989), pp. 21–2.

24 B. Lemire, 'The theft of clothes and popular consumerism in early-modern England', *Journal of Social History*, 24 (1990), 256.

25 Exhibition in Newtown Flannel Museum, summer 2011; C. Rose and V. Richmond, *Clothing, Society and Culture in Nineteenth-Century Britain* (London, 2010), 1, p. 129.

26 Rose and Richmond, *Clothing*, pp. 141–2.

27 A. Toplis, 'A stolen garment or a reasonable purchase? The male consumer and the illicit second-hand clothing market in the first half of the nineteenth century', in J. Stobart and I. Van Damme (eds), *Modernity and the Second-Hand Trade: European Consumption Cultures and Practices, 1700–1900* (Basingstoke, 2011), pp. 59–60.

28 Wilson, *Through the Looking Glass*, p. 26.

29 'Parramatta', *www.austehc.unimelb.edu.au/tia/273.html* (23 March 2012). Zedner writes about the Parramatta tweed factory in L. Zedner, *Women, Crime and Custody* (Oxford, 1991), p. 175. The factory, ironically, was operated by female convicts. See also D. Beddoe, *Welsh Convict Women: A Study of Women Transported from Wales to Australia, 1787–1852* (Cowbridge, 1979), pp. 135–42.

30 See T. C. Whitlock, *Crime, Gender and Consumer Culture in Nineteenth-Century England* (Farnham, 2005) for discussions on nineteenth-century consumerism encouraging thefts from retail outlets, especially market stalls and bazaars.

31 *NWE*, 11 March 1873.

32 G. Jenkins, *Life in the Countryside: The Photographer in Rural Wales, 1850–2010* (Talybont, 2010). See also K. Navickas, 'Political clothing and adornment in England, 1740–1840', *Journal of British Studies*, 69 (2010), 540–5.

33 See for example J. Laver, *Costume through the Ages* (London, 1963).

34 *Peterson's Magazine*, February 1875 viewed at *http://dressmakingresearch.com/petersons_overskirt_1875.htm* (15 June 2012).

35 *NWE*, 4 April 1876.

36 *NWE*, 4 July 1871.

37 *ME*, 12 March 1878.

38 D. Phillips, *Crime and Authority in Victorian England: The Black Country, 1835–1860* (London, 1997), p. 198.

39 For a comment on this issue see Jones, *Crime in Nineteenth Century Wales*, p. 127. See also B. S. Godfrey and J. P. Locker, 'The nineteenth-century decline of custom, and its impact on theories of workplace theft and white collar crime', *Northern History*, 38 (2001), 261–73.

40 Walker also found that livestock featured much more heavily as a proportion of men's thefts than women's; G. Walker, *Crime, Gender and Social Order* (Cambridge, 2003), p. 162. Godfrey identifies reduced opportunity as a reason for women's smaller range of crimes; B. S. Godfrey, D. J. Cox and S. Farrall, *Criminal Lives: Family Life, Employment and Offending* (Oxford, 2007), p. 36.

41 Godfrey discusses gendered opportunities in *Criminal Lives*, pp. 35–8.

42 See for example, Alice Roberts's theft of a bag; *NWE*, 22 October 1878; Richard Trow's and Edward Phillips's pickpocketing activities; *NWE*, 9 January 1872 and 6 July 1875 respectively.

43 *ME*, 6 July 1869.

44 *NWE*, 11 January 1870.
45 Walker, *Crime*, p. 179.
46 *NWE*: Susannah Francis, 24 October 1871; Jane Jones, 14 March 1871; Frances Evans, 22 October 1872; Fanny Robinson, Mary Edwards, 8 July 1873; Jane Jones, 11 January 1876; Elizabeth Williams, 9 July 1878; Elizabeth Lewis, 12 March 1878.
47 *NWE*: Thomas Vaughan, 16 March 1869; William Jones, 12 January 1869; Edward Jones, 26 October 1869; Thomas Brown, 6 July 1869; Moses Williams, 6 July 1869; George Middleton, 10 January 1870; Edward Mason, 14 March 1871; Thomas Davies, 9 July 1872; Thomas Turner, 11 March 1873; Edward Hughes, 27 October 1874; Edward Jones, 12 January 1875; David Thomas, 19 October 1875; Tudor Williams, 12 January 1875; Thomas Jones, 11 January 1876; John Jones, 11 January 1876; Edward Jones, 11 January 1876; Arthur Williams, 4 April 1876. For background information see B. S. Godfrey, 'Law, factory discipline and theft: the impact of the factory on workplace appropriation in mid to late nineteenth-century Yorkshire', *British Journal of Criminology*, 39 (1999), 56–71.
48 *NWE*, 6 July 1869 and 25 October 1870.
49 *NWE*, 15 March 1870.
50 *NWE*, 7 January 1873
51 Brian Short also identifies the mobility of males in B. Short, 'Environmental politics, custom and personal testimony: memory and life space on the late Victorian Ashdown Forest, Sussex', *Journal of Historical Geography*, 30 (2004), 484–5. Barry Godfrey also highlights men's mobility providing them with opportunities for theft in factories; B. Godfrey, 'Workplace appropriation and the gendering of factory "law"', in M. L. Arnot and C. Usborne (eds), *Gender and Crime in Modern Europe* (1999; London, 2003), p. 140.
52 Phillips, *Crime and Authority*, p. 197.
53 *NWE*, 24 October 1871.
54 *NWE*, 8 July 1873
55 See Zedner, *Women, Crime and Custody*, p. 25 where she argues that women's mobility was restricted by confinement to home.
56 For discussions of handicaps imposed by menstruation see J.-M. Strange, 'The assault on ignorance: teaching menstrual etiquette in England, c. 1920s to 1960s', *Social History of Medicine*, 14 (2001), pp. 247–8. Advice given to women was that they should 'avoid sudden exposure to cold or wet and avoid mental agitation' during menstruation; see E. Showalter and E. Showalter, 'Victorian women and menstruation', in M. Vicinus, *Suffer and Be Still* (Bloomington, 1973), p. 39.
57 See Jane Thomas's theft of six waistcoats, *NWE*, 21 October 1873.
58 *NWE*, 11 January 1870.
59 For this analysis, a populated area was one where people were likely to congregate, such as towns and villages, while isolated areas are country lanes, fields away from habitation, farms with few or no near neighbours, etc.

60 Mary Ann Hearne (two charges): *NWE*, 25 October 1870; Elizabeth
    Clarke and Louisa Wilson: *NWE*, 11 January 1870.
61 Anne Francis: *NWE*, 10 January 1871; Anne Goodall: *NWE*, 24 October
    1871; Frances Evans: *NWE*, 22 October 1872; Mary Edwards: *NWE*, 8
    July 1873; Elizabeth Williams: *ME*, 9 July 1878.
62 *NWE*, 9 January 1872.
63 *ME*, 9 January 1877.
64 *NWE*, 8 September 1874 and 27 October 1874.
65 *NWE*, 11 January 1870. See P. King, 'Immigrant communities, the police
    and the courts in late eighteenth and early nineteenth-century
    London', *Crime, History and Society*, 20 (2016), 39–68.
66 *NWE*, 4 July76. See R. Ireland, 'An increasing mass of heathens' for
    explanatory comments.
67 They were held at Dale Street in the city. Old maps show the police
    courts, Bridewell and detective department situated there.
68 T. Shakesheff, *Rural Conflict, Crime and Protest: Herefordshire, 1800–1860*
    (Woodbridge, 2003), pp. 69–72.
69 Nason's and Vaughan's cases both heard at the Easter 1869 sessions;
    NWE, 10 March 1869.
70 Elizabeth Gough, *ME*, 8 January 1878; Mary Ann Kinsey, *NWE*, 25
    October 1870.
71 Phillips, *Crime*, p. 237.
72 N. Woodward, 'Burglary in Wales 1730–1830: evidence from great
    sessions', *Welsh History Review*, 24 (2008), 67.
73 *NWE*, 10 March 1874.
74 *NWE*, 12 January 1869.
75 Even in trousers, the two sailors were captured during their attempted
    getaway across the hillside. It would have been easier for them to make
    their way west, across the flood plain. Witness testimony, however,
    reveals that labourers were working in that area, and the sailors tried to
    avoid them. Note Nicholas Blomley's analysis of the environment; N.
    Blomley, 'Making private property: enclosure, common right and the
    work of hedges', *Rural History*, 18/1 (2007), 1–21.
76 PCA, M/Q//SR, 1869–78.
77 PCA, M/Q/SR, midsummer 1871.
78 PCA, M/Q/SR, midsummer 1873.
79 PCA, M/Q/SR, Easter 1874.
80 PCA, M/Q/SR Easter 1869.
81 PCA, M/Q/SR Michaelmas 1873.
82 M. Clayton, 'The life and times of Charlotte Walker, prostitute and pick-
    pocket', *The London Journal*, 33 (2008), 8–9.
83 PCA, M/Q/SR, Hilary 1869. See also Chapter 8 of the present work.
84 PCA. M/Q/SR, Easter 1869.
85 PCA, M/Q/SR, midsummer 1878.
86 PCA, M/Q/SR, Hilary 1869.
87 *NWE*, 12 January 1869.
88 For a discussion on how material culture was reflected in literature, see
    A. H. Miller, *Novels behind Glass: Commodity Culture and Victorian Narrative*
    (Cambridge, 2008).

CHAPTER 8

1 F. Finnegan, *Poverty and Prostitution* (Cambridge, 1979); J. Walkowitz, *Prostitution and Victorian Society* (Cambridge, 1980); E. M. Sigsworth and T. J. Wyke, 'A study of Victorian prostitution and venereal disease', in M. Vicinus, *Suffer and Be Still* (Bloomington, 1973), pp. 77–99; P. Howell, *Geographies of Regulation: Policing Prostitution in Nineteenth-Century Britain and the Empire* (Cambridge, 2009); C. Lee, *Policing and Prostitution, 1856–1886: Deviance, Surveillance and Morality* (London, 2013).

2 National Census, 1851.

3 PCA, M/Q/SR, Hilary 1870; NWE, 11 January 1870.

4 PCA, M/Q/SR, Hilary 1869; NWE, 12 January 1869. Prostitutes commonly used aliases. Mary Davies in Shrewsbury was known as 'The Butterfly', Sarah Ann Davenall was called 'The Great Western', Elizabeth Hughes was 'Bet o' the Hank', and Margaret Colley was 'Peg o' the Match'; J. Butt, 'Red lights on Roushill', in B. Trinder (ed.), *Victorian Shrewsbury* (Shrewsbury, 1984), p. 70. In Merthyr there were 'Big Jane', 'Big Nell' and 'The Buffalo'. One of Jack the Ripper's victims was known as Long Lizzie. As the word 'alias' implies a serious alternative name, a better term in cases such as these might be 'nickname'. The definition of 'nickname' in the *Concise Oxford English Dictionary* (Oxford, 1982) is 'a name jokingly or admiringly or contemptuously added or substituted for person's proper name'. Peter King and Amanda Vickery use the term 'nickname' when discussing smugglers in nineteenth-century Sussex, 'Voices from the Old Bailey', BBC Radio 4 (14 August 2014).

5 D. V. J. Jones, *Crime in Nineteenth-Century Wales* (Cardiff, 1992), p. 171.

6 Note, however, Emsley's comment about perception: C. Emsley, *The Great British Bobby* (London, 2009), p. 133.

7 D. J. V. Jones, *Crime, Protest, Community and Police in Nineteenth-Century Britain* (Boston, 1982), p. 107.

8 Walkowitz, *Prostitution and Victorian Society*, chapter 1.

9 K. Chesney, *The Victorian Underworld* (London, 1970), p. 312. See also J. Burnette, *Gender, Work and Wages in Industrial Revolution Britain* (Cambridge, 2008).

10 R. Davies, *Secret Sins* (Cardiff, 1996), p. 162.

11 National Census, 1861.

12 M. Berg, 'Women's work, mechanization and the early phase of industrialization in England', in P. Joyce (ed.), *The Historical Meanings of Work* (Cambridge, 1987); D. Valenze, *The First Industrial Woman* (New York, 1995), pp. 85–127. See also M. Berg, *The Age of Manufactures: Industry, Innovation and Work in Britain, 1700–1820* (London, 1985).

13 B. S. Godfrey, and D. J. Cox, *Policing the Factory* (London, 2013), p. 38. For detail and discussion on women moving into textile centres for work see 'Women in the textile trades', in J. Rendall, *Women in an Industrializing Society* (Oxford, 1990), pp. 58–64. For a very interesting discussion on the relation of women's work in factories, patriarchal interests and balance of capital see G. Holloway, *Women and Work in Britain since 1940* (London, 2005), pp. 27–30.

[14] K. Powell, *The Cambridge Companion to Victorian and Edwardian Theatre* (Cambridge, 2004), p. 229.

[15] See also 'Women's paid employment', in Rendall, *Women in an Industrializing Society*, pp. 55–78.

[16] P. J. R. King, 'The summary courts and social relations in eighteenth-century England', *Past and Present*, 183 (2004), p. 139.

[17] Godfrey and Lawrence quoting Walkowitz, in B. S. Godfrey and P. Lawrence, *Crime and Justice, 1750–1950* (Cullompton, 2005), p. 145.

[18] A short description of a night-time beat patrol can be found in Emsley, *The Great British Bobby*, p. 124.

[19] See address of police office given in *ME*, 21 January 1877. From this location, which is part-way up a slope, there is a good view down Broad Street to the centre of town. Thus, this location was perhaps a better one for observation and surveillance than the ultimate location of the new building detailed in Chapter 2, which gives a poor view of Broad Street.

[20] *NWE*, 6 April 1869.

[21] *NWE*, 24 April 1869.

[22] The Picton Arms was the next pub along from The Albion, where Mary Morris was working.

[23] In the centre of York, several public houses and beer shops were apparently used as brothels; Finnegan, *Poverty and Prostitution*, p. 53.

[24] Butt, 'Red lights on Roushill', p. 69. Note that the census enumerator of this area in 1861 unusually identified each prostitute and brothel. The etymology of the phrase 'red light area' is unclear but may be from the practice of railwaymen of hanging oil lamps identifying where they were in case they were needed. Sometimes so many of these lights would be seen in any one location that it became known as a red-light area. This means that the phrase could date from the mid-nineteenth century and could have been familiar to the community studied here.

[25] These bullies often lived with the prostitutes or managed them in brothels, sometimes making their livings entirely through the proceeds of prostitution but often having part-time work; Jones, *Crime, Protest*, p. 108.

[26] *NWE*, 26 April 1870 and 5 July 1870.

[27] Jones, *Crime, Protest*, p. 107.

[28] Finnegan, *Poverty and Prostitution*, p. 117.

[29] PCA, M/Q/SR, Easter 1869; *NWE*, 2 March 1869.

[30] F. Rule, *The Worst Street in London* (Horsham, 2008), p. 80.

[31] *NWE*, 18 May 1869.

[32] PCA, M/Q/SR, midsummer 1869.

[33] For a discussion of this see B. Taithe, 'Consuming desires: prostitutes and "customers" at the margins of crime and perversion in France and Britain, c. 1836–85', in M. L. Arnot and C. Usborne (eds), *Gender and Crime in Modern Europe* (1999; London, 2003), pp. 159–60.

[34] Finnegan, *Poverty and Prostitution*, p. 54.

[35] *NWE*, 23 February 1869.

NOTES 253

36 *NWE*, 21 September 1869. William Rhys Lambert cites data from Caernarfonshire petitions to magistrates to argue that there was strong working-class support for temperance, for example nine labourers and seven shop assistants on one petition. He does not state what proportion of labourers and shop assistants these were; W. R. Lambert, *Drink and Sobriety in Victorian Wales* (Cardiff, 1983), p. 97. Lambert makes hardly any connection between public houses and prostitution; see his brief comments on pp. 18 and 132.

37 R. Wallace, 'Wales and the parliamentary reform movement', *Welsh History Review*, 11 (1983), 471–2 and 482–4.

38 Here we see a reference to the magistracy in their civil role as administrators of county business. They were superseded in this role by the new county council which was formed after the Local Government Act of 1888. Some magistrates were elected to the new council and were thereby able to continue their former roles; 'County Councils Act' in D. Hey (ed.), *The Oxford Companion to Local and Family History* (1996; Oxford, 1998), p. 252. Capt. Mytton was one such man, and served on Montgomeryshire Council from its earliest days and was chairman at one point. Obituary of Capt. Mytton: *ME*, 22 February 1910.

39 See 'I.O.G.T.: a brief history', *http://iogt-ew.org/history.html* (4 January 2013). See also Lambert's comments, *Drink and Sobriety*, p. 89. Note the comment that there was 'enormous' space in local government activity for influence and pressure from various groups pressing for social reform, and that although landowners and employers had great power, it was business, labour, religious, recreational and planning groups which wielded greatest influence. Landlords also had influence as they were the main source of council income; B. M. Doyle, 'The changing functions of urban government: councillors, officials and pressure groups', in M. Daunton (ed.), *The Cambridge Urban History of Britain* (Cambridge, 2000), pp. 307–8.

40 *NWE*, 15 April 1873.

41 P. Jenkins, *A History of Modern Wales, 1536–1990* (London, 1992), p. 202.

42 J. Walkowitz, *Prostitution*, chapter 4.

43 W. Acton, *Prostitution* (London, 1968), p. 88.

44 The 1744 Vagrancy Act listed who could be prosecuted under the law. The list was a long one and included unlicensed pedlars, men who deserted their families and all persons found wandering abroad. Prostitutes were prosecuted under this law; *www.londonlives.org/static/vagrancy.jsp*, 3 November 2010; A. J. Engel, 'Immoral intentions: The University of Oxford and the problem of prostitution 1827–1914', *Victorian Studies*, 23 (1979), 80–1.

45 The Vagrancy Act of 1824 reads: '… every common prostitute wandering in the public streets or public highways, or in any place of public resort, and behaving in a riotous or indecent manner …'; *www.statutelaw.gov.uk* (3 November 2010). The university was concerned that indecency would be difficult to prove and that incidents of riotous behaviour would be few, giving the university limited opportunities for prosecution.

[46] S. Stone, *Justices' Manual* (n.p., 1862), NLW, shelf mark KyL 40 S87.

[47] *NWE*, 6 April 1869.

[48] *NWE*, 26 October 1869.

[49] Leader, *NWE*, 6 April 1869.

[50] Jeremiah 40:1 and 31:15; Matthew 2:18.

[51] J. Hart, 'Religion and social control in the mid-nineteenth century', in A. P. Donajgrodski (ed.), *Social Control in Nineteenth-Century Britain* (London, 1977), pp. 108–38 (especially pp. 128–9).

[52] 'Henry Parry', in J. I. Davies, 'The history of printing in Montgomeryshire, 1789–1960', *Mont. Colls*, 70 (1982), 78–80.

[53] Taithe, 'Consuming desires', p. 153.

[54] A. Fried and R. Elman (eds), *Charles Booth's London* (Harmondsworth, 1971), p. 198.

[55] *NWE*, 16 November 1869. There is no evidence that Griffiths was a prostitute.

[56] *NWE*, 12 March 1872.

[57] By 17 and 18 Victoria, chapter 86 any person under sixteen convicted of any offence punishable upon indictment or summary conviction before a police or stipendiary magistrate or before two justices may, by direction of the convicting magistrate or justices, be sent at the expiration of his sentence to a reformatory school (and it is not now necessary to name the particular school at the time of passing sentence; see 19 and 20 Victoria, chapter 109, section 1) the directors of which shall be willing to receive him, and be there detained for not less than two years and not exceeding five years; but no offender shall be sent unless the sentence be one of imprisonment for fourteen days at the least; Stone, *Justices' Manual*, 1862. Oliver and Ellis were sent to the Mount Vernon institution in Liverpool. Investigation has found that this was one of the so-called Church of England 'Magdalene institutions' (named after Mary Magdalene of New Testament fame, thought by some to have been a prostitute).

[58] See J. Davies, *The Age of Consent: A Warning from History* (Newcastle, 2009); Finnegan discusses child prostitution briefly in *Poverty and Prostitution*, pp. 81–2. For a discussion on analysis of historical cases see A. Bingham, 'Historical child sexual abuse in England and Wales: the role of historians', *History of Education*, 45 (2016), pp. 411–29.

[59] For discussion about how newspapers could bring crime to public consciousness see R. Sindall, 'The London garrotting panics of 1856 and 1862', *Social History*, 12 (1987), 351–9; P. King, 'Newspaper reporting and attitudes to crime and justice in late-eighteenth- and early-nineteenth-century London', *Continuity and Change*, 22 (2007), 73–112; M. Diamond, *Victorian Sensation or the Spectacular, the Shocking and the Scandalous in Nineteenth-Century Britain* (Bath, 2003). For a fascinating method of analysing crime headlines see S. Hester and P. Eglin, *A Sociology of Crime* (London, 1992), pp. 119–28.

[60] See discussion about studies of collective action in K. Navickas, 'Whatever happened to class? New histories of labour and collective action in Britain', *Social History*, 36 (2011), 197–204. See also G. Rudé, *The Crowd*

in the French Revolution (Oxford, 1959); G. Rudé, *The Crowd in History: A Study of Popular Disturbance in France and England, 1730–1848* (New York, 1964); M. Harrison, *Crowds and History: Mass Phenomena in English Towns, 1790–1835* (Cambridge, 2002).

61 The jury consisted of seven farmers, two skilled manual workers, two retailers and a farm labourer. The grand jury consisted of eleven farmers, five skilled manual workers, one professional and one retailer. This case took place before the new method of jury selection, which included manipulation of the jury lists to restrict the number of farmers (see earlier section in Chapter 5 on jury selection).

62 See D. Bentley, *English Criminal Justice in the Nineteenth Century* (London 1998), pp. 131–2.

63 The grand jury consisted of eight farmers, six skilled manual workers, two retailers, one agent (unspecified) and one professional.

64 Eight farmers, eleven skilled manual workers and four retailers.

65 *NWE*, 11 January 1870.

66 Barry Godfrey identifies both the view of some magistrates that it was their duty to protect women from violence, and the general difficulty of convicting women. B. Godfrey, 'Workplace appropriation and the gendering of factory "law"', in M. L. Arnot and C. Usborne (eds), *Gender and Crime in Modern Europe* (1999; London, 2003), pp. 141 and 147.

67 *NWE*, 6 July 1869 and PCA, M/Q/SR, midsummer 1869. The shawl may have been valued at over £2 because in October 1860 two women in Caernarfon were charged with stealing a paisley shawl valued at fifty shillings; Caernarfonshire County Archives, XQS/1861/29. It shows that Lloyd was making a good income from prostitution and could afford good clothes. A female farm haymaker would have had to work for about seven weeks to earn fifty shillings (based on the Gregynog rates of pay used for the analysis in Chapter 2). Walkowitz explains: 'To these women, flaunting it "first rate" undoubtedly signified status, autonomy and freedom from the workaday world of their respectable sisters'; Walkowitz, *Prostitution*, p. 26.

68 Stephen Higgs was also living in the house, giving the impression that it was a brothel run by Higgs, or that Higgs was controlling both women.

69 Examination of newspaper reports shows that other defendants received similar sentences for a series of thefts taking place on different occasions. For example, Edward Edwards was convicted of stealing items on four separate occasions. He was sentenced to six months for the first offence and one day for each of the others. Lewis Hearn and John Smith stole chickens, a turkey and a cob horse on three separate occasions. They received seven years' penal servitude for the theft of the horse and one day for each of the other thefts; *NWE*, 20 October 1870.

70 In this case, Lloyd went by train to Welshpool and invited Williams to go with her. Williams declined and, on her return, Lloyd found that the shawl was gone. Williams had gone to Mrs Thomas to ask to borrow her black bonnet 'for Lloyd to wear to Welshpool', but kept it herself.

71 *NWE*, 5 July 1870.

72   In similar cases of theft, the longest sentence was given for the most valuable item. For example, the six months with hard labour that Edward Edwards received in the cases quoted in an earlier note, was for the theft of nine yards of flannel; the other thefts were of low-value items and received one day each. In the case of the theft of livestock mentioned in the same note, the cob horse theft received seven years' penal servitude whereas the less valuable turkey and chickens merited one day each. If this pattern was followed, the theft of the shawl by Ann Williams should have received the greater sentence, as it was likely to have been valued at around fifty shillings. The fact that it did not raises questions about whether the magistrates treated crimes against prostitutes, or prostitute-on-prostitute crime, as unimportant. In modern magistrates' courts, too, the value of the item taken is taken into consideration when deciding on the sentence. In the guidance given to twenty-first-century magistrates on assessing the seriousness of the theft, the Judicial Studies Board, *Adult Court Bench Book* (2005) reads: 'When assessing the harm caused by a theft offence, the starting point is normally based on the loss suffered by the victim.'

73   The chairman of the Bench told Rowlands that if she had been a few years younger (she was twenty years old at the time) she would have been sent to a reformatory.

74   *NWE*, 24 October 1871.

75   *NWE*, 19 October 1869.

76   *NWE*, 4 May 1869.

77   *NWE*, 5 October 1869.

78   See comments on expenses in D. Phillips, *Crime and Authority in Victorian England: The Black Country, 1835–1860* (London, 1997), pp.114–17. See also P. King, 'Resources available to victims: public funding, prosecution associations, print and policing', in P. King, *Crime, Justice and Discretion in England, 1740–1820* (Oxford, 2000), pp. 47–81.

79   In a modern magistrates' court, ability to pay is taken into consideration when deciding on the level of a fine. Magistrates are advised to not set up the convicted person to fail; *Adult Court Bench Book*, p. 155.

80   Butt, 'Red lights on Roushill', p. 70.

81   For comments on inter-woman violence see A. August, 'A horrible-looking woman: female violence in late-Victorian east London', *Journal of British Studies*, 54 (2015), 844–68.

82   For comments on this topic see H. M. Hyde, *The Other Love: An Historical and Contemporary Survey of Homosexuality in Britain* (London, 1970); H. M. Hyde, *The Cleveland Street Scandal* (London, 1976).

83   PCA, M/QS, midsummer 1870; *NWE*, 5 July 1870.

84   J. Weeks '"Sins and diseases": some notes on homosexuality in the nineteenth century', *History Workshop*, 1 (1976), 212.

85   *NWE*, 27 July 1874.

86   PCA, M/QS, Hilary 1872; *NWE*, 9 January 1872.

87   Taithe, 'Consuming desires', p. 153.

CONCLUSION

1   In his foreword to *Gender and Crime in Modern Europe*, Emsley writes that
    the ways in which rules and law are interpreted and enforced provide a
    valuable route into understanding the mores and values of particular
    societies; M. L. Arnot and C. Usborne (eds), *Gender and Crime in Modern
    Europe* (1999; London, 2003).
2   As well as the works already cited by C. Harrison, B. Short, B. Cowell
    and N. Blomley, see R. N. Davidson, *Crime and Environment* (London,
    1981); R. A. E. Wells, 'Social conflict and protest in the English country-
    side in the early nineteenth century: a rejoinder', *Journal of Peasant
    Studies*, 8 (1981), 514–30; W. M. Ormrod, 'Law in the landscape: crimi-
    nality, outlawry and regional identity in late medieval England', in A.
    Musson (ed.), *Boundaries of the Law: Geography, Gender and Jurisdiction in
    Medieval and Early-Modern Europe* (Aldershot, 2005), pp. 7–20.
3   One of the calls of the Chartists was for members of Parliament to be
    paid so that standing for election was not dependent on income. See
    'Chartism', in J. Cannon (ed.), *The Oxford Companion to British History*
    (1997; Oxford, 2002), p. 192.
4   This may well have had the effect now known as 'subliminal stimula-
    tion', 'exposure effect' or 'product placement'. In modern times, this
    technique is used to induce a positive effect on the viewer. See S.
    Ruggieri and S. Boca, 'At the roots of product placement: the mere
    exposure effect', *Europe's Journal of Psychology*, 9 (2013), 246–58. It has
    been found, however, that individuals are more likely to 'buy into'
    something with which they identify; therefore the majority of the Mont-
    gomeryshire community in the 1870s was unlikely to 'buy into' the
    justice system as represented in the built environment. See I.
    Zimmerman, 'Product placement can be a lot more powerful than we
    think', *Psychology Today*, viewed at *www.psychologytoday.com* (30 March
    2014).
5   See Bailey's analysis and discussion of working-class hostility being
    higher than that of middle-class shopkeepers in V. Bailey (ed.), *Policing
    and Punishment in Nineteenth-Century Britain* (London, 1981), pp. 71–2,
    and of reasons for working-class hostility, pp. 72–6.
6   Philips discusses this point, arguing against E. P. Thompson's analysis of
    the poorer classes being unwilling to invoke the law at all, in D. Philips,
    Crime and Authority in Victorian England (London, 1978), pp. 127–9.
7   In a similar way, the annual payment for seating in church or chapel
    followed a comparable pattern shared by upper- and more lower-class
    people, whereby status was determined by location of the family pew or
    an individual seat which could change year by year. This was said to
    'alienate the working classes' and to 'form divided and hostile social
    classes'; C. G. Brown, 'The costs of pew renting: church going and
    social class in nineteenth-century Glasgow', *Journal of Ecclesiastical
    History*, 38 (1987), 347. See also K. D. M. Snell, and P. S. Ell, *Rival Jerusa-
    lems: The Geography of Victorian Religion* (Cambridge, 2000), pp. 321–63,
    who point out that the pew-letting system was also pervasive in more

lower-class denominations, both for reasons of status and financial necessity.

8   See comments in A. Shubert, 'Private initiative in law enforcement: associations for the prosecution of felons', in V. Bailey, *Policing and Punishment*, p. 3.

9   Cox and Godfrey detected signs of magistrates' personalities from their actions: D. J. Cox and B. S. Godfrey (eds), *Cinderellas and Packhorses: A History of the Shropshire Magistracy* (Woonton Almeley, 2005), pp. 48–9.

10 In his study of early modern Montgomeryshire, Humphreys identified a lower-class woman taking on a squire at the court of great session; M. Humphreys, 'Harmony, crime and order', in *The Crisis of Community* (Cardiff, 1996), pp. 250–1.

11 P. Burke, *History and Social Theory* (Cambridge, 2005), p. 38.

12 Burke, *History*, p. 41. See also Muir and Ruggiero's comments that 'observation of trifles can lead to important conclusions, and that general conclusions can be drawn from local data'; E. Muir and G. Ruggiero, *Microhistory and the Lost Peoples of Europe* (Baltimore, 1991), pp. vii–viii.

13 On the issues of class, see G. Stedman Jones, *Languages of Class* (Cambridge, 1983); P. Joyce, *Visions of the People: Industrial England and the Question of Class, 1848–1914* (Cambridge, 1990); D. Cannadine, *Class in Britain* (New Haven, 1998); D. Feldman, 'Class', in P. Burke (ed.), *History and Historians in the Twentieth Century* (Oxford, 2002), pp. 181–206.

14 See P. Bourdieu, *Outline of a Theory of Practice* (Cambridge, 1977); J. Field, *Social Capital* (London, 2003).

15 J. W. Scott, 'Women's history' in P. Burke (ed.), *New Perspectives on Historical Writing* (Cambridge, 2001), pp. 43–70.

16 S. Rogers, 'The myth of male dominance', *American Ethnologist*, 2 (1975), 727–57.

17 E. Ardener, 'Belief and the problem of women', in S. Ardener (ed.), *Perceiving Women* (London, 1975), pp. 1–27.

18 Report of the first Montgomeryshire woman magistrate, *ME*, 26 October 1920.

19 Maddox does not give a date when women police officers joined the force, but mentions auxiliaries appointed at the beginning of Second World War; W. C. Maddox, *A History of the Montgomeryshire Constabulary, 1840–1948* (Carmarthen, 1982), p. 18. A photograph of the county force on p. 28 dated 1946 does not show any women. See also C. Griffiths, *The Police Forces of Mid and West Wales, 1829–1974* (Llandybie, 2004), p. 91. For details, see 'Women police', in P. J. Stead, *The Police of Britain* (London, 1985), pp. 89–90 and I. Zweiniger-Bargielowska (ed.), *Women in Twentieth-Century Britain* (2001; Abingdon, 2014), pp. 210–11.

20 For examples of pertinent Irish studies see W. Walsh, 'Hard labour, hard board and hard fare: Kilkenny's gaols, 1770–1900', *Ossory, Laois and Leinster*, 3 (2008), pp. 209–38; W. Walsh, *Kilkenny: The Struggle for the Land, 1850–82* (Thomastown, 2008); P. O. Machain, *Six Years in Galmoy: Rural Unrest in County Kilkenny, 1819–1824* (Dublin, 2004); M.

O'Hanrahan, 'The tithe war in County Kilkenny, 1930–34', in W. Nolan and K. Whelan (eds), *Kilkenny: History and Society: Interdisciplinary Essays on the History of an Irish County* (Dublin, 1990); M. Luddy, 'Abandoned women and bad characters: prostitution in nineteenth-century Ireland', *Women's History Review*, 6 (1997), 485–503; N. Howlin, 'Fenians, foreigners and jury trials in Ireland, 1865–70', *Irish Jurist*, 45 (2010), 51–81; R. B. Brown, 'A delusion, a mockery and a snare: jury selection in England and Ireland, 1800–50', *Canadian Journal of History*, 39 (2004), 126.

21 See M. Beard, *English Landed Society in the Twentieth Century* (London, 1989); J. Davies, 'The end of the great estates and the rise of freehold farming in Wales', *Welsh History Review*, 7 (1974), pp. 186–212; C. Emsley, *Crime and Society in Twentieth-Century England* (Harlow, 2011); H. Taylor, 'The politics of the rising crime statistics in England and Wales, 1914–1960', *Crime, Histoire et Sociétés*, 2 (1998), 5–28; R. Davies, 'Voices from the void: social crisis, social problems and the individual in south-west Wales, 1876–1920', in G. H. Jenkins and B. Smith (eds), *Politics and Society in Wales, 1840–1922: Essays in Honour of Ieuan Gwynedd Jones* (Cardiff, 1998), pp. 81–1; K. I. Wolpin, 'An economic analysis of crime and punishment in England and Wales, 1894–1967', *Journal of Political Economy*, 86 (1978), 815–40.

BIBLIOGRAPHY

PRIMARY SOURCES

Caernarfonshire County Archives
Court records of paisley shawl theft, Caernarfonshire County Archives, XQS/1861/29.

Leicester University: Centre for English Local History
The Imperial Gazetteer of England and Wales (Edinburgh, Glasgow and London, no date, c. 1874).

London Metropolitan Archives
Map of Montgomeryshire petty sessional divisions, ACC/2425/102.

National Archives, London
Pentonville Register, TNA, HO24/192.

National Library of Wales
Chambers English Dictionary (1879), edited by James Donald, NWL, shelf mark: 87MB135æÆ9.
Gregynog Estate labour books 186673, NWL, item no.1957112/55, 56, 57.
Johnes, J. A., *Causes of Dissent in Wales* (1832; London, 1870). No shelf mark.
Journal of PC Edward Jones, Constable of Llanfyllin, NWL, shelf mark MS 6227D.
Montgomeryshire Jury Book 1869–74, NWL, MSS 21843–4.
Report of Commission of Enquiry into the State of Education in Wales, 1847, NWL, item no. 003207204.
Richard, H., *Letters on the Social and Political Condition of the Principality of Wales* (1866), NWL, shelf mark Wb. 4585.
Stone, S., *The Justices' Manual*, 1862, NWL, shelf mark KyL 40 S87.
Stone, S., *The Justices' Manual*, 1880, NWL, item no. 94MA16717.

Newtown (Powys) Library
National Census, 1841–1911 (also viewed online).
Pigot and Co., *Directory of North Wales* (1835).
Robson, *Directory of North Wales* (1840).
Slater, *Directory of North Wales* (1850 and 1868).

County Times.
Montgomeryshire Express.
Newtown and Welshpool Express.
Ordnance Survey maps (1881 and 1902).
Worrall, *Directory* (1874).

Newspaper articles
'A Montgomeryshire magistrate and his dairymaid', *Western Mail*, 25 February 1875.
Baron Bramwell (court report), *The Times*, 21 February 1871.
Baron Bramwell, comment about, *Exeter Flying Post*, 15 March 1871.
'Charles Spencer Thorn', *Worcester Journal*, 14 June 1872.
'Habitual criminals', *The Times*, 10 March 1869, p. 9.
'In defence of Welsh juries', *Oswestry Advertiser*, reprinted in *Liverpool Mercury*, 16 March 1871.
'Landed estates court', *Freeman's Journal and Daily Commercial Advertiser*, 9 April 1876.
'Obituary of Capt Mytton', *ME*, 22 February 1910.
'Obituary of J. Blythe', *ME*, 13 September 1892.
'Obituary of John Danily', *ME*, 26 January 1915.
'Obituary of Martin Woosnam, *ME*, 2 February 1924.
'Political oppression by Welsh landlords', *Wrexham Advertiser*, 10 July 1869.
'Singular case of assault upon a tradesman', *Liverpool Mercury*, 24 December 1868.
'Territorial Tyranny in Wales', *Bradford Observer*, 9 July 1869.
'The Tarpey case', *Liverpool Mercury*, 16 March 1871.
'Welsh assize case', *Liverpool Mercury*, 18 March 1869.
'The population in Newtown, 1871', *NWE*, 23 April 1871.

Powys County Archives, Llandrindod Wells
Architect's plans of Newtown Police Station, PCA, M/Q/AC/6.
Clerk of the peace's record book, PCA, MQ/CX/2.
Journal of PC Thomas Jones, PCA, M/SOC/7/42.
Justices Qualifications Rolls, 1843–1900, PCA, M/QS/JQ/3 and 4.
Letter from C. A. Cobbe, PCA, M/Q/AC/6.
Letter from Liverpool Town Clerk, PCA, M/Q/AC/7.
Memorandum on the construction of police stations 1875, PCA, MQ/AC/7.
Montgomeryshire Militia records, PCA, M/Q/AX/1, M/Q/CR/2, M/Q/RQ.
Montgomeryshire Militia records, PCA, Ref. M/L.
Quarter sessions records, PCA, M/QS, 1869–78.

Powysland Museum, Welshpool
Photographic collection.

Shropshire Archives
Shrewsbury Chronicle.
Shropshire quarter sessions order books, 1840–89.

Textile Museum, Newtown (Powys)
Display about Pryce Pryce-Jones.

Parliamentary papers
Bill for the Appointment of a Private Prosecutor, (28), 1872, Part 4, 583.
Bill to Provide for the Appointment of Public Prosecutors, (15), 1854 Part 5, 571.
Census of Great Britain, 1851: Religious worship. England and Wales, (89), 1.
Census of England and Wales, 1871, Volume 1.
Minutes of Evidence of the Commission of Inquiry as to Disturbances Connected with Levying of Tithe Rent Charge in Wales (House of Commons, 1887).
Report of HMIC, 1870, 36.
Report of HMIC, 1871, 28.
Report of HMIC, 1872, 30.
Report of Royal Commission on Penal Servitude, 1856, 17.
Report of Royal Commission on Penal Servitude, 1863, 21.

Pictures
Architect's drawing of Welshpool's new town hall, E. Bredsdorff, *Welshpool in Old Photographs* (Stroud, 1993), p. 46.
Painting of Earl Vane, Plas Machynlleth, Machynlleth, Powys.
Cartoon of Sir George Wilshire Bramwell, *Vanity Fair,* January 1876.

Websites
Alberbury Cassey Shropshire Directory 1875 at *http://www.parishmouse.com/shropshire/2009/4/25/alberbury-cassey-shropshire-directory-1875.html* (5 February 2011).
D. Defoe, *A Tour Thro' the Whole Island of Great Britain, Divided into Circuits or Journeys* (Letter 6, Part 3: Worcester, Hereford and Wales), *http://www.visionofbritain.org.uk* (5 June 2013).
Flintshire petty sessions records viewed at *http://www.archiveswales.org.uk* (13 January 2011).
Memorial to William Wynn Ffoulkes, *http://members.tripod.com/caryl_williams/index-4.html* (3 November 2011).

Shrewsbury School Register, 1874–1908.

Stephens, H., *The Book of the Farm*, 3 (Edinburgh, 1844).

SECONDARY SOURCES

Acton, W., *Prostitution* (London, 1968).

Aitkin, J., *England Described: Being a Concise Delineation of Every County in England and Wales* (London, 1818).

Arnot, M. L. and Usborne, C. (eds), *Gender and Crime in Modern Europe* (1999; London, 2003).

Bailey, V. (ed.) *Policing and Punishment in Nineteenth-Century Britain* (London, 1981).

Barrett, A. and Harrison, C. (eds), *Crime and Punishment in England: A Sourcebook* (Keele, 1999).

Bartley, P., *Prostitution: Prevention and Reform in England, 1860–1914* (London, 2000).

Bayley, D. H. (ed.), *Police and Society* (London, 1997).

Beard, M., *English Landed Society in the Twentieth Century* (London, 1989).

Beattie, J. M., *Crime and the Courts in England 1660–1800* (Oxford, 1986).

Beddoe. D., *Welsh Convict Women Transported from Wales to Australia, 1787–1852* (Cowbridge, 1979).

Bentley, D., *English Criminal Justice in the Nineteenth Century* (London, 1998).

Berg, M., *The Age of Manufactures: Industry, Innovation and Work in Britain, 1700–1820* (London, 1985).

Berridge, K., *Waxing Mythical* (London, 2006).

Birch, H. K., *The History of Policing in North Wales* (Pwllheli, 2008).

Blocker, J. S., Fahey M. and Tyrrell, I. R. (eds), *Alcohol and Temperance in Modern History: A Global Encyclopedia* (Santa Barbara, 2003).

Bourdieu, P., *Outline of a Theory of Practice* (Cambridge, 1977).

Bourke, J., *Working-Class Cultures in Britain, 1890–1960: Gender, Class and Ethnicity* (London, 1994).

Brand, B., and Getzler, J., (eds), *Judges and Judging in the History of the Common Law and Civil Law: From Antiquity to Modern Times* (Cambridge, 2012).

Bredsdorff, E., *Welshpool in Old Photographs* (Stroud, 1993).

Briggs, J., Harrison, C., McInnes, A., and Vincent, D., *Crime and Punishment in England: An Introductory History* (London, 1996).

Brontë, E., *Wuthering Heights* (1847; London, 1992).

Brooks, S., *Why Wales Never Was: The Failure of Welsh Nationalism* (Cardiff, 2017).

Brown, L., *Victorian News and Newspapers* (Oxford, 1985).

Cannon, J. (ed.), *The Oxford Companion to British History* (1997; Oxford, 2002).

Cannadine, D., *Class in Britain* (New Haven, 1998).

Carroll, L., *Alice in Wonderland* (London, 1865).

Castleden, R., *Infamous Murders* (London, 2005).

Channing, I., *The Police and the Expansion of Public Order Law in Britain, 1829–2013* (London, 2013).

Chesney, K., *The Victorian Underworld* (London, 1970).

Clark, A., *The Struggle for Breeches: Gender and the Making of the British Working Class* (Berkeley, 1995).

Clark, A., *Women's Silence, Men's Violence: Sexual Assault in England, 1770–1845* (London, 1987).

Clark, M. and Crawford, C. (eds), *Legal Medicine in History* (Cambridge, 1994).

Clarke, P. (ed.), *The Cambridge Urban History of Britain* (Cambridge, 2000).

Cockburn, J. S. (ed.), *Crime in England, 1550–1800* (Princeton, 1977).

Cohen, A. P. (ed.), *The Symbolic Construction of Community* (Chichester, 1985).

Cohen, M. N., *Lewis Carroll: A Biography* (London, 1995).

Conley, C., *Certain Other Countries: Homicide, Gender and National Identity in Late Nineteenth-Century England, Ireland, Scotland and Wales* (Columbus, 2007).

Cooper, K. J., *Exodus from Cardiganshire: rural–urban migration in Victorian Britain* (Cardiff, 2011).

Corsby, C., *The Ends of History: Victorians and the 'Woman Question'* (London, 1991).

Council of Europe, *Crime and Economy: Reports Presented to the 11th Criminological Colloquium, 1994* (Strasbourg, 1995).

Council of Europe, *Economic Crisis and Crime* (Strasbourg, 1985).

Cowley, R., *A History of the British Police: From its Earliest Beginnings to the Present Day* (Stroud, 2011).

Cowley, R., Todd, R. and Ledger, L., *The History of Her Majesty's Inspectorate of Constabulary: The First 150 Years* (n.d, n.p.).

Cox, D. J. and Godfrey, B. S. (eds), *Cinderellas and Packhorses: A History of the Shropshire Magistracy* (Woonton Almeley, 2005).

D'Cruze, S. and Jackson, L. A., *Women, Crime and Justice in England since 1660* (Basingstoke, 2009).

D'Cruze, S., *Crimes of Outrage: Sex, Violence and Victorian Working Women* (London, 1998).

D'Cruze, S., *Everyday Violence in Britain, 1850–1950: Gender and Class* (2000; Harlow, 2004).

Dahrendorf, R., *Class and Class Conflict in Industrial Society* (Stanford, 1959).

Davey, B. J., *Lawless and Immoral: Policing a Country Town 1838–57* (Leicester, 1983).

Davidoff, L. and Hall, C., *Family Fortunes: Men and Women of the English Middle Class, 1740–1850* (Oxford, 2002).

Davidson, R. N., *Crime and Environment* (London, 1981).

Davies, A. S., *The Ballads of Montgomeryshire: Life in the Eighteenth Century* (Welshpool, 1938).

Davies, J., *The Age of Consent: A Warning from History* (Newcastle, 2009).

Davies, J., Jenkins, N., Baines, M. and Lynch, P. I., *The Welsh Academy Encyclopaedia of Wales* (Cardiff, 2008).

Davies, R., *Secret Sins* (Llandybie, 1996).

Davis, C., *Religion and Society: Essays in Social Theology* (Cambridge, 1994).

Day, G., *Community and Everyday Life* (Abingdon, 2006).

Diamond, M., *Victorian Sensation or the Spectacular, the Shocking and the Scandalous in Nineteenth-Century Britain* (Bath, 2003).

Dickens, C., *Bleak House* (1853; London, 1993).

Dickens, C., *Great Expectations* (1862; London, 1992).

Dickens, C., *Oliver Twist*, (1837; London, 1990).

Disraeli, B., *Sybil or the Two Nations* (1845; London, 1927).

Dodd, A. H., *The Industrial Revolution in North Wales* (Cardiff, 1951).

Du Maurier, D., *Jamaica Inn* (London, 1936).

Dodsworth, F., *Liberty and Order: Civil Government and the Common Good in Eighteenth-Century England, CRESC Working Paper Series*, 21 (2006), p. 5.

Donajgrodski, A. P. (ed.), *Social Control in Nineteenth-Century Britain* (London, 1977).

Edwards, J., *Language and Identity: An Introduction* (Cambridge, 2009).

Elliott, D. J., *Policing Shropshire, 1836–1967* (Studley, 1984).

Emsley, C. and Walvin, J., (eds), *Artisans, Peasants and Proletarians, 1760–1860* (Beckenham, 1983).

Emsley, C., *Crime and Society in England, 1750–1900* (1987; Harlow, 1996).

Emsley, C., *Crime and Society in Twentieth-Century England* (Harlow, 2011).

Emsley, C., *Policing and its Context* (London, 1983).

Emsley, C., *The English and Violence since 1750* (London, 2005).

Emsley, C., *The English Police: A Political and Social History* (London, 1996).

Emsley, C., *The Great British Bobby* (London, 2009).

Emsley, C. and Shpayer-Makov, H., (eds), *Police Detectives in History, 1750–1950* (Aldershot, 2006).

European Committee on Crime Problems, *Crime and Economy: Reports Presented to the 11th Criminological Colloquium, 1994* (Strasbourg, 1995).

Evans, D. G., *A History of Wales, 1815–1906* (Cardiff, 1989).

Evans, J., *Letters Written during a Tour of North Wales in the Year 1798, and at Other Times* (London, 1804).

Evans, R and Lewis, P., *Undercover: The True Story of Britain's Secret Police* (London, 2013).

Field, J., *Social Capital* (London, 2003).

Finnegan, F., *Poverty and Prostitution* (Cambridge, 1979).

Fisher, P., 'An object of ambition? The office and role of the coroner in two Midland counties, 1751–1888' (unpublished Ph.D. thesis, University of Leicester, 2003).

Foster, D., *The Rural Constabulary Act, 1839* (London, 1982).

Foucault, M., *Power/Knowledge* (London, 1980).

Fried, A., and Elman, R. (eds), *Charles Booth's London* (Harmondsworth, 1971).

Ginzberg, C., *The Cheese and the Worms: The Cosmos of a Sixteenth-Century Miller* (Baltimore, 1980).

Godfrey, B., *The Rough: Crime in England, 1880–1945* (London, 2013).

Godfrey, B. S. and Cox, D. J., *Policing the Factory* (London, 2013).

Godfrey, B. S., Cox, D. J. and Farrall, S. D., *Criminal Lives: Family Life, Employment and Offending* (Oxford, 2007).

Godfrey, B. S., Cox, D. J. and Farrall, S. D., *Serious Offenders: A Historical Study of Habitual Criminals* (Oxford, 2010).

Godfrey, B. S. and Dunstall, G. (eds), *Crime and Empire, 1840–1940: Criminal Justice in Local and Global Context* (Cullompton, 2005).

Godfrey, B. S., Emsley, C. and Dunstall, D., *Comparative Histories of Crime* (Cullompton, 2003).

Godfrey, B. S. and Lawrence, P., *Crime and Justice, 1750–1950* (Cullompton, 2005).

Gray, D. D., *Crime, Policing and Punishment in England, 1660–1914* (London, 2016).

Griffith, W. P., *Power, Politics and County Government in Wales: Anglesey, 1780–1914* (Llangefni, 2006).

Griffiths, C., *The Police Forces of Mid and West Wales, 1829–1974* (Llandybie, 2004).

Hammond, J. L. and Hammond, B., *The Town Labourer, 1760–1832* (London, 1917).

Hardwick, M., *A Literary Atlas and Gazetteer of the British Isles* (Newtown Abbot, 1973).

Hardy, T., *The Mayor of Casterbridge* (London, 1886).

Harrison, B., *Drink and the Victorians* (London, 1971).

Harrison, M., *Crowds and History: Mass Phenomena in English Towns, 1790–1835* (Cambridge, 2002).

Haslam, R., *The Buildings of Wales: Powys (Montgomeryshire, Radnorshire, Breconshire)* (New Haven and London, 2003).

Hawkings, D. T., *Criminal Ancestors* (1998; London, 2008).

Hay, D. and Craven, P. (eds), *Masters, Servants and Magistrates in Britain and the Empire* (London, 2004).

Hay, D. and Snyder, F., *Policing and Prosecution in Britain, 1750–1850* (Oxford, 1980).

Heathcote, B., *Viewing the Lifeless Body: A Coroner and his Inquests held in Nottinghamshire Public Houses during the Nineteenth Century, 1828–1866* (Nottingham 2006).

Hester, S. and Eglin, P., *A Sociology of Crime* (London, 1992).

Hey, D. (ed.), *The Oxford Companion to Local and Family History* (Oxford, 1996).

Hill, I. C. and Bowers, M., *Teeline* (London, 1983).

Hobbs, D., *Doing the Business* (Oxford, 1988).

Hobsbawm, E. J., *Primitive Rebels: Studies in Archaic Forms of Social Movement in the 19th and 20th Centuries* (Manchester, 1959).

Hoffman, D. and Rowe, J., *Human Rights in the U.K.* (2003; Harlow, 2010).

Holloway, G., *Women and Work in Britain since 1940* (London, 2005).

Howard, S., *Studies in Welsh History: Law and Disorder in Early Modern Wales, c. 1660–1730* (Cardiff, 2008).

Howell, P., *Geographies of Regulation: Policing Prostitution in Nineteenth-Century Britain and the Empire* (Cambridge, 2009).

Humphreys, M., *The Crisis of Community* (Cardiff, 1996).

Hyde, H. M., *The Cleveland Street Scandal* (London, 1976).

Hyde, H. M., *The Other Love: An Historical and Contemporary Survey of Homosexuality in Britain* (London, 1970).

Jackson, M. (ed.), *Infanticide: Historical Perspectives on Child Murders and Concealment, 1550–2000* (Aldershot, 2002).

Jenkins, D. (ed.), *Historical Atlas of Montgomeryshire* (Welshpool, 1999).

Jenkins, G., *Life in the Countryside: The Photographer in Rural Wales, 1850–2010* (Talybont, 2010).

Jenkins, G. H. (ed.), *The Welsh Language before the Industrial Revolution* (Cardiff, 1997).

Jenkins, P., *A History of Modern Wales, 1536–1990* (London, 1992).

John, A. V. (ed.), *Unequal Opportunities: Women's Employment in England, 1800–1918* (Oxford, 1986).

Johnes, J., *Causes of Dissent in Wales* (1832; London, 1870).

Jones, A., *Welsh Chapels* (Stroud, 1984).

Jones, D., *A Social History of the Welsh Language* (Cardiff, 1998).

Jones, D., *Crime, Protest, Community and Police in Nineteenth-Century Britain* (Boston, 1982).

Jones, D., *Statistical Material Relating to the Welsh Language, 1801–1911* (Cardiff, 1998).

Jones, D. J. V., *Crime in Nineteenth-Century Wales* (Cardiff, 1992).

Jones, D. J. V., *Rebecca's Children* (Oxford, 1990).

Jones, G. S., *Languages of Class* (Cambridge, 1983).

Joyce, P., *Visions of the People: Industrial England and the Questions of Class, 1848–1914* (Cambridge, 1991).

Joyce P. (ed.), *Historical Meanings of Work* (Cambridge, 1987).

Judicial Studies Board, *Adult Court Bench Book* (n.p., 2005).

Kermode, J. and Walker, G. (eds), *Women, Crime and the Courts in Early Modern England* (London, 1994).

Kilday, A.-M. and Nash, D. (eds), *Law, Crime and Deviance since 1700: Micro-studies in the History of Crime* (London, 2017).

King, P., *Crime and Law in England, 1750–1850* (Cambridge, 2006).

King, P., *Crime, Justice and Discretion in England, 1740–1820* (Oxford, 2000).

Kent, S. K., *Sex and Suffrage, 1860–1914* (1987; London, 1990).

Kretchmer, R., *Llanfyllin: A Pictorial History* (Welshpool, 1992).

Lambert, W. R., *Drink and Sobriety in Victorian Wales* (Cardiff, 1983).

Langbein, J. H., *The Origins of the Adversary Criminal Trial* (Oxford, 2003).

Laver, J., *Costume through the Ages* (London, 1963).

Lee, C., *Policing Prostitution, 1859–1886: Deviance, Surveillance and Morality* (London, 2013).

Lewis, J. R., *The Victorian Bar* (London, 1982).

Le Roy Ladurie, E., *Montaillou* (Harmondworth, 1980).

Lombroso, C. and Ferrero, W., *The Female Offender* (London, 1995).

Maddox, W. C., *A History of Radnorshire Constabulary* (Llandrindod Wells, 1959).

Maddox, W. C., *A History of the Montgomeryshire Constabulary, 1840–1948* (Carmarthen, 1982).

Marland, H., *Dangerous Motherhood: Insanity and Childbirth in Victorian Britain* (Basingstoke, 2004).

Mayhew, H. and Hemyng, B., *London Labour and the London Poor* (London, 1862).

McMahon, R. (ed.), *Crime, Law and Popular Culture in Europe, 1500–1900* (Cullompton, 2008).

Miller. A. H., *Novels behind Glass: Commodity Culture and Victorian Narrative* (Cambridge, 2008).

Moir, E., *Justice of the Peace* (Harmondsworth, 1969).

Moore, D., *Wales in the Eighteenth Century* (Swansea, 1976),

Morris, A., *Women, Crime and Criminal Justice* (Oxford, 1987).

Muir E., and Ruggiero, G., *Microhistory and the Lost Peoples of Europe* (Baltimore, 1991).

Neale, R. S. (ed.), *History and Class* (Oxford, 1983).

Newtown Local History Group, *Newtown* (Stroud, 1995).

Niall, I., *The Village Policeman* (London, 1971).

Norton, J. E., *Guide to the National and Provincial Directories of England and Wales Published before 1856* (London, 1950).

O'Leary, P., *Immigration and Integration: The Irish in Wales, 1789–1922* (Cardiff, 2000).

O'Leary, P. (ed.), *Irish Migrants in Modern Wales* (Liverpool, 2004).

O Machain, P., *Six Years in Galmoy: Rural Unrest in County Kilkenny, 1819–1824* (Dublin, 2004).

Owen, B., *Transportation by Montgomeryshire Courts, 1788–1868* (Llanidloes, 2003).

Oxford Concise English Dicitonary (Oxford, 1982).

Pennant, T., *A Tour in Wales* (1778; Caernarfon, 1883).

Phillips, D., *Crime and Authority in Victorian England: The Black Country, 1835–1860* (London, 1997).

Phillips, D. and Storch, R. D., *Policing Provincial England, 1829–1856* (London, 1999).

Phillips, P., *A View of Old Montgomeryshire* (1977; Swansea, 1978).

Plowden, A. C., *Grain or Chaff: The Autobiography of a Police Magistrate* (London, 1903).

Powell, K., *The Cambridge Companion to Victorian and Edwardian Theatre* (Cambridge, 2004).

Powysland Club, *Domesday Book of Montgomeryshire, being a Return of the Owners of Land, 1873* (London, 1876).

Radzinowicz, L. and Hood, R., *The Emergence of Penal Policy in Victorian and Edwardian England* (Oxford, 1990).

Rawlongs, P., *Policing: A Short History* (Cullompton, 2002).

Reay, B., *Microhistories: Demography, Society and Culture in Rural England, 1800–1930* (Cambridge, 1996).

Redford, A., *Labour Migration in England, 1800–1850* (Manchester, 1976).

Reed, M. and Wells, R. (eds), *Class, Conflict and Protest in the English Countryside, 1700–1880* (London, 1990).

Rees, A., *Life in a Welsh Countryside: A Social Study of Llanfihangel-yng Ngwyngfa* (1950; Cardiff, 1996).

Reich, B. and Adcock, C., *Values, Attitudes and Behaviour Change* (London, 1976).

Rendall, J., *Women in an Industrialising Society* (Oxford, 1990).

Richard, H., *Letters and Essays on Wales* (London, 1884).

Richard, H., *Letters on the Social and Political Condition of the Principality of Wales, Reprinted from the Morning and Evening Star* (London, 1866).

Rose, C. and Richmond, V., *Clothing, Society and Culture in Nineteenth-Century Britain*, 3 vols (London, 2010).

Rose, L., *The Massacre of the Innocents: Infanticide in Britain, 1800–1939* (London, 1986).

Rose, S. O., *Limited Livelihoods: Gender and Class in Nineteenth-Century England* (Berkeley, 1992).

Rowbotham, S., *Hidden from History* (London, 1977).

Rudé, G., *The Crowd in History: A Study of Popular Disturbances in France and England, 1730–1848* (New York, 1964).

Rule, F., *The Worst Street in London* (2008; Horsham, 2010).

Saville, J., *Rural Depopulation in England and Wales, 1851 to 1951* (London, 1957).

Scott, J., *Gender and the Politics of History* (New York, 1988).

Shakesheff, T., *Rural Conflict, Crime and Protest: Herefordshire, 1800–1860* (Woodbridge, 2003).

Shaw, G. B., *Mrs Warren's Profession* (Toronto, 2005).

Shore, H., *Artful Dodgers: Youth and Crime in Early 19th-Century London* (Woodbridge, 2002).

Shpayer-Makov, H., *The Ascent of the Detective* (Oxford, 2011).

Skyrme, T., *History of the Justices of the Peace* (Chichester, 1991), vol. 3.

Smart, C., *Women, Crime and Criminology: A Feminist Critique* (London, 1977).

Smith, D. W., *Aberrriw to Berriew: The Story of a Community* (Newtown, 1992).

Snell, K. D. M., *Annals of the Labouring Poor: Social Change and Agrarian England, 1660–1900* (1985; Cambridge,1987).

Snell, K. D. M., *Parish and Belonging: Community, Identity and Welfare in England and Wales, 1700–1950* (Cambridge, 2006).

Snell, K. D. M. (ed.), *The Regional Novel in Britain and Ireland, 1800–1990* (Cambridge, 1998).

Snell, K. D. M. and Ell, P. S., *Rival Jerusalems* (Cambridge, 2000).

Stead, P. J., *The Police of Britain* (London, 1985).

Stedman Jones, G., *Languages of Class* (Cambridge, 1983).

Steedman, C, *Policing the Victorian Community: The Formation of the English Provincial Police Forces, 1856–80* (London, 1984).

Stephens, H., *The Book of the Farm*, 3 vols (Edinburgh, 1844).

Strathern, M., *Kinship at the Core: An Anthropology of Elmdon, a Village in North-West Essex in the Nineteen-Sixties* (Cambridge, 1981).

Swift, R. and Gilley, S. (eds), *The Irish in Victorian Britiain: The Local Dimension* (Dublin, 1999).

Taylor, B., *Eve and the New Jerusalem: Socialism and Feminism in the Nineteenth Century* (New York, 1983).

Taylor, D., *Beerhouses, Brothels and Bobbies: Policing by Consent in Huddersfield and the Huddersfield District in the Nineteenth Century* (Huddersfield, 2016).

Taylor, D., *Crime, Policing and Punishment in England, 1750–1914* (Basingstoke, 1998).

Taylor, D., *Policing the Victorian Town: The Development of the Police in Middlesbrough c. 1840–1891* (Basingstoke, 2002).

Taylor, D., *The New Police in Nineteenth Century England* (Manchester, 1997).

The Living Bible (Wheaton, 1971).

Thompson, E. P., *The Making of the English Working Class* (London, 1963).

Thompson, F. M. L., *English Landed Society in the Nineteenth Century* (London, 1963).

Tilly, L. A. and Scott, J. W., *Women, Work and Family* (London, 1978).

Tobias, J. J., *Crime and Industrial Society in the Nineteenth Century* (Oxford, 1967).

Trant, I., *The Changing Face of Welshpool* (Welshpool, 1986).

Trinder, B. (ed.), *Victorian Shrewsbury* (Shrewsbury, 1984).

University of Wales Dictionary (n.p., 2002).

Valenze, D., *The First Industrial Woman* (New York, 1995).

Vicinus, M., *Suffer and be Still* (Bloomington, 1973).

Walker, G., *Crime, Gender and Social Order* (Cambridge, 2003).

Walkowitz, J., *Prostitution and Victorian Society* (Cambridge, 1980).

Walsh, W., *Kilkenny: The Struggle for the Land, 1850–82* (Thomastown, 2008).

Webb, S. and Webb, B., *English Local Government* (London, 1924 and1963).

White, R. and Haines, F., *Crime and Criminology* (1996; Oxford, 2008).

Whitlock, T. C., *Crime, Gender and Consumer Culture in Nineteenth Century England* (Farnham, 2005).

Wiener, M., *Men of Blood: Violence, Manliness and Criminal Justice in Victorian England* (Cambridge, 2004).

Willans, J. B., *The Byways of Montgomeryshire* (London 1905).

Williams, G. A., *When was Wales? A History of the Welsh* (Harmondsworth, 1985).

Williams, J. L. and Hughes, G. R. (eds), *The History of Education in Wales* (Swansea, 1978).

Williams, R., *The Country and the City* (London, 1973).

Wilson, E. and Taylor, L., *Through The Looking Glass: A History of Dress from 1860 to the Present Day* (London, 1989).

Wilson, J. M., *The Imperial Gazetteer of England and Wales* (Edinburgh, Glasgow and London, n.d. [c. 1874]).

Wise, S., *The Blackest Streets* (London, 2009).

Zedner, L., *Women, Crime and Custody in Victorian England* (Oxford, 1991).

I. Zweiniger-Bargielowska (ed.), *Women in Twentieth-Century Britain* (2001; Abingdon, 2014).

Chapters in books

Ardener, E., 'Belief and the problem of women', in S. Ardener (ed.), *Perceiving Women* (London, 1975), pp. 1–27.

Arnot, M. L. and Usborne, C., 'Why Gender and Crime?', in M. L. Arnot and C. Usborne (eds), *Gender and Crime in Modern Europe* (1999; London, 2003), pp. 1–43.

Arnot, M. L., 'Understanding women committing newborn child murder in Victorian England', in S. D'Cruze (ed.), *Everyday Violence in England, 1850–1950* (Harlow, 2000), pp. 55–69.

Bailey, V., 'The fabrication of deviance: "dangerous classes" and "criminal classes" in Victorian England', in J. Rule and R. Malcolmson (eds), *Protest and Survival: The Historical Experience; Essays for E. P. Thompson* (London, 1993), pp. 221–56.

Baker, J. H., 'Criminal courts and procedure at common law, 1550–1800', in J. S. Cockburn (ed.), *Crime in England, 1550–1800* (London, 1977), pp. 15–48.

Beattie, J., 'Crime and the courts in Surrey, 1736–1753', in J. S. Cockburn (ed.), *Crime in England, 1550–1800* (Princeton, 1977), pp. 155–86.

Berg, M., 'Women's work, mechanization and the early phase of industrialization in England', in P. Joyce (ed.), *The Historical Meanings of Work* (Cambridge, 1987), pp. 64–98.

Bourdieu, P., 'The forms of capital', in I. Szeman and T. Kaposy (eds), *Cultural Theory: An Anthology* (Oxford, 2011), pp. 81–93.

Briggs, A., 'The language of class in early nineteenth-century England', in A. Briggs and J. Saville (eds), *Essays in Labour History in Memory of G. D. H. Cole* (London, 1967), pp. 43–73.

Britton, D. M., 'Feminism in Criminology', in M. Chesney-Lind and L. Pasko (eds), *Girls, Women and Crime* (Los Angeles, 2004).

Clark, A., 'Domesticity and the problem of wife beating in nineteenth-century Britain: working-class culture, law and politics', in S. D'Cruze (ed.), *Everyday Violence in Britain, 1850–1950: Gender and Class* (2000; Harlow, 2004), pp. 27–40.

Cocks, R., 'Victorian barristers, judges and taxation: a study in the expansion of legal work', in G. R. Rubin and D. Sugarman (eds), *Law, Economy and Society, 1750–1914* (Abingdon, 1984), pp. 445–69.

Council of Europe, 'Earlier studies on economic crisis and crime', in *Economic Crisis and Crime* (Strasbourg, 1985), pp. 9–18.

Davies, R., 'Voices from the void: social crisis, social problems and the individual in south-west Wales, 1876–1920', in G. H. Jenkins and B. Smith (eds), *Politics and Society in Wales, 1840–1922: Essays in Honour of Ieuan Gwynedd Jones* (Cardiff, 1998), pp. 81–91.

Davis, J., 'Prosecutions and their context', in D. Hay and F. Snyder, *Policing and Prosecution in Britain 1750–1850* (Oxford, 1980), pp. 397–426.

Doyle, B. M., 'The changing functions of urban government: councillors, officials and pressure groups', in P. Clarke (ed.), *The Cambridge Urban History of Britain* (Cambridge, 2000), pp. 298–301.

Feldman, D., 'Class' in P. Burke (ed.), *History and Historians in the Twentieth Century* (Oxford, 2002), pp. 181–206.

Gattrell, V. A. C., 'Crime, authority and the policeman state'. in F. M. L. Thompson (ed.), *The Cambridge Social History of Britain*, vol. 3 (Cambridge, 1990), pp. 243–310.

Gattrell, V. A. C., 'The decline of theft and violence in Victorian and Edwardian England', in V. A. C. Gatrell, B. Lenman and G. Parker (eds), *Crime and the Law: The Social History of Crime in Western Europe since 1500* (London, 1980), pp. 238–370.

Gerrard, J. and Parrott, V., 'Craft, profession and middle-class identity: solicitors and gas engineers, c. 1850–1914', in A. Kidd and D. Nicholls, *The Making of the British Middle Class* (Stroud, 1998), pp. 148–61.

Godfrey, B., 'Workplace appropriation and the gendering of factory "law"' in M. L. Arnot and C. Usborne (eds), *Gender and Crime in Modern Europe* (1999; London, 2003), pp. 137–50.

Godfrey, B. and Dunstall, G., 'The growth of crime and crime control in developing towns: Timaru and Crewe, 1850–1920', in B. Godfrey and G. Dunstall (eds), *Crime and Empire, 1840–1940: Criminal Justice in Local and Global Context* (Cullompton, 2005), pp. 135–44.

Hart, J., 'Religion and social control in the mid nineteenth-century', in A. P. Donajgrodski (ed.), *Social Control in Nineteenth-Century Britain* (London, 1977), pp. 108–38.

Hay, D., 'England 1562–1875: the law and its uses', in D. Hay and P. Craven (eds), *Masters, Servants and Magistrates in Britain and the Empire* (London, 2004), pp. 59–116.

Hay, D., 'Property, authority and the criminal law', in D. Hay, P. Linebaugh, J. G. Rule, E. P. Thompson and C. Winslow, *Albion's Fatal Tree: Crime and Society in Eighteenth-Century England* (London, 1975), pp. 17–65.

Humphreys, M., 'Harmony, crime and order', in Humphreys, *Crisis*, pp. 217–52.

Ireland, R. W., 'A second Ireland? Crime and popular culture in nineteenth-century Wales', in R. McMahon (ed.), *Crime, Law and Popular Culture in Europe, 1500–1900* (Cullompton, 2008) pp. 239–61.

Ireland, R. W., '"Perhaps my mother murdered me": child death and the law in Victorian Carmarthenshire', in C. Brooks and M. Lobban (eds.), *Communities and Courts in Britain, 1150–1900* (Hambledon, 1997), pp. 229–43.

Ireland, R. W., 'Putting oneself in whose country? Carmarthenshire juries in the mid nineteenth century', in T. G. Watkin (ed.), *Legal Wales, Its Past, Its Future* (Cardiff, 2001), pp. 63–87.

Jackson, L. A., 'Women professionals and the regulation of violence in interwar Britain', in S. D'Cruze (ed.), *Everyday Violence in Britain, 1850–1950: Gender and Class* (Abingdon, 2000), pp. 119–35.

Jarman, M., 'The Welsh language and the courts', in T. G. Watkin and N. S. B. Cox (eds), *Canmlywddiant, Cyfraith a Chymreictod: A Celebration of the Life and Work of Dafydd Jenkins, 1911–2012* (Bangor, 2013), pp. 170–3.

Kent, C., 'The editor and the law', in J. H. Wiener (ed.), *Innovators and Preachers: The Role of the Editor in Victorian England* (Westport, 1985)

Jones, D. J. V., 'Greater and lesser men', in D. J. V. Jones, *Rebecca's Children*.

Jones, D. J. V., 'The Welsh and crime: 1801–1891', in C. Emsley and J. Walvin (eds), *Artisans, Peasants and Proletarians, 1760–1860* (Beckenham, 1983), pp. 81–103.

Jones, F. P., 'The Blue Books of 1847', in J. L. Williams and G. R. Hughes (eds), *The History of Education in Wales* (Swansea, 1978), pp. 127–44.

Jones, J. G., 'The Welsh language in local government: justices of the peace and the courts of quarter sessions, *c.*1536–1800', in G. H. Jenkins (ed.), *The Welsh Language before the Industrial Revolution* (Cardiff, 1997), pp. 181–206.

Langbein, J. H., 'The bifurcation and the bench: the influence of the jury on English conceptions of the judiciary', in P. Brand and J. Getzler (eds), *Judges and Judging in the History of the Common Law and Civil Law: From Antiquity to Modern Times* (Cambridge, 2012), pp. 67–82.

Maclaughlin, J., 'Pestilence on their backs, famine in their stomachs: the racial construction of Irishness and the Irish in Victorian Britain', in C. Graham and R. Kirkland (eds), *Ireland and Cultural Theory: The Mechanics of Authenticity* (Basingstoke, 1999), pp. 50–76.

Marland, H., 'Getting away with murder? Puerperal insanity, infanticide and the defence plea', in M. Jackson (ed.), *Infanticide* (Aldershot, 2002), pp. 168–93.

May, M., 'Violence in the family: an historical perspective', in J. P. Martin (ed.), *Violence in the Family* (Chichester, 1978), pp. 125–67.

McGowan, R., 'Cruel inflictions and the claims of humanity in early nineteenth-century England', in K. D. Watson (ed.), *Assaulting the Past: Violence and Civilisation in Historical Context* (Newcastle, 2007), pp. 38–57.

Morris, E. R., 'The Hundreds', in D. Jenkins, *Historical Atlas*, pp. 65–6.

Morris, E. R., 'Woollen Industry', in D. Jenkins (ed.), *Historical Atlas*, pp. 98–9.

Neale, R. S., 'Class consciousness in early nineteenth-century England: three classes or five?', in R. S. Neale (ed.), *History and Class* (Oxford, 1983), pp. 143–65.

Ormrod, W. M., 'Law in the landscape: criminality, outlawry and regional Identity in late medieval England', in A. Musson (ed.), *Boundaries of the Law: Geography, Gender and Jurisdiction in Medieval and Early-Modern Europe* (Aldershot, 2005), pp. 7–20.

O'Hanrahan, M., 'The tithe war in County Kilkenny, 1930–34', in W. Nolan and K. Whelan (eds), *Kilkenny: History and Society: Interdisciplinary Essays on the History of an Irish County* (Dublin, 1990), pp. 481–505.

O'Leary, P., 'The Irish and crime', in P. O'Leary (ed.), *Immigration and Integration: The Irish in Wales, 1789–1922*, pp. 161–85.

Poole, B., 'Agriculture', in D. Jenkins, *Historical Atlas*, pp. 103–7.

Pritchard, T. W., 'The Church in Wales', in D. Jenkins, *Historical Atlas*, pp. 67–73.

Pryce, W. T. R., 'Changing language geographies of Montgomeryshire', in D. Jenkins, *Historical Atlas*, pp. 118–24.

Rendall, J., 'Women's paid employment', in J. Rendall, *Women in an Industrializing Society* (Oxford, 1990), pp. 55–78.

Roberts, G. T., 'Under the hatches: English parliamentary commissioners' views of the people and language of mid nineteenth-century Wales', in B. Schwartz (ed.), *The Expansion of the English Race: Race, Ethnicity and Cultural History* (London, 1996), pp. 171–97.

Ryan, L., 'Publicising the private: suffragists' critique of sexual abuse and domestic violence', in L. Ryan and M. Ward (eds), *Irish Women and the Vote: Becoming Citizens* (Dublin, 2007), pp. 75–90.

Scott, J. W., 'Women's history', in P. Burke (ed.), *New Perspectives on Historical Writing* (Cambridge, 2001), pp. 43–70.

Showalter, E. and Showalter, E., 'Victorian women and menstruation', in M. Vicinus, *Suffer and Be Still*, pp. 38–44.

Shubert, A., 'Private initiative in law enforcement: associations for the prosecution of felons', in V. Bailey (ed.), *Policing and Punishment*, pp. 25–41.

Siedentop, L., 'Distinguishing spiritual from temporal power', in L. Siedentop (ed.), *Inventing the Individual: The Origins of Western Liberalism* (London, 2014), pp. 126–40.

Sigsworth, E. M. and Wyke, T. J., 'A study of Victorian prostitution and venereal disease', in M. Vicinus (ed.) *Suffer and Be Still*, pp. 77–99.

Smith, D. W., 'Tithe protests', *Mont. Colls*, 84 (1996), pp. 134–5.

Smith, G. T., 'Violent crime and the public weal in England, 1700–1900', in R. McMahon (ed.), *Crime, Law and Popular Culture in Europe, 1500–1900* (Cullompton, 2008).

Suggett, R., 'The Welsh language and the Court of Great Sessions', in G. H. Jenkins (ed.), *The Welsh Language before the Industrial Revolution* (Cardiff, 1997), pp. 153–80.

Storch, R. D., 'Police control of street prostitution in Victorian London: a study in the context of police action', in D. Bayley (ed.), *Police and Society* (London, 1977), pp. 49–72.

Taithe, B., 'Consuming desires: prostitutes and "customers" at the margins of crime and perversion in France and Britain, c. 1836–85', in M. L. Arnot and C. Usborne (eds), *Gender and Crime in Modern Europe* (1999; London, 2003), pp. 151–72.

Thompson, F. M. L., 'The nature of landed society', in F. M. L. Thompson, *English Landed Society in the Nineteenth Century* (London, 1963), pp. 1–24.

Tomlinson, M. H., 'Penal servitude 1846–65: a system in evolution', in V. Bailey, *Policing and Punishment*, pp. 126–49.

Toplis, A., 'A stolen garment or a reasonable purchase? The male consumer and the illicit second-hand clothing market in the first half of the nineteenth century', in J. Stobart and I. Van Damme (eds), *Modernity and the Second-Hand Trade: European Consumption Cultures and Practices, 1700–1900* (Basingstoke, 2011), pp. 59–60.

Van Damme (eds), *Modernity and the Second-Hand Trade: European Consumption Cultures and Practices, 1700–1900* (Basingstoke, 2011), pp. 59–60.

Weber, M., 'Class, status, party', in R. S. Neale (ed.), *History and Class*, pp. 56–72.

Weinberger, B., 'The police and the public in mid-nineteenth-century Warwickshire', in V. Bailey (ed.), *Policing and Punishment in Nineteenth-Century Britain* (London, 1981), pp. 65–93.

White, B., 'Training medical policemen: forensics, medicine and public health in nineteenth-century Scotland', in M. Clark and C. Crawford (eds), *Legal Medicine in History* (Cambridge, 1994), pp. 145–66.

White, E. M., 'The Established Church, dissent and the Welsh Language', in G. H. Jenkins (ed.), *The Welsh Language before the Industrial Revolution* (Cardiff, 1997), pp. 235–88.

Williams, L. H., 'Education', in D. Jenkins (ed.), *Historical Atlas*, pp. 85–91.

Articles in journals

Archer, J. E., 'Poaching gangs and violence', *British Journal of Criminology*, 39 (1999), 25–38.

Armytage, W. H. G., 'The 1870 Education Act', *British Journal of Educational Studies*, 18 (1970), 121–33.

Ashton, O. R., 'Chartism in mid Wales', *Mont. Colls*, 62 (1971), 10–57.

Auerbach, S., '"The law has no feeling for poor folks like us!" Everyday responses to legal compulsion in England's working-class communities, 1871–1904', *Journal of Social History*, 45 (2012), 686–708.

August, A., 'A horrible-looking woman: female violence in late-Victorian East London', *Journal of British Studies*, 54 (2015), pp. 844–68.

Ballinger, A., 'Masculinity in the dock: legal responses to male violence and female retaliation in England and Wales, 1900–1965', *Social and Legal Studies*, 16 (2007), 459–81.

Barrow, R. J., 'Rape on the railway: women, safety, and moral panic in Victorian newspapers', *Journal of Victorian Culture*, 20 (2015), 341–56.

Bauer, M. and Patzelt, D., 'Evaluation of mRNA markers for the identification of menstrual blood', *Journal of Forensic Science*, 47 (2002), 1278–82.

Bauer, M. and Patzelt, D., 'Identification of menstrual blood by real time RT-PCR: technical improvements and the practical value of negative test results', *Forensic Science International*, 174 (2008), 54–8.

Beattie, J., 'The criminality of women in eighteenth-century England', *Journal of Social History*, 8 (1975), 80–116.

Beattie, J. M., 'The pattern of crime in England', *Past and Present*, 62 (1974), 47–95.

Behlmer, G. K., 'Deadly motherhood: infanticide and medical opinion in mid-Victorian England', *Journal of Historical Medicine and Allied Sciences*, 34 (1979), 403–27.

Beier, A. L., 'Identity, language and resistance in the making of the Victorian "Criminal Class": Mayhew's convict revisited', *Journal of British Studies*, 44 (2005), 927–42.

Bellanta, M., 'Looking flash: disreputable women's dress and "modernity", 1870–1910', *History Workshop Journal*, 78 (2014), 58–81.

Bennison, B., 'Drunkenness in turn-of-the-century Newcastle upon Tyne', *Local Population Studies*, 52 (1994), 14–22.

Bingham, A., 'Historical child sexual abuse in England and Wales: the role of historians', *History of Education*, 45 (2016), pp. 411–29.

Blomley, N., 'Making private property: enclosure, common right and the work of hedges', *Rural History*, 18 (2007), 1–21.

Boritch, H. and Hagan, J., 'A century of crime in Toronto: gender, class and patterns of social control 1859 to 1955', *Criminology*, 28 (1990), 567–600.

Boyer, G. R. and Hatton, T. J., 'Migration and labour market integration in late nineteenth-century England and Wales', *Economic History Review*, 50 (1997), 697–734.

Brown, C. G., 'The costs of pew renting: church going and social class in nineteenth-century Glasgow', *Journal of Ecclesiastical History*, 38 (1987), 347–61.

Brown, R. B., 'A delusion, a mockery and a snare: jury selection in England and Ireland, 1800–50', *Canadian Journal of History*, 39 (2004), 1–26.

Brown, R. L. 'The Reverend David Davies, Rector of Llansilin, 1876–1901', *Mont. Colls*, 101 (2013), 109–16.

Charlesworth, A., 'An agenda for historical studies of rural protest in Britain, 1750–1850', *Rural History*, 11 (1991), 231–40.

Clapham, J. H., 'The transference of the worsted industry from Norfolk to the West Riding', *Economic Journal*, 20 (1910), 195–210.

Clay, J., 'On the relation between crime, popular instruction, attendance at religious worship and beer-house', *Journal of the Statistical Society*, 20 (1857), 22–32.

Clayton, M., 'The life and times of Charlotte Walker, prostitute and pick-pocket', *London Journal*, 33 (2008), 3–19.

Clements, F., 'Vagrancy in Victorian Denbighshire', *Transactions of the Denbighshire Historical Society*, 58 (2010), 56–64.

Clements, F., 'Sergeant W. R. Breese: a policeman in rural nineteenth-century Denbighshire', *Transactions of the Denbighshire Historical Society*, 56 (2008).

Coleman, J., 'Incorrigible offenders: media representations of female habitual criminals in the late Victorian and Edwardian press', *Media History*, 22 (2016), pp. 143–58.

Conley, C. C., 'Rape and justice in Victorian England', *Victorian Studies*, 29 (1986), 519–36.

Cowell, B., 'The Commons Preservation Society and the campaign for Berkhamsted Common, 1866–70', *Rural History*, 13 (2002), 145–61.

Davies, J., 'The end of the great estates and the rise of freehold farming in Wales', *Welsh History Review*, 7 (1974), 186–212.

Davies, J. I., 'The history of printing in Montgomeryshire, 1789–1960', *Mont. Colls*, 70 (1982), 71–98.

Davis, J., 'A poor man's system of justice: the London police courts in the second half of the nineteenth century', *Historical Journal*, 27 (1984), 309–35.

Devereaux, S., 'From sessions to newspaper? Criminal trial reporting, the nature of crime and the London press, 1770–1800', *The London Journal*, 32 (2007), 1–17.

Emsley, C., 'A typology of nineteenth-century police', *Crime, History and Society*, 3 (1991), 29–44.

Emsley, C., 'Mother, what did policemen do when there weren't any motors? The law, the police and the regulation of motor traffic in England, 1900–1939', *Historical Journal*, 36 (1992), 357–81.

Engel, A. J., 'Immoral intentions: the University of Oxford and the problem of prostitution 1827–1914', *Victorian Studies*, 23 (1979), 79–107.

Feeley, M. M. and Little, D. L., 'The vanishing female: the decline of women in the criminal process, 1687–1912', *Law and Society Review*, 25 (1991), 719–57.

Finlayson, G. B. A., 'The politics of municipal reform, 1835', *English Historical Review*, 81 (1966), 673–92.

Friedlander, D. and Roshier, R. J., 'A study of internal migration in England and Wales: part 1', *Population Studies*, 19 (1966), 239–79.

Godfrey, B. S., 'Changing prosecution practices and their impact on crime figures, 1857–1940', *British Journal of Criminology*, 48 (2008), 171–89.

Godfrey, B. S., 'Law, factory discipline and "theft": the impact of the factory on workplace appropriation in mid to late nineteenth-century Yorkshire', *British Journal of Criminology*, 39 (1999), 56–71.

Godfrey, B. S. and Cox, D. J., 'Policing the industrial north of England, 1777–1877: the control of labour at work, and in the streets', *Crime, History and Society*, 20 (2016), pp. 129–47.

Godfrey, B. S., Farrall, S. and Karstedt, S., 'Explaining gendered sentencing patterns', *British Journal of Criminology*, 45 (2005), 696–720.

Godfrey, B. S. and Locker, J. P., 'The nineteenth-century decline of custom, and its impact on theories of workplace theft and white collar crime', *Northern History*, 38 (2001), 261–73.

Golan, T., 'The history of scientific expert testimony in the English courtroom', *Science in Context*, 12 (1999), 1–12.

Griffiths, C. C., 'The Prisoner's Counsel Act, 1836: doctrine, advocacy and the criminal trial', *Law, Crime and History*, 2 (2014), 28–47.

Hamlin, C., 'Sanitary policing and the local state, 1873–4: a statistical study of English and Welsh towns', *Social History of Medicine*, 18 (2005), 39–61.

Handler, P., 'The law of felonious assault in England, 1803–61', *Journal of Legal History*, 28 (2007), 183–206.

Harrison, R. D., 'Royal Montgomery Regiment of Militia', *Mont. Colls*, 17 (1884), 181–232.

Howard, S., 'Investigating responses to theft in early modern Wales: communities, thieves and the courts', *Continuity and Change*, 19 (2004), 409–30.

Howells, C. E., 'The association for the prosecution of felons, Welshpool', *Mont. Colls*, 33 (1904), 95–105.

Howlin, N., 'Fenians, foreigners and jury trials in Ireland, 1865–70', *Irish Jurist*, 45 (2010), 51–81.

Hudson, P., 'The limits of wool', *Cardiff Historical Papers* (2007), 1–40.

Hunt, K., 'Gender and labour history in the 1990s', *Mitteilungsblatt des Instituts für soziale Bewegungen*, 27 (2002), 185–200.

Hurren, E. T., 'Remaking the medico-legal scene: a social history of the late-Victorian coroner in Oxford', *Journal of the History of Medicine and Allied Sciences*, 65 (2010), 207–52

Ireland, R., 'An increasing mass of heathens in the bosom of a Christian land: the railway and crime in the nineteenth century', *Continuity and Change*, 12 (1997), 55–78.

Jenkins, J. G., 'The woollen industry in Montgomeryshire', *Mont. Colls*, 58 (1963–4), 50–69.

Johnston, H., 'The Shropshire magistracy and local imprisonment: networks of power in the nineteenth century', *Midland History*, 30 (2005), 67–91.

Jones, D. J. V., 'A dead loss to the community: the nineteenth-century vagrant in mid-nineteenth-century Wales', *Welsh History Review*, 8 (1977), 312–44.

Jones, D. J. V., 'Crime, protest and community in nineteenth-century Wales', *Llafur*, 3 (1974), 110–20.

Jones, D. J. V., 'The new police in England and Wales', *Transactions of the Royal Historical Society*, 33 (1983), 151–68.

Jones, D. J. V., 'The poacher: a study in Victorian crime and protest', *Historical Journal*, 22 (1979), 825–60.

Jones, D. J. V., 'Where did it all go wrong? Crime in Swansea, 1938–68', *Welsh History Review*, 15 (1990), 240–74.

Jones, E., 'Missing out on an industrial revolution', *World Economics*, 9 (2008), 101–28.

Jones, P., 'Finding Captain Swing: protest, parish relations and the state of the parish mind in 1830', *Southern History*, 22 (2010), 429–58.

Jones, R., 'A Montgomeryshire magistrate and his dairymaid', *Mont. Colls*, 101 (2013), 101–8.

Jones, R., 'Maria Humphreys-Owen: Montgomeryshire's champion of women's rights', *Mont. Colls*, 99 (2011), 109–21.

Jones, R., 'Victorian schools in nineteenth-century Montgomeryshire', *Mont. Colls*, 102 (2014), 121–31.

Kelly, C., 'Reforming juvenile justice in nineteenth-century Scotland: the subversion of the Scottish day industrial school movement', *Crime, History and Society*, 20 (2016), pp. 129–47.

King, P., 'The impact of urbanization on murder rates and on the geography of homicide in England and Wales, 1780–1850', *Historical Journal*, 53 (2010), 671–98.

King, P., 'Immigrant communities, the police and the courts in late eighteenth and early nineteenth-century London', *Crime, History and Society*, 20 (2016), pp. 39–68.

King, P. J. R., 'Decision-makers and decision-making in the English criminal law, 1750–1800', *Historical Journal*, 27 (1984), 25–58.

King, P. J. R., 'Making crime news: newspapers, violent crime and the selective reporting of Old Bailey trials in the late eighteenth century', *Crime, History and Societies*, 13 (2009), 91–116.

King, P. J. R., 'Newspaper reporting and attitudes to crime and justice in late eighteenth- and early nineteenth-century London', *Continuity and Change*, 22 (2007), 73–112.

King, P. J. R., 'Punishing assault: the transformation of attitudes in the English courts', *Journal of Interdisciplinary History*, 27 (1996), 43–74.

King, P. J. R., 'The summary courts and social relations in eighteenth-century England', *Past and Present*, 183 (2004), 125–72.

Koditschek, T., 'The gendering of the British working class', *Gender and History*, 5 (1997), 333–63.

Landau, N., 'Appearances at the quarter sessions of eighteenth-century Middlesex', *London Journal*, 23 (1998), 30–52.

Landau, N., 'Indictment for fun and profit', *Law and History Review*, 17 (1999), 507–36.

Landsman, S., 'One hundred years of rectitude: medical witnesses at the Old Bailey, 1717–1817', *Law and History Review*, 16 (1998), 445–94.

Langbein, J. H., 'Albion's fatal flaws', *Past and Present*, 98 (1983), 96–120.

Lemire, B., 'The theft of clothes and popular consumerism in early modern England', *Journal of Social History*, 24 (1990), 255–76.

Lemmings, D., 'Criminal trial procedure in eighteenth-century England: the impact of lawyers', *Journal of Legal History*, 26 (2005), 73–82.

Lewis, E. A., 'A schedule of the quarter sessions records of the county of Montgomery at the National Library of Wales', *Mont. Colls*, 46 (1940), 156–82.

Lloyd, D. J. K., 'The Lieutenants of Montgomeryshire', *Mont. Colls*, 63 (1973), 114–18.

Logan, A., 'A suitable person for suitable cases? The gendering of the juvenile courts in England, 1910–39', *Twentieth-Century British History*, 16 (2005), 129–45.

Logan, A., 'In search of equal citizenship: the campaign for women magistrates in England and Wales, 1910–1939', *Women's History Review*, 16 (2007), 501–18.

Logan, A., 'Professionalism and the impact of the first women justices, 1920–1950', *Historical Journal*, 49 (2006), 833–50.

Logan, A., 'Women and the provision of criminal justice advice: lessons from England and Wales, 1944–1964', *British Journal of Criminology*, 50 (2010), 1077–93.

Luddy, M., 'Abandoned women and bad characters: prostitution in nineteenth-century Ireland', *Women's History Review*, 6 (1997), 485–503.

MacKay, L., 'Why they stole: women in the Old Bailey, 1779–1789', *Journal of Social History*, 32 (1999), 623–639.

Margerey, S., 'The invention of juvenile delinquency in early nineteenth-century London', *Labour History*, 34 (1978), 11–25.

May, M., 'Innocence and experience: the evolution of the concept of juvenile delinquency in the mid-nineteenth century', *Victorian Studies*, 17 (1973), 7–29.

McDonagh, B., 'Subverting the ground: private property and public protest in the sixteenth-century Yorkshire Wolds', *Agricultural History Review*, 57 (2009), 191–206.

Middleton, J., 'Thomas Hopley and mid-Victorian attitudes to corporal punishment', *History of Education*, 24 (2005), 599–615.

Minkes, J., 'Wales and the Bloody Code', *Welsh History Review*, 22 (2006), 673–704.

Moody, T. W., 'Michael Davitt in penal servitude', *Irish Quarterly Review*, 30 (1941), 517–30.

Moore-Colyer, R., 'Gentlemen, horses and the turf in nineteenth-century Wales', *Welsh History Review*, 16 (1992), 47–62.

Morris, E. R., 'Who were the Montgomeryshire Chartists?', *Mont. Colls*, 58 (1963–4), 27–49.

Morris, E. R., 'Hugh Jerman', *Mont. Colls*, 72 (1984), 47–52.

Munsche, P. B., 'The gamekeeper and English rural society', *Journal of British Studies*, 20 (1981), 82–105.

Navickas, K., 'Political clothing and adornment in England, 1740–1840', *Journal of British Studies*, 69 (2010), 540–65.

Navickas, K., 'Whatever happened to class? New histories of labour and collective action in Britain', *Social History*, 36 (2011), 192–204.

Neale, R. S., 'Class and class consciousness in early nineteenth-century England: three classes or five?', *Victorian Studies*, 12 (1968), 4–32.

Newby, H., 'The deferential dialectic', *Comparative Studies in Society and History*, 17 (1975), 139–64.

O'Leary, P., 'Masculine histories: gender and the social history of modern Wales', *Welsh History Review*, 22 (2004), 252–77.

Osborne, H., 'The seasonality of nineteenth-century poaching', *Agricultural History Review*, 45 (2000), 27–41.

Owen, B., 'The Newtown and Llanidloes poor law union workhouse, Caersws, 1837–1847', *Mont. Colls*, 78 (1990), 115–60.

Owen, W. S., 'A parochial history of Tregynon', *Mont. Colls*, 30 (1898), 14–15.

Parry, E., 'The bloodless wars of Montgomeryshire: law and disorder, 1837–41', *Mont. Colls*, 97 (2009), 123–64.

Pavlich, G., 'The emergence of habitual criminals in nineteenth-century Britain', *Journal of Theoretical and Philosophical Criminology*, 2 (2010), 1–62.

Pearson, J. M., 'The decayed and decaying industries of Montgomeryshire', *Mont. Colls*, 37 (1915), 15–30.

Phillips, D. 'The Black Country magistracy, 1835–60', *Midland History*, 3 (1976), 161–90.

Pugsley, D., 'The Western Circuit', *Bracton Law Journal*, 26 (1994), 43–54.

Rabin, D., 'Drunkenness and responsibility for crime', *Journal of British Studies*, 44 (2005), 457–77.

Rademan, G., 'The Cedewain Lodge of Freemasons', *Newtonian*, 32 (2008), 8–14.

Rademan, G., 'The story of Milford Road', *Newtonian*, 30 (2007), 10–17.

Riva, M. A., Tremolizzo, L., Spicci, M., Ferrarese, C., De Vito, G., Cesana, G. C., Sironi, V. A., 'The disease of the moon: the linguistic and pathological evolution of the English term "lunatic"', *Journal of the History of the Neurosciences*, 20 (2011), 65–73.

Robinson, D. J., 'Crime, police and the provincial press: a study of Victorian Cardiff', *Welsh History Review*, 25 (2011), 551–75.

Rock, P., 'Victims, prosecutors and the state in nineteenth-century England and Wales', *Criminal Justice*, 4 (2004), 331–54.

Rogers, S., 'The myth of male dominance', *American Ethnologist*, 2 (1975), 727–57.

Rowbotham, J., 'Turning away from criminal intent: a reflection on Victorian and Edwardian strategies for promoting distance amongst petty offenders', *Theoretical Criminology*, 13 (2009), 105–28.

Ruggieri, S. and Boca, S., 'At the roots of product placement: the mere exposure effect', *Europe's Journal of Psychology*, 9 (2013), 246–58.

Sharpe, J., 'Reporting crime in the north of England eighteenth-century newspaper: a preliminary investigation', *Crime, Histoire et Société*, 16 (2012), 25–45.

Short, B., 'Conservation, class and custom: lifespace and conflict in a nineteenth-century forest environment', *Rural History*, 10 (1999), 127–54.

Short, B., 'Environmental politics, custom and personal testimony: memory and lifespace on the late Victorian Ashdown Forest, Sussex', *Journal of Historical Geography*, 30 (2004), 470–95.

Sindall, R., 'The London garrotting panics of 1856 and 1862', *Social History*, 12 (1987), 351–9.

Smith, D. W., 'The tithes to their end in Montgomeryshire: an introduction', *Mont. Colls*, 84 (1996), 123–36.

Snell. K. D. M., 'Belonging and community: understandings of "home" and "friends" among the English poor, 1750–1850', *Economic History Review*, 65 (2012), 1–25.

Spencer, N. and Gatley, D. A., 'Investigating population mobility in nineteenth-century England and Wales', *Local Population Studies*, 65 (2000), 47–57.

Storch, R. D., 'The plague of the Blue Locusts: police reform and popular resistance in northern England, 1840–57', *International Review of Social History*, 20 (1975), 61–90.

Storch, R. D., 'The policeman as domestic missionary: urban discipline and popular culture in Northern England, 1850–1880', *Journal of Social History*, 9 (1976), 481–509.

Strange, J.-M., 'The assault on ignorance: teaching menstrual etiquette in England c. 1920s to 1960s', *Social History of Medicine*, 14 (2001), 247–65.

Sudeley, Lord, 'Gregynog before 1900', *Mont. Colls*, 62 (1972), 116–82.

Taylor, H., 'The politics of the rising crime statistics in England and Wales, 1914–1960', *Crime, Histoire et Sociétés*, 2 (1998), 5–28.

Thomas, J., 'Women and capitalism: oppression or emancipation?', *Comparative Studies in Society and History*, 30 (1988), 534–49.

Tilley, P., 'Creating life histories and family trees from nineteenth-century census records, parish registers and other sources', *Local Population Studies*, 68 (2002), 63–81.

Tomes, N., '"A Torrent of Abuse": crimes of violence between working-class men and women in London, 1840–1875', *Journal of Social History*, 11 (1978), 328–45.

Virkler, K. and Lednev, I. K., 'Analysis of body fluids for forensic purposes: from laboratory testing to non-destructive rapid confirmatory identification at a crime scene', *Forensic Science International*, 188 (2009), 1–17.

Wallace, R., 'Wales and the parliamentary reform movement', *Welsh History Review*, 11 (1983), 469–87.

Wolpin, K. I., 'An economic analysis of crime and punishment in England and Wales, 1894–1967', *Journal of Political Economy*, 86 (1978), 815–40.

Walsh, W., 'Hard labour, hard board and hard fare: Kilkenny's gaols, 1770–1900', *Ossory, Laois and Leinster*, 3 (2008), 209–38.

Ward, D., 'Environs and neighbours in the two nations: residential differentiation in mid nineteenth-century Leeds', *Journal of Historical Geography*, 6 (1980), 133–62.

Warner, J. H., 'Therapeutic explanation and the Edinburgh bloodletting controversy: two perspectives on the medical meaning of science in the mid-nineteenth century', *Medical History*, 24 (1980), 241–58.

Weeks, J., '"Sins and diseases": some notes on homosexuality in the nineteenth century', *History Workshop*, 1 (1976), 211–19.

Wiener, M. J., 'Judges v. jurors: courtroom tensions in murder trials', *Law and History Review*, 17 (199), 467–506.

Wells, R. A. E., 'Social conflict and protest in the English countryside in the early nineteenth century: a rejoinder', *Journal of Peasant Studies*, 8 (1981), 514–30.

Williams, R., 'Montgomeryshire Nonconformity: extracts from gaol files, with notes', *Mont. Colls*, 27 (1893), 55–76.

Woodall, R., 'The Ballot Act of 1872', *History Today*, 24 (1974), 464–71.

Woodward, N., 'Burglary in Wales, 1730–1830: evidence from Great Sessions', *Welsh History Review*, 24 (2008), 60–91.

Woodward, N., 'Horse stealing in Wales, 1730–1830', *Agricultural History Review*, 57 (2009), 70–108.

Woodward, N., 'Infanticide in Wales, 1730–1830', *Welsh History Review*, 23 (2007), 94–125.

Woodward, N., 'Seasonality and sheep stealing in Wales, 1730–1830', *Agricultural History Review*, 56 (2008), 23–47.

Woodward, N., 'Transportation convictions during the great Irish famine', *Journal of Interdisciplinary History*, 37 (2006), 59–87.

Wynter, R., 'Good in all respects: appearance and dress at Staffordshire County Lunatic Asylum, 1818–54', *History of Psychiatry*, 22 (2011), 40–57.

Zangerl, C. H. E., 'The social composition of the county magistracy in England and Wales, 1831–1887', *Journal of British Studies*, 11 (1971), 113–25.

Web pages

'A brief history of Welshpool', *www.cpat.org.uk/ycom/wpool/wplhis.htm* (15 May 2010).

'A short history of the police', *www.adam-matthew-publications.co.uk/digital_guides/a.aspx* (11 November 2010).

'Augusta Hall, Baroness Llanover', *http://en.wikipedia.org/wiki/Lady_Llanover* (1 August 2011).

'British Listed Buildings', *www.britishlistedbuildings.co.uk* (viewed many times).

'Charles Hanbury-Tracy, 1st Baron Sudely' viewed at *http://en.wikipedia.org/wiki/Charles_Hanbury-Tracy,_1st_Baron_Sudeley* (5 May 2011).

'Crime, punishment and protest through time', *http://www.learnhistory.org.uk/cpp/met.htm* (10 November 2010).

'Decker Hall', *www.anatpro.com/index_files/Annie_Augusta_Garnett_Botfield.htm* (15 March 2014).

'Flying Scotsman', *www.bbc.co.uk/ahistoryoftheworld* (5 August 2012).

'Forensics Timeline', *www.umbc.edu/tele/canton/studentproj/May.A/timeline.htm* (15 December 2010).

'High Sheriff of Montgomeryshire', *http://en.wikipedia.org/wiki/High_Sheriff_of_Montgomeryshire* (10 October 2010).

Highways Act 1835, *www.legislation.gov.uk* (5 May 2011).

'History of Warwickshire', *http://en.wikipedia.org/wiki/History_of_Warwickshire* (12 December 2010.).

'IOGT: A brief history', *http://iogt-ew.org/history.html* (4 January 2013).

Information about legislation, *www.legislation.gov.uk* (viewed many times).

Information about legislation, *www.statutelaw.gov.uk* (viewed many times).

'Jasper More', *www.british-history.ac.uk* (11 March 2011).

'Jasper More', *http://en.wikipedia.org/wiki/Robert_Jasper_More* (11 March 2011).

'John Bartholomew Gough', *http://en.wikipedia.org/wiki/John_Bartholomew_Gough* (1 August 2011).

'Lords Lieutenant of Montgomeryshire', *http://en.wikipedia.org/wiki/Lord_Lieutenant_of_Montgomeryshire* (9 September 2012).

'Municipal Corporations Act 1835', *http://en.wikipedia.org/wiki/Municipal_Corporations_Act_1835* (10 November 2010).

Online Etymology Dictionary, *www.etymonline.com* (20 July 2014).

Offences against the Person Act (1861), *www.legislation.gov.uk* (11 November 2011).

'Parramatta', *www.austehc.unimelb.edu.au/tia/273.html* (23 March 2012).

'Product placement can be a lot more powerful than we think', *www.psychologytoday.com* (30 March 2014).

'Pryce-Jones: pioneer of the mail-order industry', *www.bbc.co.uk/legacies/work/wales/w_mid/ article_1.shtml* (14 April 2012).

'Repeal of turnpike laws', *www.lawcom.gov.uk/docs/turnpikes.pdf*, p. 11 (18 November 2010).

'Sergeant James Owen', *www.owen.cholerton.org* (4 November 2010).

'Shropshire Royal Infirmary', *www.geograph.org.uk/photo/1220231* and *www.paradeshops.co.uk/default.asp?id=124andsC=page39* (11 December 2010).

'Sir Ellis Jones Ellis Griffiths', *http://wbo.llgc.org.uk/en/s-elli-jon-1860.html* (13 January 2012).

'Sir George Willshire Bramwell', *http://en.wikipedia.org* (1 November 2001).

'Sir Thomas Artemus Jones', *http://yba.llgc.org.uk/en/s2-jone-art-1871.html* (13 January 2012).

'Student Riot', *www.youtube.com/watch?v=MmudJafnQh0* (11 November 2010).

'Technology in Australia, 1888–1988', *www.austehc.unimelb.edu.au/tia/273.html* (2 May 2010)

'Temperance Movement', *http://en.wikipedia.org/wiki/Temperance_movement* (1 August 2011).

'The Chartist outbreak, 1839', *http://history.powys.org.uk/history/llani/ chart1.html* (11 November 2010).

'The Victorian medico-legal autopsy', *www.casebook.org/dissertations/rip-victorian-autopsy.html* (1 May 2010).

'Timeline of UK Railways', *www.stationbuffet.co.uk/history4.html* (5 August 2012).

'Turnpikes', *www.lawcom.gov.uk/docs/turnpikes.pdf* (18 November 2010).

'Vagrancy', *www.londonlives.org/static/Vagrancy.jsp* (3 November 2010).

'white collar', *http://en.wikipedia.org/wiki/White-collar_worker* (29 November 2010).

Wikipedia, *www.en.wikipedia.org* (viewed many times).

Other sources

'A Montgomeryshire magistrate and his dairymaid', *Western Mail*, 25 February 1875.

'Angus Bethune Reach', *DNB*.

Appeal hearing at Mold Crown Court, 16 August 2013.

Bowlby, C., 'Do difficult areas need special police attention?', *BBC History* (September 2012), 49.

'Be polite to the public, police told', *Daily Telegraph*, 9 July 2013.

Criminal Justice Act of 1855, Phillips, *Crime and Authority*, p. 97.

'Equality laws should aid the working classes', *Daily Telegraph*, 13 December 2013.

Juvenile Offenders Acts of 1847 and 1850, in Phillips, *Crime and Authority*, p. 97.

'Landed estates court', *Freeman's Journal and Daily Commercial Advertiser*, 29 April 1876.

'Law relating to killing a pigeon', *Law Journal*, 32 (1863), 186.

'Lists of Deputy Lieutenants, and Correspondence', *Mont. Colls*, 16 (1883), 120–1.

'New rent rules to impact on commercial landlords', *Agricultural Group News*, 1 (2014), 4.

'Obituary of Walter John Nash Millard', *Collections Historical and Architectural Relating to Montgomeryshire*, 44 (1936), 176–7.

'Political oppression by Welsh landlords', *Wrexham Advertiser*, 10 July 1869.

'Riot on the Mid-Wales Railway', reprinted in G. Roberts (ed.), *Pencambria*, 23 (2013).

'Sir William Fry Channell', *DNB*.

'Territorial Tyranny in Wales', *Bradford Observer*, 9 July 1869.

'The eclipse of *mens rea*', *Law Quarterly Review*, 60 (1936).

'The Western Circuit', *Bracton Law Journal*, 26 (1994).

'Voices from the Old Bailey', BBC Radio 4, 14 August 2014.

Colley, L., 'Acts of union and disunion: Wales', BBC Radio 4, 15 January 2014.

Emsley, C., 'Lessons from history: how worried should we be when the police close ranks?', *BBC History*(Christmas 2013), 12.

Jones, R., 'The Gregynog estate, 1880–1920' (unpublished MA dissertation, University of Leicester, 2007).

Morris, R. J., 'Middle classes', *Oxford Guide to British History* (1997; Oxford, 2002), pp. 639–40.

Personal communication, Richard Jones, Wern Ddu Farm, Aberhafesp, 12 February 2013.

Personal correspondence, A. Pugh, 15 April 2013.

Personal correspondence, Clive Emsley, 18 February 2013.

Personal correspondence, Peter King, 9 May 2012.

Personal correspondence, Thomas Glyn Watkin, 6 February, 2017.

Personal correspondence, Thomas Glyn Watkin, 20 June 2013.

Personal correspondence, Thomas Glyn Watkin, 29 October 2012.

S. Howard, 'Crime, communities and authority in early modern Wales: Denbighshire, 1660–1713' (unpublished Ph.D. thesis, University of Wales, Aberystwyth, 2003).

'Singular case of assault upon a tradesman', *Liverpool Mercury*, 24 December 1868.

'The Ballot Act of 1872', *History Today*, 24 (1974), 464–71.

'The Tarpey Case', *Liverpool Mercury*, 16 March 1871.

'Welsh assize cases', *Liverpool Mercury*, 18 March 1869.

'What about the public being told to be polite to the police?', *Daily Telegraph*, 10 July 2013.

INDEX

Fight, against perceived injustice
    98, 146, 245
Fines *see* sentencing
Forensic investigations 3, 72–5, 221
Freemasons 78, 81

Good Templars 78, 175
Grand jury 48, 74, 109–12, 115–16,
    124, 126–8, 136, 141, 143,
    144–5, 174, 181, 184, 186, 193

Habitual offenders 122
High sheriff 37, 112–14, 125, 127,
    135, 156, 192

Imprisonment *see* sentencing
Incomers 17, 20–1, 25
Infanticide 138, 141, 201, 241
Inspector of constabulary 46, 51,
    54, 213, 216
Irish 8, 22, 29, 137, 197, 207

Judges 48, 127, 129, 238, 243
    assisting witnesses 130, 133
    Bramwell, Sir George Willshere
        141–2, 242–3
    Channell, Sir William Fry 127,
        132, 240
    Kelly, Sir Fitzroy 127, 240
    Mellor 143, 145
    Parade 126–7
    Piggott, Sir Gillery 127, 240
    pompous 149, 195
Juries 138, 144
    grand 48, 74, 109–16, 124, 126,
        127, 128, 136, 141, 143–5,
        174, 181, 184, 186, 193, 232,
        233, 237, 242, 255
    petty 48, 109, 112, 126, 140–1,
        149, 181, 193, 232, 242
    perverse decisions 120
    Welsh, characteristics of 140
Juvenile offenders 115–16, 160,
    199, 231, 233

Landscape 1, 3, 4, 8, 31, 46, 51, 257
Language 173, 178, 184, 193, 194,
    197, 205

Legal system 31, 35, 37, 41, 100,
    107, 131, 139, 149, 230, 242
Lord lieutenant 28, 36–7, 87, 113

Magistrates
    attendance 34–6, 210
    backgrounds 31–2
    discretion 81–96, 115–17, 123,
        186, 191, 192, 194, 195
    parade 58
    personalities 182–7
    Welsh-speaking 85–6
Map, Montgomeryshire/
    neighbouring counties 11
Map, Montgomeryshire/rivers and
    towns 12
Marxist theory 7, 195–6
Medical experts *see* Expert
    witnesses
Menstrual blood 74, 221, 249
Methodology 4–9, 202
Middle classes 21, 23, 26, 28, 51, 58,
    59, 65, 70, 75, 83, 89, 100,
    110, 124, 126, 133, 134, 141,
    192, 195, 200, 205, 220, 232,
    237
Midwife 138, 139, 241
Millbank 121
Militia 22, 29, 32, 61, 69–70, 86–70,
    87, 117, 177
Montgomeryshire
    Anglican nature 27, 28, 32, 50,
        148, 175, 236
    occupations 10–18
    flannel industry 5, 13–18, 20, 25,
        29, 204
    geographical characteristics
        11–13
    map 12

Neighbours 22, 49, 97, 100, 133,
    136, 194, 237, 242, 249
Newspapers 5, 41, 155, 244, 254
    analysis of headlines 254
    letters to 54–8, 63–4, 71, 132,
        174, 178, 190
    reports 20, 31, 33, 38, 42, 55, 59,
        65, 69, 70, 79, 80, 82–3, 85,